Fodor's InF[...]

D0208111

SAVANNAH & CHARLESTON

1st Edition

**Where to Stay and Eat
for All Budgets**

**Must-See Sights
and Local Secrets**

Ratings You Can Trust

Excerpted from *Fodor's The Carolinas & Georgia*

Fodor's Travel Publications   New York, Toronto, London, Sydney, Auckland

www.fodors.com

FODOR'S IN FOCUS SAVANNAH & CHARLESTON

Series Editor: Douglas Stallings

Editor: Mark Sullivan

Editorial Production: Evangelos Vasilakis

Editorial Contributors: Eileen Robinson Smith

Maps & Illustrations: David Lindroth, *cartographer*; Bob Blake and Rebecca Baer, *map editors*

Design: Fabrizio LaRocca, *creative director*; Guido Caroti, Siobhan O'Hare, *art directors*; Ann McBride, *designer*

Photography: Melanie Marin, *senior photo editor*

Cover Photo (Drayton Hall, Charleston): Jeff Greenberg/Omni-Photo Communications

Production/Manufacturing: Matthew Struble

COPYRIGHT

1st Edition

ISBN 978-1-4000-1871-0

ISSN 1939-9863

SPECIAL SALES

This book is available for special discounts for bulk purchases for sales promotions or premiums. Special editions, including personalized covers, excerpts of existing books, and corporate imprints, can be created in large quantities for special needs. For more information, write to Special Markets/ Premium Sales, 1745 Broadway, MD 6-2, New York, New York, NY 10019, or e-mail specialmarkets@randomhouse.com.

AN IMPORTANT TIP & AN INVITATION

Although all prices, opening times, and other details in this book are based on information supplied to us at press time, changes occur all the time in the travel world, and Fodor's cannot accept responsibility for facts that become outdated or for inadvertent errors or omissions. **So always confirm information when it matters,** especially if you're making a detour to visit a specific place. Your experiences—positive and negative—matter to us. If we have missed or misstated something, **please write to us.** We follow up on all suggestions. Contact the Savannah & Charleston editor at editors@fodors.com or c/o Fodor's at 1745 Broadway, New York, NY 10019.

PRINTED IN THE UNITED STATES OF AMERICA

10 9 8 7 6 5 4 3 2 1

Be a Fodor's Correspondent

Your opinion matters. It matters to us. It matters to your fellow Fodor's travelers, too. And we'd like to hear it. In fact, we *need* to hear it. When you share your experiences and opinions, you become an active member of the Fodor's community. Here's how you can help improve Fodor's for all of us.

Tell us when we're right. We rely on local writers to give you an insider's perspective. But our writers and staff editors also depend on you. Your positive feedback is a vote to renew our recommendations for the next edition.

Tell us when we're wrong. We update most of our guides every year. But things change. If any of our descriptions are inaccurate or inadequate, we'll incorporate your changes in the next edition and will correct factual errors at fodors. com *immediately*.

Tell us what to include. You probably have had fantastic travel experiences that aren't yet in Fodor's. Why not share them with a community of like-minded travelers? Share your discoveries and experiences with everyone directly at fodors.com. Your input may lead us to add a new listing or a higher recommendation.

Give us your opinion instantly at our feedback center at www.fodors.com/feedback. You may also e-mail editors@ fodors.com with the subject line "Savannah & Charleston Editor." Or send your nominations, comments, and complaints by mail to Savannah & Charleston Editor, Fodor's, 1745 Broadway, New York, NY 10019.

Happy Traveling!

Tim Jarrell, Publisher

CONTENTS

ABOUT THIS BOOK

Our Ratings

We wouldn't recommend a place that wasn't worth your time, but sometimes a place is so experiential that superlatives don't do it justice: you just have to be there to know. These sights, properties, and experiences get our highest rating, Fodor's Choice, indicated by orange stars throughout this book. Black stars highlight sights and properties we deem Highly Recommended places that our writers, editors, and readers praise again and again.

Credit Cards

Want to pay with plastic? **AE, D, DC, MC, V** following restaurant and hotel listings indicate whether American Express, Discover, Diners Club, MasterCard, and Visa are accepted.

Restaurants

Unless we state otherwise, restaurants are open for lunch and dinner daily. We mention dress only when there's a specific requirement and reservations only when they're essential or not accepted—it's always best to book ahead.

Hotels

Unless we tell you otherwise, you can assume that the hotels have private bath, phone, TV, and air-conditioning. We always list facilities but not whether you'll be charged an extra fee to use them, so when pricing accommodations, find out what's included.

Many Listings
- ★ Fodor's Choice
- ★ Highly recommended
- ⊠ Physical address
- ✛ Directions
- ⌂ Mailing address
- ☎ Telephone
- ⎕ Fax
- ⊕ On the Web
- ✉ E-mail
- 💲 Admission fee
- ☉ Open/closed times
- Ⓜ Metro stations
- ⊟ Credit cards

Hotels & Restaurants
- ☒ Hotel
- ⬐ Number of rooms
- ⌂ Facilities
- ⍟ Meal plans
- ✕ Restaurant
- ⬐ Reservations
- ⬎ Smoking
- ⍋ BYOB
- ✕☒ Hotel with restaurant that warrants a visit

Outdoors
- ⛳ Golf
- ⛺ Camping

Other
- ♨ Family-friendly
- ⇨ See also
- ⊠ Branch address
- ☞ Take note

WHEN TO GO

There's really no bad time to visit either Charleston or Savannah, but spring is undoubtedly the most attractive season. Throughout the region, the blooming of cherry-blossoms is followed by a profusion of azaleas, dogwoods, and camellias in April and apple blossoms in May. Art shows, craft fairs, and music festivals (including the famous Spoleto USA festival) take place in summer, which is also high season in Hilton Head and Georgia's Coastal Isles. Things are certainly much quieter on the islands in the winter season, but the weather is mild enough that you can visit year-round, and golfers may appreciate Hilton Head's mild winter weather.

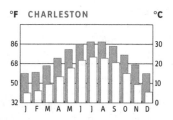

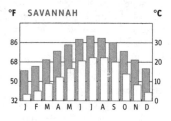

Climate

Spring and fall temperatures are delightful during the day, and mild at night. Summer can be hot and humid, though temperatures are a bit more temperate on the coastal islands. Mild winter weather can be punctuated by brief bouts of frigid conditions. Thunderstorms are common in the spring and summer. Hurricane season stretches from May through November, and storms occasionally strike the area.

Forecasts The Weather Channel (⊕ *www.weather.com*).

Savannah

WORD OF MOUTH

"Stroll, stroll, stroll the squares. Spend very little time on River Street. It's become too commercial. Do step in one of the candy shops for a sample of a praline. You'll probably buy some to take home. Here's your homework assignment: Read 'The Book' or watch the movie. Everywhere you turn in Savannah you will hear a reference to 'The Book,' which is of course, Midnight in the Garden of Good and Evil."

—starrville

Updated
by Eileen
Robinson
Smith

GENERAL JAMES OGLETHORPE, Savannah's founder, set sail for England in 1743, never to return. His last instructions, it's said, were, "Don't change a thing until I get back." That local joke holds more than a bit of truth. Savannah's elegant mansions, dripping Spanish moss, and sticky summer heat can make the city seem sleepy and stubbornly resistant to change. Which is exactly why many folks like the place.

Savannah, Georgia's oldest city, began its modern history on February 12, 1733, when Oglethorpe and 120 colonists arrived at Yamacraw Bluff on the Savannah River to found the 13th and last of the British colonies. As the port city grew, more settlers from England and Ireland arrived, joined by Scottish Highlanders, French Huguenots, Germans, Austrian Salzburgers, Sephardic and Ashkenazic Jews, Moravians, Italians, Swiss, Welsh, and Greeks.

In 1793 Eli Whitney of Connecticut, who was tutoring on a plantation near Savannah, invented a mechanized means of "ginning" seeds from cotton bolls. Cotton soon became king, and Savannah, already a busy seaport, flourished under its reign. Waterfront warehouses were filled with "white gold," and brokers trading in the Savannah Cotton Exchange set world prices. The white gold brought in hard currency; the city prospered.

General William Tecumseh Sherman's army rampaged across Georgia in 1864, setting fire to railroads, munitions factories, bridges, and just about anything else between them and the sea. Rather than see the city torched, Savannahians surrendered to the approaching Yankees.

As the cotton market declined in the early 20th century, the city's economy collapsed. For decades, Savannah's historic buildings languished; many were razed or allowed to decay. Cobwebs replaced cotton in the dilapidated riverfront warehouses. The tide turned in the 1950s, when residents began a concerted effort—which continues to this day—to restore and preserve the city's architectural heritage.

That link to the past is Savannah's main draw for travelers: the 2½-square-mi Historic District is the nation's largest. But Savannah's attraction also lies in its people, who give Southern charm their own special twist. As John Berendt's wildly popular book *Midnight in the Garden of Good and Evil* amply demonstrates, eccentricities can flourish in this hothouse environment.

Savannah Historic District

Savannah River

Riverfront Plaza

River St.

Factors Walk

W. Bay St.   E. Bay St.

W. Bryan St.   E. Bryan St.

Ellis Sq.   W. Julian   Johnson Sq.   E. Julian   Reynolds Sq.   Warren Sq.

W. Congress St.   E. Congress St.

W. Broughton St.   E. Broughton St.

W. State St.   E. State St.

Telfair Sq.   W. President   Wright Sq.   E. President   Oglethorpe Sq.   Columbia Sq.

W. York St.   E. York St.

W. Oglethorpe Ave.   E. Oglethorpe St.

Orleans Sq.   W. Hull   Chippewa Sq.   E. Hull   Colonial Park Cemetery

W. Perry   E. Perry

0   1/4 mile

0   400 meters

E. Liberty St.

Pulaski Sq.   Madison Sq.   W. Harris St.   Lafayette Sq.   E. Harris St.   Troup Sq.

W. Charlton   St. John's Episcopal Church   E. Macon St.   E. Charlton

W. Jones St.   E. Jones St.

Chatham Sq.   W. Taylor St.   Monterey Sq.   Calhoun Sq.   E. Taylor St.   Whitefield Sq.

W. Wayne St.   E. Wayne St.

W. Gordon St.   E. Gordon St.

King-Tisdell Cottage

E. Gaston St.

W. Broad   W. Bryan St.   Whitaker St.   Barnard St.   Jefferson St.   Montgomery St.   Drayton St.   Abercorn St.   Lincoln St.   Habersham St.   Bull St.   Tattnall St.

Andrew Low House, 18
Armstrong House, 25
Beach Institute, 15
Cathedral of St. John the Baptist, 16
Chippewa Square, 14
City Hall, 5
City Market, 2
Emmet Park, 7
Factors Walk, 4

First African Baptist Church, 3
Forsyth Park Apartments, 28
Green-Meldrim House, 19
Hamilton-Turner House, 17
Isaiah Davenport House, 8
Jepson Center for the Arts, 11

Joe Odom's First House, 20
Juliette Gordon Low Birthplace, 10
Lee Adler's Home, 21
Mercer House, 22
Ralph Mark Gilbert Civil Rights Museum, 23
Riverfront Plaza, 6
Savannah History Museum, 13

Scarborough House, 1
Serena Dawes's House, 24
Telfair's Owens-Thomas House, 9
Telfair Museum of Art, 12
Temple Mickve Israel, 26
Wesley Monumental Church, 27

SAVANNAH TOP 5

Intriguing Architecture:
Close to half of the 2,500 buildings in Savannah have architectural or historical significance. The many building styles—Georgian, Gothic revival, Italianate, federal, and Romanesque—make strolling the tree-lined neighborhoods a delight. The 19th-century Telfairs's Owens-Thomas house is a particular highlight. Like some other historic homes, it's open to the public.

Strolling the Squares: In the historic district, the city's famous squares are distinctive and thoroughly charming. Fountains, statues, and trees give each a different character, and all have stories to tell about different eras. To appreciate Savannah's unique appeal, take time to explore a few.

Gail Thurmond: Described as the female counterpart to Tony Bennett, Gail is a melodic fixture at Savannah's cozy Planters Tavern. Expect to hear many schmoozing favorites from a repetoire that rivals her mentor, the late, great Emma Kelly who earned the moniker "lady of 6,000 songs." Gail's CD "Savannah Moon" is a great keepsake.

Midnight in the Garden of Good and Evil: John Berendt's famous 1994 book about a local murder and the city's eccentric characters still draws many travelers eager to visit the places mentioned. It's a good read, and you can still enjoy retracing some of the scenes.

Melon Bluff: If you want to see the coast with nary a hint of development, this is one of the few remaining places to do so. Explore it by kayak, by canoe, or simply by walking beneath the canopies of live oaks and soaking up the pristine landscape.

EXPLORING SAVANNAH

THE HISTORIC DISTRICT

Georgia's founder, General James Oglethorpe, laid out the city on a perfect grid. The Historic District is neatly hemmed in by the Savannah River, Gaston Street, East Street, and Martin Luther King Jr. Boulevard. Streets are arrow-straight, public squares of varying sizes are tucked into the grid at precise intervals, and each block is sliced in half by narrow, sometimes unpaved streets. Bull Street, anchored on the north by City Hall and the south by Forsyth Park, charges down the center of the grid and maneuvers around the five public squares that stand in its way. The layout means the area is easy to explore, and is best appreciated on foot. All the squares have some historical significance; many have fountains and shady resting areas; and all are bordered by beautiful houses and mansions that speak to another era.

Numbers in the margin correspond to numbers on the Savannah Historic District map.

MAIN ATTRACTIONS

⑱ Andrew Low House. This residence was built in 1848 for Andrew Low, a native of Scotland and one of Savannah's merchant princes. The home later belonged to his son William, who married Juliette Gordon. After her husband's death, she founded the Girl Scouts in this house on March 12, 1912. The house has 19th-century antiques, stunning silver, and some of the finest ornamental ironwork in Savannah. ⊠*329 Abercorn St., Historic District* ☎*912/233–6854* ☜*$7.50* ☺*Mon.–Wed., Fri., and Sat. 10–4:30, Sun. noon–4.*

⑭ Chippewa Square. Daniel Chester French's imposing bronze statue of General James Edward Oglethorpe, founder of Savannah and Georgia, anchors the square. The bus-stop scenes of *Forrest Gump* were filmed on the north end of the square. Also note the **Savannah Theatre,** on Bull Street, which claims to be the oldest continuously operated theater site in North America. ⊠*Bull St. between Hull and Perry sts., Historic District.*

❷ City Market. Although the 1870s City Market was razed years ago, city fathers are enacting a three-year plan to capture the authentic atmosphere and character of its bustling origins. Already a lively destination for art studios, open-air cafés, theme shops, and jazz clubs, this popular pedestrian-only area will become the ever more vibrant, youthful heart of Savannah's Historic District. ⊠*Between Franklin Sq. and Johnson Sq. on W. St. Julian St., Historic District* ☎*912/525–2489 for current events.*

★ Colonial Park Cemetery. The park is the final resting place for Savannahians who died between 1750 and 1853. You may want to stroll the shaded pathways and read some of the old tombstone inscriptions. Local legend story tells that when Sherman's troops set up camp here, they moved some of the headstones around for fun. ⊠*Oglethorpe and Abercorn sts., Historic District.*

Columbia Square. When Savannah was a walled city (1757–90), Bethesda Gate (one of six) was at this location. The square, which was laid out in 1799, was named "Columbia," the female personification of the U.S. Liberty Square, now lost to urban sprawl. It was the only other square named in honor of the United States and the concept of freedom that stoked the fires of the American Revolution. Davenport House and Kehoe House are on Columbia Square. ✉*Habersham St. between E. State and E. York sts., Historic District.*

❹ **Factors Walk.** A network of iron crosswalks connects Bay Street with the multistory buildings that rise up from the river level, and iron stairways descend from Bay Street to Factors Walk. The area was originally the center of commerce for cotton brokers, who walked between and above the lower cotton warehouses. Cobblestone ramps lead pedestrians down to River Street. ■TIP➔**These are serious cobblestones, so wear comfortable shoes.** ✉*Bay St. to Factors Walk, Historic District.*

NEED A BREAK? The best place for an ice-cream soda is at **Leopold's** (✉*212 E. Broughton St., Historic District* ☎*912/234–4442*), a Savannah institution since 1919. It's currently owned by Stratton Leopold, grandson of the original owner and a Hollywood producer whose films include *Mission Impossible 3, The General's Daughter,* and *The Sum of All Fears.* Movie paraphernalia makes for an entertaining sideline to the selection of ice creams and sorbets. Famed lyricist Johnny Mercer grew up a block away from Leopold's and was a faithful customer.

Forsyth Park. The park forms the southern border of Bull Street. On its 30 acres are a glorious white fountain dating to 1858, Confederate and Spanish–American War memorials, and the Fragrant Garden for the Blind, a project of Savannah garden clubs. There are tennis courts and a tree-shaded jogging path. Outdoor plays and concerts often take place here. At the northwest corner of the park, in **Hodgson Hall,** a 19th-century Italianate Greek–revival building, you can find the **Georgia Historical Society,** which shows selections from its collection of artifacts and manuscripts. The park's 1-mi perimeter is among the prettiest walks in the city, and takes you past many beautifully restored and historic homes. ✉*501 Whitaker St.,*

Historic District ☎912/651–2128 ⊕*www.georgiahistory. com* ⊘*Tues.–Sat. 10–5.*

⑲ Green-Meldrim House. Designed by New York architect
★ John Norris and built in 1850 for cotton merchant Charles Green, this Gothic-revival mansion cost $90,000 to build—a princely sum back then. The house was bought in 1892 by Judge Peter Meldrim, whose heirs sold it to **St. John's Episcopal Church** to use as a parish house. General Sherman lived here after taking the city in 1864. Sitting on **Madison Square,** the house has Gothic features such as a crenellated roof, oriels, and an external gallery with filigree ironwork. Inside are mantels of Carrara marble, carved blackwalnut woodwork, and doorknobs and hinges of either silver plate or porcelain. ⊠*1 W. Macon St., Historic District* ☎912/233–3845 ☜*$7* ⊘*Tues., Thurs., and Fri. 10–4, Sat. 10–1. Closed last 2 wks of Jan. and 2 wks before Easter.*

❽ Isaiah Davenport House. The proposed demolition of this
★ historic Savannah structure galvanized the city's residents into action to save their treasured buildings. Semicircular stairs with wrought-iron trim lead to the recessed doorway of the redbrick federal mansion that master builder Isaiah Davenport built for himself between 1815 and 1820. Three dormered windows poke through the sloping roof of the stately house, and the interior has polished hardwood floors, fine woodwork and plasterwork, and a soaring elliptical staircase. Furnishings, from the 1820s, are Hepplewhite, Chippendale, and Sheraton. ⊠*324 E. State St., Historic District* ☎912/236–8097 ⊕*www.davenporthousemuseum.org* ☜*$8* ⊘*Mon.–Sat. 10–4, Sun. 1–4.*

⓫ Jepson Center for the Arts. In **Telfair Square** is Telfair's newest gallery, an unexpectedly modern building amid so many 18th- and 19th-century structures that are the city's hallmark. Inside you can find permanent hangings of Southern art, African-American art, and photography. There's a sculpture gallery and an outdoor sculpture terrace in addition to interactive, kid-friendly exhibits. ⊠*207 W. York St., Historic District* ☎912/232–1177 ⊕*www.telfair.org* ☜*$9* ⊘*Mon. noon–5, Tues.–Sat. 10–5, Sun. 1–5.*

Johnson Square. The oldest of James Oglethorpe's original 24 squares was laid out in 1733 and named for South Carolina governor Robert Johnson. A monument marks the grave of Nathanael Greene, a hero of the Revolutionary War. The square was once a popular gathering place:

Spa Savannah

As with the rest of the world, spa-ing is catching on in the city of Spanish Moss. **Vanilla Day Spa** (⊠1 E. Broughton St., Downtown ☎912/232–0040) is inside the Downtown Athletic Club—with access to steam rooms, saunas, and whirlpools—and offers a full menu of professional services for men and women such as manicures, pedicures, facials, and body treatments. In addition to traditional spa services, **Savannah Day Spa** (⊠18 E. Oglethorpe St., Downtown ☎912/234–9100) also offers a complete line of skin-care products, accessories for your home spa, and a new line of vegan body products. The very chic **Poseidon Spa** (⊠700 Drayton St., Historic District ☎912/721–5004) at the Mansion on Forsyth Park is another first-class European-style spa, with a number of rejuvenating treatments and refinement services.

Savannahians came here to welcome President Monroe in 1819, to greet the Marquis de Lafayette in 1825, and to cheer for Georgia's secession in 1861. ⊠Bull St. between Bryan and Congress sts., Historic District.

🔟 Juliette Gordon Low Birthplace/Girl Scout National Center. This majestic Regency town house, attributed to William Jay (built 1818–21), was designated in 1965 as Savannah's first National Historic Landmark. "Daisy" Low, founder of the Girl Scouts, was born here in 1860, and the house is now owned and operated by the Girl Scouts of America. Mrs. Low's paintings and other artwork are on display in the house, restored to the style of 1886, the year of Mrs. Low's marriage. ⊠142 Bull St., Historic District ☎912/233–4501 ⊕www.girlscouts.org/birthplace ☜$8 ⊙Mon.–Sat. 10–4, Sun. 11–4.

Madison Square. A statue on the square, laid out in 1839 and named for President James Madison, depicts Sergeant William Jasper hoisting a flag and is a tribute to his bravery during the Siege of Savannah. Though mortally wounded, Jasper rescued the colors of his regiment in the assault on the British lines. A granite marker denotes the southern line of the British defense during the 1779 battle. The Green-Meldrim House is here. ⊠Bull St. between W. Harris and W. Charlton sts., Historic District.

9 Telfair's Owens-Thomas House and Museum. English architect William Jay's first Regency mansion in Savannah is widely considered the country's finest example of that architectural style. Built in 1816–19, the English house was constructed mostly with local materials. Of particular note are the curving walls of the house, Greek-inspired ornamental molding, half-moon arches, stained-glass panels, and Duncan Phyfe furniture. The carriage house includes a gift shop and rare urban slave quarters, which have retained the original furnishings and "haint-blue" paint made by the slave occupants. ⊠*124 Abercorn St., Historic District* ☎*912/233–9743* ⊕*www.telfair.org* ≅*$9* ⊙*Mon. noon–5, Tues.–Sat. 10–5, Sun. 1–5; last tour at 4:30.*

Reynolds Square. John Wesley, who preached in Savannah and wrote the first English hymnal in the city in 1736, is remembered here. A monument to the founder of the Methodist Church is shaded by greenery and surrounded by park benches. The **Olde Pink House** (⊠*23 Abercorn St.*), built in 1771, is one of the oldest buildings in town. Now a restaurant, the portico pink-stucco Georgian mansion has been a private home, a bank, and headquarters for a Yankee general during the Civil War. ⊠*Abercorn St. between E. Bryant and E. Congress sts., Historic District.*

6 Riverfront Plaza. Amid this nine-block brick concourse, you can watch a parade of freighters and pug-nose tugs. Youngsters can play in the tugboat-shape sandboxes. There are a plethora of outlets for shopping and eating. River Street is the main venue for many of the city's celebrations, including the First Saturday festivals, when flea marketers, artists, and artisans display their wares and musicians entertain the crowds. ⊠*River St. between Abercorn and Barnard sts., Historic District.*

13 Savannah History Museum. This museum in a restored railway station is an excellent introduction to the city. Exhibits range from old locomotives to a tribute to Savannah-born songwriter Johnny Mercer. Built on the **site of the Siege of Savannah,** it marks the spot where in 1779 the colonial forces, led by Polish count Casimir Pulaski, laid siege to Savannah in an attempt to retake the city from the redcoats. They were beaten back, and Pulaski was killed while leading a cavalry charge against the British. The dead lie underneath the building. ⊠*303 Martin Luther King Jr. Blvd., Historic District* ☎*912/238–1779*

⊕www.chsgeorgia.org/shm/home.htm 🖹$4.25 ☉ Weekdays 8:30–5, weekends 9–5.

GUNS OF PEACE George and Martha are the affectionate names of the two bronze cannons that stand at the corner of Bay and Drayton streets. The guns were taken at the battle of Yorktown and presented to the Chatham Artillery as a dramatic "bread-and-butter" peace offering by General George Washington when he visited Savannah in May 1791.

❶ ★ **Scarborough House.** This exuberant Greek-revival mansion, built during the 1819 cotton boom for Savannah merchant prince William Scarborough, was designed by English architect William Jay. Scarborough was a major investor in the steamship *Savannah*. The house has a Doric portico capped by one of Jay's characteristic half-moon windows. Four massive Doric columns form a peristyle in the atrium entrance hall. Inside is the **Ships of the Sea Museum,** with displays of ship models, including steamships, and a nuclear-power ship. ✉*41 Martin Luther King Jr. Blvd., Historic District* 🕿*912/232–1511* *⊕www.shipsofthesea. org* 🖹*$7* ☉*Tues.–Sun. 10–5.*

⓬ **Telfair Museum of Art.** The oldest public art museum in the Southeast was designed by William Jay in 1819 for Alexander Telfair and sits across the street from **Telfair Square.** Within its marble rooms are American, French, and Dutch impressionist paintings; German tonalist paintings; a large collection of works by Kahlil Gibran; plaster casts of the Elgin Marbles, the Venus de Milo, and the Laocoön, among other classical sculptures; and some of the Telfair family furnishings, including a Duncan Phyfe sideboard and Savannah-made silver. ✉*121 Barnard St., Historic District* 🕿*912/232–1177* *⊕www.telfair.org* 🖹*$9* ☉*Mon. noon–5, Tues.–Sat. 10–5, Sun. 1–5.*

THE WAVING GIRL This charming statue at River Street and East Board Ramp is a symbol of Savannah's Southern hospitality, and commemorates Florence Martus, the lighthouse keeper's sister who waved to ships in Savannah's port for more than 44 years.

ALSO WORTH SEEING

⓯ **Beach Institute African-American Cultural Center.** Works by African-American artists from the Savannah area and around the country are on display in this building, which once housed the first school for African-American children

1

in Savannah, established in 1867. On permanent exhibit are more than 230 wood carvings by folk artist Ulysses Davis. ✉*502 E. Harris St., Historic District* ☏*912/234–8000* ⊕*www.kingtisdell.org* 🖅*$4* ⊙*Tues.–Sat. noon–5.*

⑯ Cathedral of St. John the Baptist. Soaring over the city, this French Gothic–style cathedral, with pointed arches and free-flowing traceries, is the seat of the diocese of Savannah. It was founded in 1799 by the first French colonists to arrive in Savannah. Fire destroyed the early structures; the present cathedral dates from 1874. ✉*222 E. Harris St., Historic District* ☏*912/233–4709* ⊙*Weekdays 9–5.*

❺ City Hall. Built in 1905 on the site of the Old City Exchange (1799–1904), this imposing structure anchors Bay Street. Notice the bench commemorating Oglethorpe's landing on February 12, 1733. ✉*1 Bay St., Historic District* ☏*912/651–6410* ⊙*Weekdays 8:30–5.*

❼ Emmet Park. Once an Indian burial ground, the lovely tree-shaded park is named for Robert Emmet, a late-18th-century Irish patriot and orator. The park contains monuments to German Salzburgers, Vietnam's fallen soldiers, and the Celtic Cross, among others. ✉*Borders E. Bay St., Historic District.*

❸ First African Baptist Church. This church was built by slaves at night by lamplight, after they worked the plantations during the day. The basement floor still shows signs of its time as a stop on the Underground Railroad. Designs drilled in the floor are thought to actually have been air holes for slaves hiding underneath, waiting to be transported to the Savannah River for their trip to freedom. ✉*23 Montgomery St., Historic District* ☏*912/233–6597* ⊕*www.firstafricanbc.org* 🖅*Donations requested* ⊙*Tours: Tues.–Thurs. at 11, 1, and 3.*

Lafayette Square. Named for the Marquis de Lafayette who aided the Americans during the Revolutionary War, the square contains a graceful three-tier fountain donated by the Georgia chapter of the Colonial Dames of America. The Cathedral of St. John the Baptist and the childhood home of author Flannery O'Conner are on the square. ✉*Abercorn St. between E. Harris and E. Charlton sts., Historic District.*

Monterey Square. Commemorating the victory of General Zachary Taylor's forces in Monterrey, Mexico, in 1846, this is the fifth and southernmost of Bull Street's squares.

Moss Mystique

Spanish moss—the silky, snake-like garlands that drape over the branches of live oaks—has come to symbolize the languorous sensibilities of the Deep South. A relative of the pineapple, the moisture-loving plant requires an average year-round humidity of 70%, and thus thrives in subtropical climates—including Georgia's coastal regions.

Contrary to popular belief, Spanish moss is not a parasite; it's an epiphyte, or "air plant," taking water and nutrients from the air and photosynthesizing in the same manner as soil-bound plants. It reproduces using tiny flowers. When water is scarce, it turns gray, and when the rains come it takes on a greenish hue. The old saying "Good night, sleep tight, don't let the bed bugs bite," is thought to come from the past practice of stuffing mattresses with Spanish moss, which often harbored the biting menaces commonly known as chiggers.

A monument honors General Casimir Pulaski, the Polish nobleman who lost his life in the Siege of Savannah during the Revolutionary War. Also on the square is Temple Mickve Israel. ⊠*Bull St. between Taylor and Gordon sts., Historic District.*

㉓ Ralph Mark Gilbert Civil Rights Museum. In Savannah's Historic District, this history museum has a series of 15 exhibits on segregation, from emancipation through the civil rights movement. The role of black and white Savannahians in ending segregation in their city is detailed in these exhibits, largely derived from archival photographs. The museum also has touring exhibits. ⊠*460 Martin Luther King Jr. Blvd., Historic District* ☎*912/231–8900* 🖷*912/234–2577* 🖾*$4* ☉*Mon.–Sat. 9–5.*

㉖ Temple Mickve Israel. A Gothic-revival synagogue on Monterey Square houses the third-oldest Jewish congregation in the United States; its founding members settled in town five months after the establishment of Savannah in 1733. The synagogue's collection includes documents and letters (some from George Washington, James Madison, and Thomas Jefferson) pertaining to early Jewish life in Savannah and Georgia. ⊠*20 E. Gordon St., Historic District* ☎*912/233–1547* ⊛*www.mickveisrael.org* 🖾*Free; tour $3* ☉*Weekdays 10–noon and 2–4.*

㉗ Wesley Monumental Church. This Gothic-revival style church memorializing the founders of Methodism is patterned after Queen's Kerk in Amsterdam. It dates from 1868 and is particularly noted for its magnificent stained-glass windows. ✉ *429 Abercorn St., Historic District* ☎ *912/232–0191 ⊙ By appointment only.*

Wright Square. Named for James Wright, Georgia's last colonial governor, this square has an elaborate monument in its center that honors William Washington Gordon, founder of the Central of Georgia Railroad. A slab of granite from Stone Mountain adorns the grave of Tomo-Chi-Chi, the Yamacraw chief who befriended General Oglethorpe and the colonists. ✉ *Bull St. between W. State and W. York sts., Historic District.*

OTHER AREA ATTRACTIONS

Ebenezer. When the Salzburgers arrived in Savannah in 1734, Oglethorpe sent them up the Savannah River to establish a settlement. The first effort was assailed by disease, and they sought his permission to move to better ground. Denied, they moved anyway and established Ebenezer. Here, they engaged in silkworm production and, in 1769, built the Jerusalem Church, which still stands. After the revolution, the silkworm operation never resumed, and the town faded into history. Descendants of these Protestant religious refugees have preserved the church and assembled a few of the remaining buildings, moving them to this site from other locations. Be sure to follow Route 275 to its end and see Ebenezer Landing, where the Salzburgers came ashore. ✉ *Ebenezer Rd., Rte. 21–Rte. 275, 25 mi north of Savannah, Rincon.*

Old Fort Jackson. About 2 mi east of Broad Street via President Street, you can see a sign for the fort, which is 3 mi from the city. Purchased in 1808 by the federal government, this is the oldest standing fort in Georgia. It was garrisoned in the War of 1812 and was the Confederate headquarters of the river batteries. The fort guards Five Fathom Hole, the 18th-century deep-water port in the Savannah River. The brick edifice is surrounded by a tidal moat, and there are 14 exhibit areas. Battle reenactments, blacksmithing demonstrations, and programs of 19th-century music are among the fort's activities for tour groups. ✉ *1 Fort Jackson Rd., Fort Jackson* ☎ *912/232–3945* ⊕ *www.chsgeorgia. org/jackson/home.htm* 🖃 *$4.25 ⊙ Daily 9–5.*

CLOSE UP

Famous Faces in Savannah

Here's a sampling of the figures who have etched themselves into Savannah's collective memory.

Actor Robert Mitchum (1917–97) gave one of his finest performances as a psychotic ex-convict in 1961's *Cape Fear*, which was filmed in and around Savannah. The shooting wasn't Mitchum's first visit to the city. In 1934, as a wayward 17-year-old, he roamed across America and was arrested on charges of vagrancy and begging while panhandling in Savannah. Six days after he was jailed, he escaped. When he returned to Savannah as a Hollywood star, his earlier transgressions were never mentioned.

James L. Pierpont (1822–93) wrote the Christmas classic "Jingle Bells" in Savannah—at least that's what locals will tell you. A native of Medford, Massachusetts, Pierpont became music director of Savannah's Unitarian church in the 1850s. In 1857 he obtained a copyright for "The One Horse Open Sleigh," (known as "Jingle Bells"). In the 1980s, tempers boiled when Medford claimed that Pierpont had written the song in their city. This dispute has never been resolved.

John Wesley (1703–91), the founder of Methodism, arrived in 1735, and fell in love with Sophia Hopkey. But Wesley wasn't prepared to marry and Sophia found another suitor, William Williamson. The jealous Wesley charged Sophia with neglect of public church services and refused to let her participate in communion. Sophia's uncle, Thomas Causton, Savannah's chief magistrate, charged Wesley with defamation, claiming he was unfit to be a minister. Wesley, found guilty on some of the counts, fled to England. By the time he died, at 88, he had become one of the towering figures in religious history.

Names of note also include Johnny Mercer (1909–76), a fourth generation Savannah native and one of America's most popular and successful songwriters of the 20th century. He is buried in Bonaventure Cemetery.

Fiction writer Flannery O'Connor (1925–64) spent the first 13 years of her life in Savannah. Her novels *Wise Blood* and *The Violent Bear It Away* amply convey her unique take on the Southern-Gothic style, but her greatest achievement is found in her short stories, published in the collections *A Good Man Is Hard to Find* and *Everything That Rises Must Converge.*

Savannah is also the proud hometown of Supreme Court Justice Clarence Thomas, America's second African-American Supreme Court Justice.

Fort Pulaski National Monument. Named for Casimir Pulaski,
★ a Polish count and Revolutionary War hero, this must-see
sight for Civil War buffs was designed by Napoléon's military engineer and built on Cockspur Island between 1829
and 1847. Robert E. Lee's first assignment after graduat-
ing from West Point was as an engineer here. During the
Civil War the fort fell, on April 11, 1862, after a mere 30
hours of bombardment by newfangled rifled cannons. The
restored fortification, operated by the National Park Service, has moats, drawbridges, massive ramparts, and towering walls. The park has trails and picnic areas. It's 14
mi east of downtown Savannah; you can see the entrance
on your left just before U.S. 80 reaches Tybee Island. ⊠*U.
S. 80, Fort Pulaski* ☎*912/786–5787* ⊕*www.nps.gov/fopu*
⊆*$3* ⊙*Daily 9–7.*

Melon Bluff. On land obtained with a Kings Grant in 1745,
this 9,500 acre plantation has been in the same family
ever since, and is one of the few remaining stretches of
pristine Georiga coastline. ■TIP➔**Archaeological finds and
historical records indicate that Melon Bluff is 37 years older
than St. Augustine (long considered the oldest community in
the United States).** You can find a nature center here and
facilities for canoeing, kayaking, bird-watching, hiking,
and other outdoor activities. You can camp here or stay at
one of three B&Bs ($$–$$$): Palmyra Plantation, an 1850s
cottage; the Ripley Farmhouse, a classic rural house with
a tin-covered roof; and an old barn, renovated to contain
nine guest rooms. From Melon Bluff you can visit nearby
Seabrook Village, a small but growing cluster of rural
buildings from an African-American historic community;
Old Sunbury, whose port made it a viable competitor to
Savannah until the Revolutionary War ended its heyday;
Fort Morris, which protected Savannah during the revolution; and **Midway,** an 18th-century village with a house
museum and period cemetery. To reach Melon Bluff, take
Interstate 95 south from Savannah (about 30 mi) to Exit 76
(Midway/Sunbury), turn left, and go east for 3 mi. ⊠*2999
Islands Hwy., Midway* ☎*912/884–5779 or 888/246–8188*
🖷*912/884–3046* ⊕*www.melonbluff.com.*

Mighty Eighth Air Force Heritage Museum. The famous World
War II squadron the Mighty Eighth Air Force was formed
in Savannah in January 1942 and shipped out to the United
Kingdom. Flying Royal Air Force aircraft, the Mighty
Eighth became the largest air force of the period. Exhibits
at this museum begin with the prelude to World War II

and the rise of Adolf Hitler and continue through Desert Storm. You can see vintage aircraft, fly a simulated bombing mission with a B-17 crew, test your skills as a waist gunner, and view interviews with courageous World War II vets. The museum also has three theaters, an art gallery, a 1940s-era English pub, a 7,000-volume library, archives, memorial garden, chapel, and museum store. ⊠ *175 Bourne Ave., I-95, Exit 102, to U.S. 80, 14 mi west of Savannah, Pooler* ☎ *912/748–8888* ⊕ *www.mightyeighth.org* ⊡ *$10* ⊙ *Daily 9–5.*

☉ **Skidaway Marine Science Complex.** On the grounds of the former Modena Plantation, Skidaway has a 14-panel, 12,000-gallon aquarium with marine and plant life of the continental shelf. Other exhibits highlight coastal archaeology and fossils of the Georgia coast. Nature trails overlook marsh and water. ⊠ *30 Ocean Science Circle, 8 mi south of Savannah, Skidaway Island* ☎ *912/598–2496* ⊡ *$2* ⊙ *Weekdays 9–4, Sat. noon–5.*

Tybee Island. *Tybee* is an Indian word meaning "salt." The Yamacraw Indians came to this island in the Atlantic Ocean to hunt and fish, and legend has it that pirates buried their treasure here. The island is about 5 mi long and 2 mi wide, with seafood restaurants, chain motels, condos, and shops—most of which sprang up during the 1950s and haven't changed much since. The entire expanse of white sand is divided into a number of public beaches, where you can shell and crab, charter fishing boats, and swim. **Tybee Island Lighthouse and Museum** (⊠ *30 Meddin Dr.* ☎ *912/786–5801*) has been well restored; the Head Keeper's Cottage is the oldest building on the island, and should be on your list. Kids will enjoy the **Marine Science Center** (⊠ *1510 Strand Ave.* ☎ *912/786–5917*), which houses local marine life such as the Ogeechee corn snake, turtles, and American alligator. Tybee Island is 18 mi east of Savannah; take Victory Drive (U.S. 80), sometimes called Tybee Road, onto the island. Nearby, the misnamed Little Tybee Island, actually larger than Tybee Island, is entirely undeveloped. Contact **Tybee Island Convention and Visitors Bureau** (✆ *Box 491, Tybee Island, 31328* ☎ *800/868–2322* ⊕ *www.tybeevisit.com*) for information and maps.

SPORTS & THE OUTDOORS

BOATING

At the **Bull River Yacht Club Marina** (✉8005 Old Tybee Rd., Tybee Island ☎912/897–7300), you can arrange a dolphin tour, a deep-sea fishing expedition, or a jaunt through the coastal islands. **Lake Mayer Park** (✉Montgomery Crossroads Rd. and Sallie Mood Dr., Cresthill ☎912/652–6780) has paddleboats, sailing, and canoeing, as well as an in-line skating and hockey facility. Capt. Judy Helmley, a long-time and legendary guide of the region, heads up **Miss Judy Charters** (✉124 Palmetto Dr., Wilmington Island ☎912/897–4921 or 912/897–2478) and provides packages ranging from two-hour sightseeing tours to 13-hour deep-sea fishing expeditions. **Savannah Islands Expressway** (✉Adjacent to Frank W. Spencer Park, Skidaway Island ☎912/231–8222) offers boat ramps on the Wilmington River. **Savannah Marina** (✉Thunderbolt) provides boat ramps on the Wilmington River.

GOLF

Bacon Park (✉1 Shorty Cooper Dr., Southside ☎912/354–2625) is a public facility with 27 holes of golf and a lighted driving range. **Crosswinds Golf Club** (✉232 James Blackburn Dr., Pooler ☎912/966–1909), located north of town, has an 18-hole championship course as well as a nine-hole course that is lighted for night play. **Henderson Golf Club** (✉1 Al Henderson Dr., at I–95, Exit 94 to Rte. 204, Southside ☎912/920–4653) is an 18-hole, par-71 course about 15 mi from downtown Savannah. The **Mary Calder Golf Course** (✉W. Lathrop Ave., West Chatham ☎912/238–7100) is par 35 for its nine holes.

TENNIS

Bacon Park (✉6262 Skidaway Rd., Southside ☎912/351–3850) has 16 lighted asphalt courts. Fees are $3 per person, and you can reserve courts in advance. **Forsyth Park** (✉Drayton St. and Park Ave., Historic District ☎912/652–6780) contains four lighted courts available until about 10 PM; there's no charge to use them. **Lake Mayer Park** (✉Montgomery Crossroads Rd. and Sallie Mood Dr., Southside ☎912/652–6780) has eight asphalt lighted courts avail-

No-Hills Workout

Savannah is table flat—bad news indeed for any mountaineers who find themselves in coastal Georgia—but great for bicyclists. One favorite spot for local bikers is the 28,000-acre Savannah Wildlife Refuge, where alligators bask alongside the trail. Another possibility is Rails-to-Trails, a 3-mi route that starts 1 mi east of the Bull River Bridge on Highway 80 and ends at the entrance to Fort Pulaski. Tom Triplett Park, east of town on U.S. 80, offers three bike loops—3.5 mi, 5 mi, and 6.3 mi. Though much of downtown is fairly unfriendly to bikers, several of the suburbs—Windsor Forest, Ardsley Park, the Isle of Hope—are fine for riding relatively free of traffic hassles.

able at no charge and open 8 AM to 10 PM; until 11 PM May through September.

WHERE TO EAT

Savannah has excellent seafood restaurants, though locals also have a passion for spicy barbecued meats. The Historic District yields a culinary cache, especially along River Street. Several of the city's restaurants—such as Elizabeth on 37th, the Olde Pink House, and Sapphire Grill—are beacons that have drawn members of the culinary upper crust to the region for decades. And there are others, such as Johnny Harris and Mrs. Wilkes' Dining Room, which remain treasured mainstays. If you explore a bit, you'll soon discover that such divine dining isn't isolated to Savannah's Historic District, as nearby Thunderbolt, Skidaway, Tybee, and Wilmington islands also have a collection of remarkable restaurants.

WHAT IT COSTS				
AT DINNER				
$$$$	$$$	$$	$	¢
over $22	$17–$22	$12–$16	$7–$11	under $7

Restaurant prices are for a main course at dinner.

1

$$$$ ✕**Elizabeth on 37th.** Regional specialties are the hallmark at this acclaimed restaurant that goes so far as to credit local produce suppliers on its menu. Although original chef and owner Elizabeth Terry has now retired, the kitchen hasn't faltered one iota. Dishes such as Maryland crab cakes or the plate of roasted shiitake and oyster mushrooms sit comfortably beside Southern-fried grits and honey roasted–pork tenderloin and roasted shiitake and oyster mushroom over dried tomatoes, black-eyed peas, and carrot ragout. The extravagant Savannah cream cake is the way to finish your meal in this elegant turn-of-the-20th-century mansion with hardwood floors and spacious rooms. ✉*105 E. 37th St., Victorian District* ☎*912/236–5547* ⚄*Reservations essential* ▭*AE, D, DC, MC, V* ⊘*No lunch.*

$$$–$$$$ ✕**Belford's Steak and Seafood.** In the heart of City Market, Belford's is great for brunch on Sunday, when so many of the downtown venues are closed. A complimentary glass of sparkling wine arrives at your table when you place your order. Brunch entrées include egg dishes, such as smoked salmon Florentine and crab frittatas. The lunch and dinner menus focus on seafood, including Georgia pecan grouper and Lowcountry shrimp and grits. The building used to be a wholesale grocery company; modern tweaks include huge windows, wooden floors, exposed brick walls, and an expansive outdoor patio. ■TIP➔**Some have called the crab cakes the best in the city.** ✉*315 W. St. Julian St., Historic District* ☎*912/233–2626* ▭*AE, D, DC, MC, V.*

$$$–$$$$ ✕**Il Pasticcio.** Sicilian Pino Venetico turned this former department store into his dream restaurant—a bistro-style place gleaming with steel, glass, and tile. The menu changes frequently, but fresh pasta dishes are a constant, and excellent desserts include a superior tiramisu. The signature filet mignon with melted gorgonzola is superb. As the evening progresses—particularly on weekends when live jazz ensembles start up around 10 PM—the scene gets ever more lively and hip. A lower level caters to private parties; the upper level, separate from the restaurant, is a hip-hop club. ✉*2 E. Broughton St., Historic District* ☎*912/231–8888* ▭*AE, D, DC, MC, V* ⊘*No lunch.*

$$$–$$$$ ✕**The Lady & Sons.** Expect to take your place in line, along with locals, here. Everyone patiently waits to attack the buffet, which is stocked for both lunch and dinner with specials such as moist, crispy fried chicken; crab stew; chicken potpie; the best baked spaghetti in the South;

green beans cooked with ham and potatoes; tender, sweet creamed corn; and homemade lemonade. (The quality can sometimes suffer because of the volume.) Look for owner Paula H. Deen on the Food Channel or pick up a copy of her cookbook that includes recipes for the most popular dishes. She also holds cooking classes year-round here and at her other restaurant, Uncle Bubba's Oyster House. ⊠ *102 W. Congress St., Historic District* ☎ *912/233–2600* ⊟ *AE, D, MC, V* ⊘ *No dinner Sun.*

$$$–$$$$ ✕ **Sapphire Grill.** Savannah's young and restless pack this trendy haunt nightly. Chef Chris Nason focuses his seasonal menus on local ingredients, such as Georgia white shrimp, crab, and fish. The Grill features succulent choices of steak, poultry, and fish, with a myriad of interesting à la carte accompaniments such as jalapeño tartar, sweet soy-wasabi sauce, and lemongrass butter. Vegetarians will delight in the elegant vegetable presentations—perhaps including roasted sweet onions, spicy peppers, rice-marinated watercress, or fried green tomatoes with grilled ginger. Chocoholics should try the delicious, potent chocolate flan. ■ **TIP→ Downstairs the decor is hip with gray brick walls alongside those painted a deep sapphire and a stone bar; upstairs is quieter and more romantic.** ⊠ *110 W. Congress St., Historic District* ☎ *912/443–9962* ⟞ *Reservations essential* ⊟ *AE, D, DC, MC, V* ⊘ *No lunch.*

$$$–$$$$ ✕ **17 Hundred 90.** In a rustic structure dating to colonial days,
    ★   tucked in among ancient oaks dripping with Spanish moss, you'll find a very creative kitchen. Entrées include pan-seared veal medallions with artichoke hearts and capers in lemon butter; roasted half duckling with a port-wine lingonberry sauce; and local shrimp stuffed with scallops and crabmeat and served with a lemon beurre-blanc sauce. ■ **TIP→ There's a ghost story to go with dinner, so make sure the waiter fills you in.** ⊠ *307 E. Presidents St., Historic District* ☎ *912/237–7122* ⊟ *AE, D, DC, MC, V* ⊘ *No lunch weekends.*

$$–$$$$ ✕ **Bistro Savannah.** High ceilings, burnished heart-pine
    ★   floors, and gray-brick walls lined with local art contribute to the bistro qualities of this spot by City Market. The menu has specialties such as seared beef tenderloin with fingerling potatoes, portobello mushrooms, red chard in a cabernet sauce, and shrimp and *tasso* (seasoned cured pork) on stone-ground grits. Another treat is the crispy roasted duck. ⊠ *309 W. Congress St., Historic District* ☎ *912/233–6266* ⊟ *AE, MC, V* ⊘ *No lunch.*

Where to Stay & Eat in Savannah

Savannah River

Restaurants

Belford's Steak and Seafood, **1**
Bella's Italian Cafe, **15**
Bistro Savannah, **3**
Elizabeth on 37th, **14**
Firefly Cafe, **11**
Georges' of Tybee, **8**
Hunter House, **7**
Il Pasticcio, **5**

Johnny Harris, **13**
The Lady & Sons, **2**
Mrs. Wilkes' Dining Room, **12**
Olde Pink House, **6**
Sapphire Grill, **4**
17 Hundred 90, **9**
Soho South Cafe, **10**
Toucan Café, **16**

Hotels

Ballastone Inn, **10**
Bed & Breakfast Inn, **13**
Eliza Thompson House, **12**
Foley House Inn, **11**
Gastonian, **14**
Green Palm Inn, **8**
Hyatt Regency Savannah, **1**

Kehoe House, **7**
Mansion on Forsyth Park, **15**
Marshall House, **6**
Mulberry Inn, **4**
Planters Inn, **5**
The President's Quarters, **9**
River Street Inn, **2**
17th Street Inn, **3**

$$–$$$$ ✗**Georges' of Tybee.** There's a romantic ambience in this upscale restaurant with a warmly lighted interior, a lovely stone fireplace, and dark rose-painted walls. Chef Robert Wood puts a refreshing spin on favorites such as a grilled rack of lamb, served with spinach, olives, and mushrooms tossed with Israeli couscous and apricot and fig chutney. The sautéed black grouper is a treat, served over bamboo rice with Asian slaw and coconut curry. ■TIP→ **The restaurant's beachfront sister, North Beach Grill, is way more casual, serving burgers by day and jerk chicken and pork in the evening.** ⊠ *1105 E. U.S. 80, Tybee Island* ☎ *912/786–9730* ⊟ *AE, MC, V* ⊘ *Closed Mon. No lunch.*

$$–$$$$ ✗**Hunter House.** When owner John Hunter followed the lady he loved to Georgia several years ago, he wasn't expecting to fall in love again—with Tybee Island—let alone create one of the region's finest dining rooms. Built in 1910 as a family beach house, this totally renovated home offers an intimate dining experience with a Victorian ambience. Seafood dominates the menu and includes deliciously creative dishes such as a cognac-laced seafood bisque and baked Chilean sea bass topped with apple bark–smoked bacon and served over Boursin cheese–garlic-chive mashed potatoes. Meat eaters need not despair; chicken and steak options are available and the restaurant boasts a pot roast as the house special. ■TIP→ **Though the restaurant is the primary business, the house also has a quality B&B with four guest rooms.** ⊠ *1701 Butler Ave., Tybee Island* ☎ *912/786–7515* ⊟ *AE, D, DC, MC, V* ⊘ *Closed Sun. Nov.–Apr.*

$$–$$$$ ✗**Olde Pink House.** This pink-brick Georgian mansion was built in 1771 for James Habersham, one of the wealthiest Americans of his time, and the old-time atmosphere comes through in the original Georgia pine floors of the tavern, the Venetian chandeliers, and the 18th-century English antiques. The she-crab soup with sherry is a light but flavorful version of a Lowcountry specialty. Regional ingredients find their way into many of the dishes, including the black grouper stuffed with blue crab and served with a Vidalia onion sauce. ⊠ *23 Abercorn St., Historic District* ☎ *912/232–4286* ⊟ *AE, MC, V* ⊘ *No lunch.*

$$–$$$ ✗**Firefly Cafe.** Chef and owner Sharon Stinogel offers a fresh twist on Southern fare at this upbeat neighborhood spot, on the corner of Troup Square, in a cozy residential area. The menu has something for everyone, including vegetarians and vegans, and offers a myriad of salads with intrigu-

ing dressings (the lemon chicken is especially good), as well as flavorful pork chops with garlic mashed potatoes. The outdoor tables are often taken by couples with their dogs in tow—perhaps that's because of the homemade dog biscuits. ✉*321 Habersham St.* ☎*912/234–1971* ═*MC, V* ⊘*Closed Mon. No dinner Sun.*

$$–$$$ ✕**Johnny Harris.** What started as a small roadside stand in 1924, across from Grayson Stadium, has grown into one of the city's beloved mainstays, with a menu that includes Brunswick stew, steaks, fried chicken, seafood, and meats spiced with the restaurant's famous tomato-and-mustard sauces. The hickory smoked barbecue pork is a treat, and their sauces are now so famous that they bottle them for take-home and shipping. ■**TIP➔Originally, the booths had doors and catered to business and romantic tête-à-têtes. The privacy doors have long gone though the old service bell's still there, and they're still the most comfortable seats in the house.** ✉*1651 E. Victory Dr., Eastside* ☎*912/354–7810* ═*AE, D, DC, MC, V* ⊘*Closed Sun.*

$$–$$$ ✕**Soho South Cafe.**Get set to have your palate treated to a palette of sensory delights in this restaurant cum art gallery cum coffee shop cum bakery cum library. If you do have to wait for a table, the time passes by quickly with so much to absorb. The food is great: from Mom's meat loaf sandwich and a portobello "pizza" to jumbo lump crab cakes. If nothing else, try the signature tomato-basil bisque. ✉*12 W. Liberty St.* ☎*912/233–1633* ⌖*Reservations not accepted* ═*MC, V* ⊘*Closed Mon. No dinner Sun.*

$–$$$ ✕**Bella's Italian Café.** From its unpretentious spot in a Mid-
★ town shopping center, Bella's serves up simple, wildly popular fare, including scampi, ziti, pizza, and panini as well as a particularly good manicotti. Desserts are also standout versions of classics, such as Italian wedding cake, tiramisu, and cannoli. The genial, hospitable service makes this a perfect place to relax over a glass of wine. ✉*4408 Habersham St., Midtown* ☎*912/354–4005* ⌖*Reservations not accepted* ═*AE, D, DC, MC, V* ⊘*No lunch weekends.*

$–$$$ ✕**Toucan Café.** This colorful café is well worth a trip a bit
★ off the beaten path to Savannah's Southside. It's a favorite for Savannahians entertaining out-of-town visitors; no one, it seems, leaves unsatisfied. The menu defines the term "eclectic," with plenty of appealing options for both vegetarians and meat eaters, including wasabi pea–encrusted tuna, tempura portobello, black-bean burgers, spanako-

pita, Jamaican jerk chicken, and rib-eye steaks. ⊠*531 Stephenson Ave., Southside* ☎*912/352–2233* ⊟*AE, D, MC, V* ⊘*Closed Sun. and Mon.*

$$ ✕**Mrs. Wilkes' Dining Room.** Folks line up for an orgy of fine
★ Southern fare, served family-style at big tables. For breakfast there are eggs, sausage, piping-hot biscuits, and grits. At lunch try fried or roast chicken, beef stew, collard greens, okra, mashed potatoes, and corn bread. Mrs. Wilkes made this place somewhat of a legend, and her granddaughter and great-grandson are keeping it a family affair in more ways than one. Menus are a set price; kids under age eight eat for half price. ⊠*107 W. Jones St., Historic District* ☎*912/232–5997* ⚐*Reservations not accepted* ⊟*No credit cards* ⊘*Closed Jan. and weekends. No dinner.*

WHERE TO STAY

Although Savannah has its share of chain hotels and motels, the city's most distinctive lodgings are the more than two dozen historic inns, guesthouses, and B&Bs gracing the Historic District.

If the term *historic inn* brings to mind images of roughing it in shabby-genteel mansions with antiquated plumbing, you're in for a surprise. Most of these inns are in mansions with the requisite high ceilings, spacious rooms, and ornate carved millwork. And most do have canopy, four-poster, or Victorian brass beds. But amid all the antique surroundings, there's modern luxury: enormous baths, many with whirlpools or hot tubs; film libraries for in-room VCRs; and turndown service with a chocolate, a praline, even a discreet brandy on your nightstand. Continental breakfast and afternoon refreshments are often included in the rate. Special seasons and holidays, such as St. Patrick's Day, push prices up a bit. On the other hand, weekdays and the off-season can yield excellent bargains.

WHAT IT COSTS				
HOTELS				
$$$$	$$$	$$	$	¢
over $220	$161– $220	$111– $160	$70– $110	under $70

Hotel prices are for two people in a standard double room in high season.

INNS & GUESTHOUSES

$$$$ ⓣ**Foley House Inn.** Two town houses, built 50 years apart,
★ form this elegant inn. Most rooms have king-size beds,
and all have fireplaces and reproduction antique furnishings; four rooms have whirlpool tubs; three have balconies. A carriage house to the rear of the property has
less expensive rooms. ⊠ *14 W. Hull St., Historic District,
31401* ☎ *912/232–6622 or 800/647–3708* ☐ *912/231–
1218* ⊕ *www.foleyinn.com* ⇆ *17 rooms, 2 suites* ⚄ *In-
room: VCR* ⊟ *AE, MC, V* ⏍ *BP.*

$$$$ ⓣ**Gastonian.** The entire inn, built in 1868, underwent an
★ extensive remodeling in 2005. Guest rooms are lavishly
decorated with antiques from the Georgian and Regency
periods; all have fireplaces and most have whirlpool tubs.
The Caracalla Suite is named for the oversize whirlpool tub
built in front of the fireplace. At breakfast you can find such
specialty items as lemon cheese or ginger pancakes. Afternoon tea, evening cordials, and complimentary wine are
other treats. ⊠ *220 E. Gaston St., Historic District, 31401*
☎ *912/232–2869 or 800/322–6603* ☐ *912/232–0710*
⊕ *www.gastonian.com* ⇆ *14 rooms, 3 suites* ⚄ *In-room
DVD. In-hotel: public Wi-Fi* ⊟ *AE, D, MC, V* ⏍ *BP.*

$$$$ ⓣ**Kehoe House.** A fabulously appointed 1890s B&B, the
Victorian Kehoe House has brass-and-marble chandeliers,
a courtyard garden, and a music room. Guest rooms have
a modern Victorian feel with a mix of antiques and modern linens. On the main floor a double parlor holds two
fireplaces and sweeps the eye upward with its 14-foot ceilings, creating an elegant setting for a beautifully served full
breakfast. Rates include access to the Downtown Athletic
Club. A charming glass armoire displays Victorian and
one-of-a-kind artisan jewelry for sale. ⊠ *123 Habersham
St., Historic District, 31401* ☎ *912/232–1020 or 800/820–
1020* ☐ *912/231–0208* ⊕ *www.kehoehouse.com* ⇆ *13
rooms* ⚄ *In-room: DVD. In-hotel: public Wi-Fi* ⊟ *AE, D,
DC, MC, V* ⏍ *BP.*

$$$–$$$$ ⓣ**Ballastone Inn.** This sumptuous inn occupies an 1838 man-
★ sion that once served as a bordello. Rooms are handsomely
furnished, with luxurious linens on canopy beds, antiques
and fine reproductions, and a collection of original framed
prints from *Harper's* scattered throughout. On the garden
level rooms are small and cozy, with exposed brick walls,
beam ceilings, and, in some cases, windows at eye level
with the lush courtyard. Most rooms have working gas

fireplaces, and three have whirlpool tubs. ■TIP→**Afternoon tea and free passes to a nearby health club are included.** ⊠*14 E. Oglethorpe Ave., Historic District, 31401* ☎*912/236–1484 or 800/822–4553* 🖷*912/236–4626* ⊕*www.ballastone.com* ↪*16 rooms, 3 suites* ⚫*In-room VCR. In-hotel: bicycles* ▭*AE, MC, V* ⊚*BP.*

$$$–$$$$ ⊡**Eliza Thompson House.** Eliza Thompson was a socially prominent widow when she built her fine town house around 1847; today the lovely Victorian edifice is one of the oldest B&Bs in Savannah. A peaceful garden courtyard provides a quiet respite. The rooms are luxuriously decorated with marble baths, rare antiques, plush bedding, and other designer accents. A full breakfast, afternoon wine and cheese, and evening desserts are served in the parlor or on the patio, which has a fine Ivan Bailey sculpture. ⊠*5 W. Jones St., Historic District, 31401* ☎*912/236–3620 or 800/348–9378* 🖷*912/238–1920* ⊕*www.elizathompsonhouse.com* ↪*25 rooms* ⚫*In-hotel: public Wi-Fi* ▭*MC, V* ⊚*BP.*

$$$–$$$$ ⊡**The President's Quarters.** You'll be impressed even before
★ you enter this lovely inn, which has an exterior courtyard so beautiful and inviting it has become a popular wedding-reception spot. Each room in this classic Savannah inn, fashioned out of a pair of meticulously restored 1860s town houses, is named for an American president. Some rooms have four-poster beds, working fireplaces, and private balconies. Expect to be greeted with wine and fruit, and a complimentary afternoon tea will tempt you with sweet cakes. Turndown service includes a glass of port or sherry. There are also rooms in an adjacent town house. Breakfast is served in the adjoining 17 Hundred 90 restaurant. ■TIP→**Room 204 is said to be haunted by a lady with a broken heart.** ⊠*225 E. President St., Historic District, 31401* ☎*912/233–1600 or 800/233–1776* 🖷*912/238–0849* ⊕*www.presidentsquarters.com* ↪*11 rooms, 8 suites* ⚫*In-room: DVD. In-hotel: public Wi-Fi* ▭*D, DC, MC, V* ⊚*BP.*

$$–$$$ ⊡**Bed & Breakfast Inn.** So called, the owner claims, because it was the first such property to open in Savannah almost 30 years ago, the inn is a restored 1853 federal-style row house on historic Gordon Row near Chatham Square. The courtyard garden is a lovely cluster of potted tropical flowers surrounding an inviting koi pond. All rooms have private baths and retain many elements of the home's original

1

charm, such as beamed ceilings and exposed-brick walls. There are four self-contained cottages, and some rooms also have kitchens. Afternoon pastries, lemonade, coffee, and tea are served. ⊠*117 W. Gordon St., Historic District, 31401* ☎*912/238–0518* 🖷*912/233–2537* ⊕*www.savannahbnb. com* ⬩*14 rooms, 2 suites, 4 cottages* ✧*In-room: some kitchens* ⊟*AE, D, MC, V* ⦿*BP.*

$$–$$$ 🏠**Green Palm Inn.** This inn is a pleasing little discovery.
★ Originally built in 1897 but renovated top to bottom, it's now a delightful B&B. The elegant furnishings of the cottage-style rooms were inspired by Savannah's British-colonial heritage. All rooms have fireplaces and a couple even have fireplaces in the bathrooms. Breakfasts are generous and served with style, and in the evening, you'll be treated to homemade desserts. ⊠*548 E. President St., Historic District, 31401* ☎*912/447–8901 or 888/606–9510* 🖷*912/236–4626* ⊕*www.greenpalminn.com* ⬩*4 suites* ⊟*AE, MC, V* ⦿*BP.*

$$–$$$ 🏠**17th Street Inn.** You're steps from the beach at this Tybee Island inn dating from 1920. The front deck, adorned with plants, palms, and swings, is a gathering place where you can chat, sip wine, and enjoy breakfast. The inn's rooms each offer a queen bed, efficiency kitchen, private bath, and private entrance. A Continental breakfast is served each morning. A self-catering, two-bedroom condo next door sleeps six. ⊠*12 17th St., Box 114, Tybee Island, 31328* ☎*912/786–0607 or 888/909–0607* 🖷*912/786–0602* ⊕*www.tybeeinn.com* ⬩*8 rooms, 1 condo* ✧*In-room: some kitchens. In-hotel: public Wi-Fi* ⊟*AE, D, MC, V* ⦿*CP.*

HOTELS & MOTELS

$$$$ 🏠**Mansion on Forsyth Park.** Sophisticated, chic, and artsy only begin to describe this Kessler property, which was purposely built to blend with its historic surroundings. Sitting on the edge of Forsyth Park, its dramatic design, opulent interiors, and magnificently diverse collection of art creates a one-of-a-kind experience. Every turn delivers something unexpected—a canopied patio by the pool that feels like it's out of *Arabian Nights*; a Nordic-looking full-service spa; back-lighted onyx panels and 100-year-old Italian Corona–marble pillars. The 700 Drayton Restaurant offers fine dining and very attentive service. Upstairs, Casimir's Lounge, with live piano and jazz, is one of the city's hot spots.

✉*700 Drayton St., 31401* ☎*912/238–5158 or 888/711–5114* 🖷*912/238–5146* ⊕*www.mansiononforsythpark.com* ⚬*126 rooms* ⚐*In-hotel: restaurant, bar, spa, no smoking rooms* ▤*AE, D, DC, MC, V.*

\$\$\$–\$\$\$\$ 🏨**Hyatt Regency Savannah.** You definitely won't get the feel of old Savannah here, despite the location in the Historic District: the seven-story structure, built in 1981, has marble floors, a towering atrium, and glass elevators. Rooms have balconies overlooking either the atrium or the Savannah River. The Vu Lounge is an appealing spot to have a drink and watch the river traffic drift by. Windows Chophouse, the hotel's restaurant, serves a fine pasta and salad buffet on weekdays and specializes in steak and seafood in the evening. ✉*2 W. Bay St., Historic District, 31401* ☎*912/238–1234 or 800/233–1234* 🖷*912/944–3673* ⊕*www.savannah.hyatt.com* ⚬*325 rooms, 22 suites* ⚐*In-room: Wi-Fi. In-hotel: restaurant, bar, pool, gym, public Wi-Fi* ▤*AE, D, MC, V* ⦿*EP.*

\$\$\$–\$\$\$\$ 🏨**River Street Inn.** The interior of this 1817 converted warehouse is so lavish that it's hard to believe the five-story building once stood vacant in a state of disrepair. Today the 86 guest rooms are filled with antiques and reproductions from the era of King Cotton. French-style balconies overlook both River Street and Bay Street. One floor has charming souvenir and gift shops, and the elevator takes you directly down to the buzz and activity of the waterfront. ✉*124 E. Bay St., Historic District, 31401* ☎*912/234–6400 or 800/253–4229* 🖷*912/234–1478* ⊕*www.riverstreetinn.com* ⚬*86 rooms* ⚐*In-room: dial-up. In-hotel: 2 restaurants, bars, gym, public Wi-Fi* ▤*AE, D, DC, MC, V* ⦿*EP.*

\$\$–\$\$\$\$ 🏨**Mulberry Inn.** This 1860s livery stable later became a ★ cotton warehouse and then a Coca-Cola bottling plant. Gleaming heart-pine floors and antiques, including a handsome English grandfather clock and an exquisitely carved Victorian mantel, make it unique. The pianist hitting the keyboard of a baby grand every afternoon adds to the elegant flair. The café is a notch nicer than most other Holiday Inn restaurants. An executive wing, at the back of the hotel, is geared to business travelers. ✉*601 E. Bay St., Historic District, 31401* ☎*912/238–1200 or 877/468–1200* 🖷*912/236–2184* ⊕*www.savannahhotel.com* ⚬*145 rooms, 24 suites* ⚐*In-room: VCR, dial-up. In-*

hotel: restaurant, bar, pool, gym, public Wi-Fi ▭*AE, D, DC, MC, V* ⦿*EP.*

$$$ ⊞**Marshall House.** This restored hotel, with original pine floors, woodwork, and brick, caters to business travelers while providing the intimacy of a B&B. Different spaces reflect different parts of Savannah's history, from its founding to the Civil War. Artwork is mostly by local artists. Guests get free passes to a downtown health club. ⊠*123 E. Broughton St., Historic District, 31401* ☎*912/644–7896 or 800/589–6304* ☎*912/234–3334* ⊕*www.marshallhouse. com* ⌁*65 rooms, 3 suites* ⟟*In-hotel: restaurant, bar* ▭*AE, D, MC, V* ⦿*EP.*

$$–$$$ ⊞**Planters Inn.** Formerly the John Wesley Hotel, this inn is
★ housed in a structure built in 1812, and though it retains the regal tone of that golden age, it still offers all the intimate comforts you would expect from an upscale inn. The inn's 60 guest rooms are all decorated in the finest fabrics and Baker furnishings (a 1920s design named for the Dutch immigrant cabinetmaker). ∎**TIP→According to lore, a (good) ghost inhabits the hotel, floating through the hallways and straightening skewed paintings hanging in the hallway.** ⊠*29 Abercorn St., Historic District, 31401* ☎*912/232–5678* ☎*912/236–2184* ⊕*www.plantersinnsavannah.com* ⌁*60 rooms* ▭*AE, D, DC, MC, V* ⦿*EP.*

NIGHTLIFE & THE ARTS

Savannah's nightlife reflects the city's laid-back personality. Some clubs have live reggae, hard rock, and other contemporary music, but most stick to traditional blues, jazz, and piano-bar vocalists. After-dark merrymakers usually head for watering holes on Riverfront Plaza or the south side.

BARS & NIGHTCLUBS

The **Bar Bar** (⊠*219 W. St. Julian St., Historic District* ☎*912/231–1910*), a neighborhood hangout, has pool tables, games, and a varied beer selection. Once a month at **Club One Jefferson** (⊠*1 Jefferson St., Historic District* ☎*912/232–0200*), a gay bar, the Lady Chablis bumps and grinds her way down the catwalk, lip-synching disco tunes in a shimmer of sequin and satin gowns; the cover is $5. **Kevin Barry's Irish Pub** (⊠*114 W. River St., Historic District* ☎*912/233–9626*) has a friendly vibe, a full menu until

1 AM, and traditional Irish music seven days a week. It's *the* place to be on St. Patrick's Day. The rest of the year there's a mix of tourists and locals of all ages. **Savannah Smiles** (⊠*314 Williamson St., Historic District* ☎*912/527–6453*) is a dueling piano saloon in which the battles heat up the humor. The place promises good fun—though perhaps not for the prudish.

SAVANNAH SOUL Planters Tavern (⊠ *23 Abercorn St., Historic District* ☎*912/232–4286*), in the basement of the Olde Pink House, is one of Savannah's most romantic late-night spots for a martini serenade. Pianist, vocalist, and composer Gail Thurmond has been a fixture here since 1993 and her vast repertoire includes interpretations of favorites from Gershwin, Porter, Ellington, Mercer, Billie Holiday, Ella Fitzgerald, Lena Horne, and others. You name it, and she'll be able to play it.

COFFEEHOUSES

Thanks to a substantial student population, the city has sprouted coffeehouses as if they were spring flowers. Tearooms also abound and seem fitting in a city with so many English influences. The **Express** (⊠*39 Barnard St., Historic District* ☎*912/233–4683*) is a warm, unassuming bakery and café that serves specialty coffees along with decadent desserts and tasty snacks. **Gallery Espresso** (⊠*234 Bull St., Historic District* ☎*912/233–5348*) is a combined coffee haunt and art enclave, with gallery shows and free Internet access to customers. It stays open until 10 PM. For traditional afternoon high tea, you can't beat the lavishly outfitted **Gryphon Tea Room** (⊠*337 Bull St., Historic District* ☎*912/525–5880*) with its expansive range of teas, from English breakfast to Apricot Arabesque to Black Dragon Choicest Oolong. The tearoom also serves specialty coffees alongside a full menu of scones, baklava, biscotti, and healthier salads and sandwiches. The **Tea Room** (⊠*7 E. Broughton St, Historic District* ☎*912/239–9690*) serves a formal afternoon tea, by reservation, daily at 2:30.

JAZZ & BLUES CLUBS

Bayou Café and Blues Bar (⊠*14 N. Abercorn St., at River St., Historic District* ☎*912/233–6411*) has acoustic music during the week and the Bayou Blues Band on the weekend. There's also Cajun food. **Café Loco** (⊠*1 Old Hwy. 80,*

Tybee Island ☎*912/786–7810*), a few miles outside Savannah, looks like a shack of a place from the outside, but showcases local blues and acoustic acts that make it well worth the trip. **Jazz'd Tapas Bar** (✉*52 Barnard St., Historic District* ☎*912/236–7777*), is a chic basement venue. Gourmet grazing is the vogue and a range of local jazz artists are featured Tuesday through Saturday.

MUSIC FESTIVALS

For four days in October, the free **Savannah Folk Music Festival** (⊕*www.savannahfolk.org*) becomes the city's main musical attraction. The **Savannah Jazz Festival** (⊕*www.savannahjazzfestival.org*) is a free event held each September in Forsyth Park featuring artists from around the region.

NONSTOP MUSIC Georgia's largest and most acclaimed music festival, the **Savannah Music Festival** (⊕*www.savannahmusicfestival.org*) begins on infamous St. Patrick's Day weekend and runs for 18 days, with four to six performances daily at some 20 downtown venues. The music ranges from foot-stomping gospel to mournful blues to frenetic Cajun zydeco.

SHOPPING

Find your own Lowcountry treasures among a bevy of handcrafted wares—handmade quilts and baskets; wreaths made from Chinese tallow trees and Spanish moss; preserves, jams, and jellies. The favorite Savannah snack, and a popular gift item, is the benne wafer. It's about the size of a quarter and comes in different flavors. Savannah has a wide collection of colorful businesses—revitalization is no longer a goal but an accomplishment. Antiques malls and junk emporiums beckon you with their colorful storefronts and eclectic offerings, as do the many specialty shops and bookstores clustered along the moss-embossed streets.

SHOPPING DISTRICTS

City Market (✉*W. St. Julian St. between Ellis and Franklin sqs., Historic District*) takes its origins from a farmers' market back in 1755. Today it's a four-block emporium in the middle of a renaissance program, and an eclectic mix of artists' studios, sidewalk cafés, jazz haunts, shops, and art galleries. **Riverfront Plaza/River Street** (⊠*Historic District*) is nine blocks of renovated waterfront warehouses (once the city's cotton exchange) where more than 75 boutiques, galleries, restaurants, and pubs deliver everything from popcorn to pottery, and even voodoo spells! Leave your stilettos at home or you'll find the street's cobblestones hard work.

PARK & SAVE Drivers be warned: Savannah patrollers are quick to dole out parking tickets. Tourists may purchase two-day parking passes ($8) at the Savannah Visitors Center and at some hotels and inns. Passes are valid in metered spots as well as in the city's lots and garages; they allow parkers to exceed the time limit in time-limit zones.

SPECIALTY SHOPS

ANTIQUES

Arthur Smith Antiques (⊠*402 Bull St., Historic District* ☎*912/236–9701*) has four floors showcasing 18th- and 19th-century European furniture, porcelain, rugs, and paintings. Near beautiful Monterey Square, the store is both a good destination shop and worth a detour while exploring the neighborhood.

ART GALLERIES

Compass Prints, Inc./Ray Ellis Gallery (⊠*205 W. Congress St., Historic District* ☎*912/234–3537*) sells original artwork, prints, and books by internationally acclaimed artist Ray Ellis. **Gallery Espresso** (⊠*6 E. Liberty St., Historic District* ☎*912/233–5348*) has a new show every two weeks focusing on work by local artists. A true coffeehouse, it stays open until the wee hours. **Gallery 209** (⊠*209 E. River St., Historic District* ☎*912/236–4583*) is a co-op gallery, with paintings, watercolors, pottery, jewelry, batik, stained glass, weavings, and sculptures by local artists. **Savannah College of Art and Design (SCAD)** (⊠*516 Abercorn St., Historic District* ☎*912/525–5200*), a private art college, has restored at least 40 historic buildings in the city, including 12 galleries. Work by faculty and students is often for sale, and touring exhibitions are frequently in the on-campus galleries. Stop by Exhibit A, Pinnacle Gallery, and the West Bank Gallery, and ask about other student galleries. Garden for the Arts has an amphitheater and shows performance art.

BENNE WAFERS

Byrd Cookie Company & Gourmet Marketplace (⊠*6700 Waters Ave., Highland Park* ☎*912/355–1716*), founded in 1924, sells picture tins of Savannah and gourmet foodstuffs such as condiments and dressings. It's the best place to get benne wafers, "the seed of good luck" and trademark Savannah cookies, which are also sold in numerous gift shops around town.

BOOKS

E. Shaver Booksellers (⊠*326 Bull St., Historic District* ☎*912/234–7257*) is the source for 17th- and 18th-century maps and new books on regional subjects; the shop occupies 12 rooms. **"The Book" Gift Shop** (⊠*127 E. Gordon St., Historic District* ☎*912/233–3867*) sells all things related to *Midnight in the Garden of Good and Evil,* including souvenirs and author-autographed copies. **V. & J. Duncan** (⊠*12 E. Taylor St., Historic District* ☎*912/232–0338*) specializes in antique maps, prints, and books.

SAVANNAH ESSENTIALS

TRANSPORTATION

BY AIR

Savannah is served by AirTran Airways, Continental Express, Northwest Airlink, Delta, Independence Air, United Express, and US Airways/Express for domestic flights.

Savannah/Hilton Head International Airport is 18 mi west of downtown. Despite the name, international flights are nonexistent. The foreign trade zone, a locus for importing, constitutes the "international" aspect.

Airport Information **Savannah/Hilton Head International Airport** (⊠*400 Airways Ave., West Chatham* ☎*912/964–0514* ⊕*www. savannahairport.com*).

BY BOAT & FERRY

On the Savannah River, the Port of Savannah is the busiest port from New Orleans to New York. Belles Ferry provides a regular service from the City Hall dock in the Historic District to the Westin Savannah Harbor Golf Resort & Spa at the Convention Center, on Hutchinson Island. Ferries are part of the transit system and run daily 7 AM to 11 PM with departures every 10 to 15 minutes. The crossing takes two minutes and costs $1 round-trip (in exact change). Guests staying in the convention district ride for free.

Contact Belles Ferry (✉ *900 E. Gwinnett St.* ☎ *912/233–5767* ⊕ *www.catchacat.org*).

BY BUS

Chatham Area Transit (CAT) operates buses in Savannah and Chatham County Monday through Saturday from 6 AM to 11 PM, Sunday from 9 to 7. Some lines may stop running earlier or may not run on Sunday. The CAT Shuttle operates throughout the Historic District and is free. For other Savannah buses, the fare is $1. Savannah and Brunswick are the coastal stops for Greyhound Bus.

Contacts Chatham Area Transit (☎ *912/233–5767* ⊕ *www. catchacat.org*). **Greyhound/Trailways** (✉ *610 W. Oglethorpe Ave., Downtown* ☎ *912/232–2135 or 800/231–2222* ⊕ *www.greyhound. com*).

BY CAR

Interstate 95 slices north–south along the eastern seaboard, intersecting 10 mi west of town with east–west Interstate 16, which dead-ends in downtown Savannah. U.S. 17, the Coastal Highway, also runs north–south through town. U.S. 80, which connects the Atlantic to the Pacific, is another east–west route through Savannah.

BY TAXI

AAA Adam Cab Co. is a reliable 24-hour taxi service. Calling ahead for reservations could yield a flat rate. Yellow Cab Company is another dependable taxi service. Standard taxi fare is $1.50 a mile. The standard flat rate between Savannah's Historic District and the airport is $25, which can rise to as much as $38 if you're staying in Savannah's South Side.

Contacts AAA Adam Cab Incorporated (☎ *912/927–7466*). **Yellow Cab Company** (☎ *912/236–1133*).

BY TRAIN

Amtrak runs its Silver Service/Palmetto route down the East Coast from New York to Miami, stopping in Georgia at Savannah. The station is about 6 mi from downtown.

Contacts Amtrak (☎ *800/872–7245* ⊕ *www.amtrak.com*).

CONTACTS & RESOURCES

BANKS & EXCHANGE SERVICES

Bank of America and other major financial outlets have branches in Savannah; most operate normal office hours weekdays, with half days on Saturday. ATM machines are numerous.

Contacts Bank of America (⊠ *22 Bull St., Historic District* ☎ *912/651–8250*). **Trust Company Bank** (⊠ *702 W. Oglethorpe Ave., Historic District* ☎ *912/944–1072*).

EMERGENCIES

Candler Hospital and Memorial Health University Medical Center are the area hospitals with 24-hour emergency rooms.

Emergency Services Ambulance, police (☎ *911*).

Hospitals Candler Hospital (⊠ *5353 Reynolds St., Kensington Park* ☎ *912/692–6000*). **Memorial Health University Medical Center** (⊠ *4700 Waters Ave., Fairfield* ☎ *912/350–8000*).

24-Hour Pharmacies CVS Pharmacy (⊠ *Medical Arts Shopping Center, 4725 Waters Ave., Fairfield* ☎ *912/355–7111*).

INTERNET, MAIL & SHIPPING

Savannah provides free wireless services and most hotels and inns offer complimentary access to the Internet. Consequently, although there are some cafés such as Café Espresso that provide customers with access to terminals, such establishments are getting few and far between. The Live Oak Public Library offers free Internet access on a first-come, first-served basis. The main branch is open 9 to 9 weekdays; 9 to 6 Saturday, and 2 to 6 on Sunday. Postal services in the Historic District include an outlet at Telfair Square. There's also a handy UPS Store in the heart of downtown at W. Bryan and Bull streets.

Contacts Gallery Espresso (⊠ *234 Bull St., Historic District* ☎ *912/233–5348*). **Live Oak Public Libary** (⊠ *2002 Bull St., Savannah* ☎ *912/652–3600*). **UPS Store** (⊠ *22 W. Bryan St., Savannah* ☎ *912/233–7807*). **U.S. Post Office** (⊠ *118 Barnard St., Savannah* ☎ *912/232–2952*).

MEDIA

Savannah's intriguing socioeconomic profile supports various media from student journals to upscale lifestyle publications. The *Herald* and *Savannah Morning News* are favorites and the *Savannah Magazine* is a nice glossy lifestyle piece that includes listings of various events about town. It publishes bimonthly. *Connect Savannah* is more detailed and youth-oriented, and lists all manner of arts and entertainment with snappy reviews and the lowdown on the current buzz.

Contacts *Connect Savannah* (✉ *1800 E. Victory Dr., Savannah* ☎ *912/233–6128*). **The** *Herald* (✉ *1803 Barnard St., Savannah* ☎ *912/232–4505*). *Savannah Morning News* (✉ *1375 Chatham Pkwy., Savannah* ☎ *912/238–2040*). *Savannah Magazine* (✉ *Box 1088, Savannah* ☎ *912/652–0293*).

TOUR OPTIONS

HISTORIC DISTRICT TOURS

Beach Institute African-American Cultural Center is the headquarters for the Negro Heritage Trail Tour. A knowledgeable guide traces the city's more than 250 years of black history. Tours, which begin at the Savannah Welcome Center, are at 10 and noon and cost $19.

Carriage Tours of Savannah takes you through the Historic District by day or by night at a 19th-century clip-clop pace, with coachmen spinning tales and telling ghost stories along the way. A romantic evening tour in a private carriage costs $85; regular tours are a more modest $20 per person.

Old Town Trolley Tours has narrated 90-minute tours traversing the Historic District. Trolleys stop at 13 designated stops every half hour daily 9 to 4:30; you can hop on and off as you please. The cost is $23.

One of the most fun ways to explore Savannah's history-laden streets is with Kinetic Tours, which offers guided tours on individual electric-propelled Segways (self-balancing, stand-up, two-wheel scooters). Tours are two hours and cost $65. Coastal Scooters has traditional scooters as well as three-wheel "scoot-coupes," which seat two people side-by-side in what looks like a tiny car. They cost $160 for eight hours.

Contacts Beach Institute African-American Cultural Center (☎ *912/234–8000*). **Coastal Scooters** (☎ *912/232–5513*).

Savannah Area Welcome Center (✉ *301 Martin Luther King Blvd., 31401* ☎ *912/944–0455* 🖷 *912/786–5895* ⊕ *www.savannahvisit. com*). **Carriage Tours of Savannah** (☎ *912/236–6756*). **Kinetic Tours** (☎ *912/233–5707*). **Old Town Trolley Tours** (☎ *912/233–0083*).

SPECIAL-INTEREST TOURS

Historic Savannah Foundation, a preservation organization, leads tours of the Historic District and the Lowcountry. Preservation, *Midnight in the Garden of Good and
Evil,* the Golden Isles, group, and private tours are also
available. In addition, the foundation leads specialty excursions to the fishing village of Thunderbolt; the Isle of Hope,
with its stately mansions lining Bluff Drive; the much-pho-
tographed Bonaventure Cemetery, on the banks of the
Wilmington River; and Wormsloe Plantation Site, with its
mile-long avenue of arching oaks. Fees for the specialty
tours start at $75 per hour, with a two-hour minimum for
a private group of up to five people.

Personalized Tours of Savannah is a small company offering upscale and intimate tours of the city, with customized themes covering movies filmed in Savannah, the city's
extraordinary architecture, ghost tours, and a very good
Jewish heritage tour. The owner is a longtime Savannah
resident, and tours are peppered with history, anecdotes,
and insider knowledge. Tours have a two-hour minimum,
are highly individualized, and start at $65 per hour.

Contacts **Historic Savannah Foundation** (☎ *912/234-4088 or
800/627-5030*). **Personalized Tours of Savannah** (☎ *912/234-
0014 or 800/627-5030*).

WALKING TOURS

Much of the downtown Historic District can easily be
explored on foot. Its grid shape makes getting around
a breeze, and you can find any number of places to stop
and rest.

A Ghost Talk Ghost Walk tour should send chills down
your spine during an easy 1-mi jaunt through the old colonial city. Tours, lasting 1½ hours, leave from the middle of
Reynolds Square, at the John Wesley Memorial. Call for
dates, times, and reservations; the cost is $10.

Savannah-by-Foot's Creepy Crawl Haunted Pub Tour is a
favorite. According to the true believers there are so many
ghosts in Savannah they're actually divided into subcat-
egories. On this tour, charismatic guide and storyteller
Greg Proffit specializes in those ghosts that haunt taverns
only, regaling you with tales from secret sub-basements
discovered to house skeletal remains, possessed gum-ball
machines, and animated water faucets. Tours traditionally
depart from the Six Pence Pub, where a ghost named Larry

likes to fling open the bathroom doors, but routes can vary, so call for departure times and locations; the cost is $15.

Contacts A Ghost Talk Ghost Walk Tour (⊠ *Reynolds Sq., Congress and Abercorn Sts., Historic District* ☎ *912/233–3896*). **Savannah-By-Foot's Creepy Crawl Haunted Pub Tour** (☎ *912/238–3843*). **Six Pence Pub** (⊠ *245 Bull St., Historic District* ☎ *912/233–3151*).

VISITOR INFORMATION

The Savannah Area Convention & Visitors Bureau does a grand job in providing quality information. The welcome center is easily accessed from U.S. 17 and Highway 80. It's open daily weekdays 8:30 to 5 and weekends 9 to 5. The center has a useful audiovisual overview of the city and is the starting point for a number of guided tours. For detailed information about Tybee Island, drop by the island's visitor center, just off Highway 80. It's open daily 10 to 6.

Contacts Savannah Area Convention & Visitors Bureau (⊠ *101 E. Bay St., Historic District, 31401* ☎ *912/644–6401 or 877/728–2662* 🖷 *912/944–0468* ⊕ *www.savannahvisit.com*). **Savannah Area Welcome Center** (⊠ *301 Martin Luther King Blvd., 31401* ☎ *912/944–0455* 🖷 *912/786–5895* ⊕ *www.savannahvisit.com*). **Tybee Island Visitor Information Center** (⊠ *Campbell Ave. and Hwy. 80, Tybee Island, 31328* ☎ *912/786–5444 or 800/868–2322* ⊕ *www.tybeevisit.com*).

The Coastal Isles

WORD OF MOUTH

"The day I spent on Cumberland Island was one of the best days I've had in my whole life! (And I'm 46.) Seeing several herds of wild horses, deer, wild turkeys, and miles of wilderness was just incredible. How about walking two miles of beach along the ocean and seeing only four other people? It was unbelievable."

—Postal

Updated
by Eileen
Robinson
Smith

GEORGIA'S COASTAL ISLES ARE A STRING of lush barrier islands meandering down the Atlantic coast from Savannah to the Florida border. Notable for their subtropical beauty and abundant wildlife, the isles also strike a unique balance between some of the wealthiest communities in the country and some of the most jealously protected preserves found anywhere. Until recently large segments of the coast were in private hands, and as a result much of the region remains as it was when the first Europeans set eyes on it 450 years ago. The marshes, wetlands, and waterways teem with birds and other wildlife, and they're ideal for exploring by kayak or canoe. Though the islands have long been a favorite getaway of the rich and famous, they no longer cater only to the well-heeled. There's mounting pressure to develop these wilderness shores and make them even more accessible.

The Golden Isles—St. Simons Island, Sea Island, and Jekyll Island—are the more developed of the coastal isles, although by Georgia law, Jekyll is only able to develop 35% of its land. Little St. Simons Island draws those well-heeled types who like to get away from it all, even if it means roughing it. Sea Island caters primarily to wealthy folks who love exclusivity and their creature comforts. Though it has only a few hundred full-time residents, it has one of the wealthiest zip codes in America. St. Simons Island and Jekyll Island are diverse havens with something for everyone from beach bums to family vacationers to the jacket-and-tie old guard. Except for Little St. Simons, the Golden Isles are connected to the mainland by bridges around Brunswick and are the only coastal isles accessible by car. Little St. Simons, a private island with accommodations for a limited number of overnight guests and day-trippers, is accessible by private launch from the northern end of St. Simons.

Sapelo Island and the Cumberland Island National Seashore can only be reached by ferry from Meridian and St. Marys, respectively. Generally unmarred by development, these remote islands with their near-pristine ecology are alluring for anyone seeking an authentic getaway. Both are excellent for camping, with sites ranging from primitive to (relatively) sophisticated. Noncamping accommodations are limited and require booking well in advance. Miles of untouched beaches, forests of gnarly live oak draped with Spanish moss, swamps and marshlands teeming with birds and wildlife combine to make these islands unique.

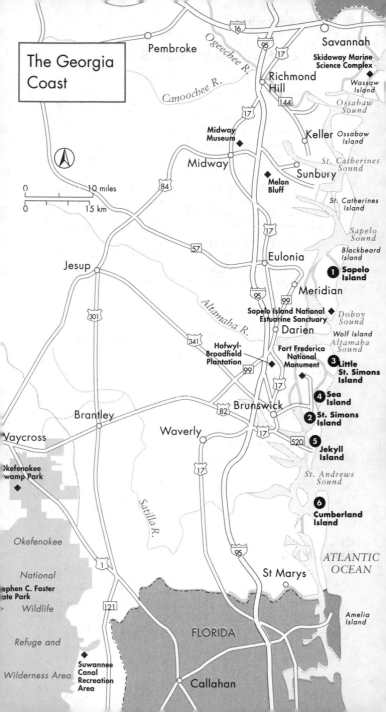

The Georgia Coast

Savannah
Skidaway Marine Science Complex
Pembroke
Richmond Hill
Wassaw Island
Ossabaw Sound
Midway Museum
Keller
Ossabaw Island
Midway
St. Catherines Sound
Melon Bluff
Sunbury
St. Catherines Island
Sapelo Sound
Eulonia
Blackbeard Island
Jesup
1 Sapelo Island
Meridian
Sapelo Island National Estuarine Sanctuary
Doboy Sound
Darien
Wolf Island
Altamaha Sound
Hofwyl-Broadfield Plantation
Fort Frederica National Monument
3 Little St. Simons Island
4 Sea Island
Brunswick
2 St. Simons Island
Brantley
Waverly
5 Jekyll Island
St. Andrews Sound
Waycross
6 Cumberland Island
Okefenokee Swamp Park
Okefenokee
ATLANTIC OCEAN
National
St Marys
Stephen C. Foster State Park
Wildlife
Amelia Island
Refuge and
FLORIDA
Wilderness Area
Suwannee Canal Recreation Area
Callahan

0 — 10 miles
0 — 15 km

Ogeechee R.
Canoochee R.
Altamaha R.
Satilla R.

COASTAL ISLES TOP 5

The Saltwater Marshes: Fringing the coastline, waist-high grasses transform both sunlight and shadow with their lyrical textures and shapes. This landscape inspired Georgia poet Sidney Lanier to describe the marshes as "a silver-wrought garment that clings to and follows the firm sweet limbs of a girl."

Sapelo Island: When land was set aside as an independent state of freed slaves, it became known as Georgia's Black Republic. Vestiges of that community remain at Sapelo, and have made it an island of contrasts—rich in history and ecowilderness, and home to Hog Hammock, a one-of-a-kind community that echoes the culture and practices of its African slave heritage.

The Horses of Cumberland: Cumberland Island is about as far removed from civilization as you can get, and seeing the majesty of these horses run wild across the shore is worth every effort of planning ahead. There are some 200 feral horses, descendants of those that were abandoned by the Spanish in the 1500s.

Jekyll Island Club: Originally the winter retreat of the exceptionally rich, this Millionaire's Village of mansion-size "cottages" is an elegant exposé of how the royalty of corporate America once played. Once an exclusive club, today you can wander around the community at your leisure.

Go for a ride: The level terrain on all the islands makes for great biking, though the most scenic is Jekyll Island. It offers 20 mi of paved bike paths that traverse salt marshes, maritime forest, and beach, as well as the island's National Historic Landmark District.

The best way to visit them is on either public or private guided tours.

EXPLORING THE COASTAL ISLES

Visiting the region is easiest by car, particularly Sapelo Island, because many of the outer reaches of Georgia are remote places with little in the way of transportation options. Touring by bicycle is an option for most of the region, but note that the ferries at Sapelo and Cumberland do not allow bicycles on board.

Coastal Georgia is a complex jigsaw wending its way from the ocean and tidal marshes inland along the intricate network of rivers. U.S. 17, the old coastal highway, gives you a taste of the slower, more rural South. But because of the subtropical climate, the lush forests tend to be dense along the mainland and there are few opportunities to glimpse the broad vistas of salt marsh and islands. To truly appreciate the mystique of Georgia's coastal salt marshes and islands, make the 40-minute ferry crossing from Meridian to Sapelo Island.

ABOUT THE RESTAURANTS

Restaurants range from fish camps—normally rustic dockside affairs connected to marinas where the food is basic but good, plentiful, and reasonably priced—to the more upscale eateries that tend to spawn around the larger towns. A series of restaurants has sprung up in the Golden Isles and Brunswick that are defying the stereotype that equates beach vacations with fast food. And though there's still room for growth, the area now has several menus gaining not only local but nationwide attention. The rising tide of quality has begun to lift all boats.

"Family style" is a dining method you're likely to encounter in this part of the world. It's a traditional, "pass-the-peas-please" approach where diners, both from your group and sometimes others as well, sit together at large tables with courses already set out for you to serve yourself at will.

ABOUT THE HOTELS

Hotels vary, from Victorian mansions to Spanish-style bed-and-breakfasts to some of the most luxurious hotel–spa accommodations found anywhere. Outside the Golden Isles and Brunswick, some towns have only a few places to stay the night, so if you plan on visiting, book as far in advance as possible. Most hotels offer the full range of guest services but, as a matter of philosophy, many B&Bs do not provide televisions or telephones in the rooms. When that's the case, you can find them in the common areas.

Lodging prices quoted here may be much lower during nonpeak seasons, and specials are often available on weekdays in high season.

TIMING

Early spring and late fall are ideal for visiting the coastal isles. By February, temperatures often reach into the 70s, while nights remain cool and even chilly, which keeps the bugs at bay. Because of the high demand to visit these areas before the bugs arrive and after they depart, you should book ferry reservations to Sapelo Island and Cumberland Island National Seashore months in advance in spring and fall: without a reservation, you risk having to wait days for a cancellation. If you plan to stay in the immediate vicinity of St. Marys or Meridian, the docking points for the Cumberland and Sapelo ferries, it's advisable to book rooms well in advance for spring, as accommodations are scarce and the demand is high. The Cumberland Island ferry accepts reservations six months in advance. If you go during the warmer months, always remember to bring water because these areas generally offer minimal services.

By May, deerflies and mosquitoes swarm the coast and islands in abundance. Don't underestimate their impact: during peak times in some areas they are so thick they sound like hail hitting your car. And though many localities spray, it's imperative to have a good repellent handy, especially when traveling to outlying areas. Despite the subtropical heat and humidity, summer is busy and you can count on crowds flocking to the beaches, so you'll want to make reservations at least a couple of months in advance. The season lasts until Labor Day, but you can still count on many travelers making weekend getaways until October or late November, when the weather begins to turn cooler. Hurricane season officially runs from June through the end of November, but August and September are typically the peak months.

WHAT IT COSTS				
RESTAURANTS				
$$$$	$$$	$$	$	¢
over $22	$17–$22	$12–$16	$7–$11	under $7
HOTELS				
over $220	$161–$220	$111–$160	$70–$110	under $70

Restaurant prices are for a main course at dinner. Hotel prices are for two people in a standard double room in high season.

SAPELO ISLAND

🌑 8 mi northeast of Darien.

The fourth largest of Georgia's coastal isles—and bigger than Bermuda—Sapelo Island is a unique community in North America. It still bears evidence of the early-Paleo-Indians who lived here some 4,500 years ago, and is home to the Geechee, direct descendants of African slaves who speak a creole of English and various African languages. This rapidly dwindling community maintains many traditional African practices, including the making of sweetgrass baskets and the use of herbal medicines made from recipes passed down for generations. It's also a nearly pristine barrier island with miles of undeveloped beaches and abundant wildlife. To take the 40-minute ferry ride from Meridian on the mainland through the expanse of salt marshes to Sapelo Island is to enter a world seemingly forgotten by time.

You can explore many historical periods and natural environments here, but facilities on the island are limited. Note that you can't simply walk up to the dock and catch the ferry—you need to have a reservation for a tour, a campsite, or one of the island's lodgings (or have prearranged plans to stay with island residents). Bring insect repellent, especially in summer, and leave your pets at home. You can rent a bicycle on the island, but you cannot bring a bicycle on the ferry.

Start your visit at the **Sapelo Island Visitor Center** in Meridian on the mainland near the Sapelo Island ferry docks. Here you can see exhibits on the island's history, culture, and ecology, and you can purchase tickets for a round-trip ferry ride and bus tour of the island. The sights that make up the bus tour vary depending on the day of the week but always included are the marsh, the sand-dune ecosystem, and the wildlife management area. On Friday and Saturday the tour includes the 80-foot **Sapelo Lighthouse,** built in 1820, a symbol of the cotton and lumber industry once based out of Darien, a prominent shipping center of the time. To see the island's **Reynolds Mansion,** schedule your tour for Wednesday or Saturday. To get to the visitor center and Meridian Ferry Dock from downtown Darien, go north on Route 99 for 8 mi, following signs for the Sapelo Island National Estuarine Research Reserve. Turn right onto Landing Road at the Elm Grove Baptist Church in

Meridian. The visitor center is about ½ mi down the road. ⊠*Rte. 1, Box 1500, Meridian* ☎*912/437–3224, 912/485–2300 for group tours, 912/485–2299 for camping reservations* ⊕*www.sapelonerr.org.*

Hog Hammock Community is one the few remaining sites on the south Atlantic coast where ethnic African-American culture from the slave era has been preserved. The "Salt Water Geechee," Georgia's sea island equivalent to the Gullah, are descendants of slaves who worked the island's plantations during the 19th century. Hog Hammock's 40 residents are the last members of a disappearing culture with its own distinct language and customs. **The Spirit of Sapelo Tours** (✑*Box 7, Sapelo Island, 31327* ☎*912/485–2170*) provides private guided bus tours led by an island native who discusses island life, culture, and history. **Sapelo Culture Day** (☎*912/485–2197* ⊕*www.sapeloislandgeorgia.org*), a celebration of Geechee folklore, music, food, handcrafts, and art takes place in Hog Hammock every year on the third weekend in October. Reservations are required.

OFF THE BEATEN PATH **Colonial Coast Birding Trail.** Georgia's vast network of rivers, marshes, and barrier islands provides ideal habitat for hundreds of species of birds, from nesting wood storks to red painted buntings. This "trail" is a string of 18 sites along the coast from the border of South Carolina to Florida, straddling U.S. 17 and Interstate 95. Several have been designated Important Birding Areas (IBAs) by the Georgia Audubon Society. With more than 330 species of birds to watch for, the staffs of visitor centers along the way have maps and plenty of bird-watching suggestions for both skilled and novice birders. ☎*478/994–1438* ⊕*georgiawildlife.dnr.state.ga.us.*

SPORTS & THE OUTDOORS

CANOEING & KAYAKING

The Altamaha River, the largest undammed river on the East Coast, runs inland from near Darien. You can take expeditions along it with **Altamaha Coastal Adventures** (⊠*112 Witcher Rd., Carlton* ☎*912/437–6010*), which rents equipment and conducts guided trips from the waterfront in Darien. With them you can explore tidal swamps, marshlands, and Queen and Sapelo islands.

CLOSE UP

The Nile of the East Coast

The Altamaha River is a national treasure. Formed by the confluence of the Ocmulgee and Oconee rivers near Hazelhurst, it's the longest undammed river and the second largest watershed in the eastern United States, covering almost 15,000 square mi. After running its 137-mi course, it spills into the Altamaha Sound, between Sapelo Island and Little St. Simons, at a rate of 100,000 gallons every second, or more than 3 trillion gallons a year—a flow comparable to Egypt's Nile.

The Altamaha's greatest value lies in the 170,000 acres of river swamps that shoulder the length of its course, serving as refuge to at least 130 endangered plants and animals, including several freshwater mussels found nowhere else in the world. The swamps are also incubators for life-giving organic matter such as leaves, twigs, and other detritus. Spring floods flush this matter downstream, where it's trapped by the salt marshes that stretch between the mouth of the river and Georgia's barrier islands. This natural fertilizer feeds marsh grasses, which in turn feed fungi and phytoplankton, and so on up the food chain.

2

WHERE TO STAY & EAT

$$–$$$ ✕**Mudcat Charlie's.** This tabby-and-wood restaurant on the
★ Altamaha River sits right in the middle of the Two Way Fish Camp and is a favorite haunt of locals from nearby Darien. The restaurant overlooks the boats moored in the marina, and the seafood is local. Crab stew, fried oysters, and shrimp are the specialties, and the peach and apple pies are made in-house. It's 1 mi south of Darien on U.S. 17, just after the third bridge. Look for the Two Way Fish Camp sign. ✉ *250 Ricefield Way* ☎ *912/261–0055* ▭ *AE, D, MC, V.*

$–$$$ ✕**Skipper's Fish Camp.** You can find this upscale take on
★ the fish camp theme at the foot of Skipper's dock on the Darien River, where the working shrimp boats moor. It has a beautiful courtyard pond that uses water from the river and an open-air oyster bar. Popular menu items include Georgia white shrimp, ribs, and fried flounder. There's usually a wait on the weekends, so get there early. At the southern end of Darien, turn right at Broad just before the river bridge, then take the first left down to the docks. ✉ *85*

Scriven St. ☎912/437–3474 ⚓*Reservations not accepted* ☐*AE, D, MC, V.*

$–$$ ⊡**The Blue Heron Inn.** Bill and Jane Chamberlain's airy, Spanish-style home sits on the edge of the marsh and is only minutes from the ferry at the Sapelo Island Visitors Center. The downstairs dining and living areas have an open, Mediterranean feel, with a large, rustic fireplace and a sweeping view of the marsh. Guest rooms are simply decorated with colorful quilts; most have four-poster beds, and all have a view of the marsh. The proprietor, an Athens native, provides drinks and hors d'oeuvres on the third-floor terrace overlooking the Doboy Sound every evening, and his breakfast specialties include lime French toast and sweet Georgia shrimp omelets. ✉*1 Blue Heron Lane, Meridian, 31319* ☎☎*912/437–4304* ⊕*www.blueheroninngacoast. com* ⇝*4 rooms, 2 suites* &*In room: no phone, no TV. In-hotel: public Wi-Fi* ☐*MC, V* ☉|*BP.*

$–$$ ⊡**Open Gates.** Built by a timber baron in 1876, this two-story, white-frame house on Darien's Vernon Square is filled with antiques and Victorian atmosphere. Each room is beautifully decorated, and the library has an excellent collection of books of local historic interest. Innkeepers Kelly and Jeff Spratt hold master degrees in biology and arrange guided tours of the Altamaha River and surrounding area. A full Southern breakfast and evening cocktails are included in your stay. ✉*301 Franklin St., Box 662, Darien, 31305* ☎*912/437–6985* 🖷*912/882–9427* ⊕*www. opengatesbnb.com* ⇝*5 rooms, 4 with bath* &*In room: no TV. In-hotel: pool* ☐*MC, V* ☉|*BP.*

¢–$$ ✕**The Tabby Cottage.** There are lots of novelties—from sweetgrass baskets to roadkill jewelry—prominently displayed at this tabby souvenir shop in Hog Hammock, but the main attraction is the small dining area in the corner. There Nancy and Ceaser Banks work their magic with fresh local shrimp; smothered pork chops; and slow-cooked, open-pit ribs. The secrets of Sapelo cooking are on full display here, and the "killer bread pudding" is as advertised. The old Wurlitzer jukebox by the bathrooms has everything from James Brown to Marvin Gaye to Harold Melvin and the Blue Notes—and it's still just a quarter. ✉*400 E. Autobahn, Hog Hammock* ☎*912/485–2199* ☉*Closed Sun. and Mon. No dinner.*

¢ ⊡**The Wallow Lodge.** Cornelia Walker Bailey's memoir of life growing up Geechee on Sapelo, *God, Dr. Buzzard,* *and the Bolito Man*, has made her a folk hero and focused awareness on the disappearing communities of descendants of African slaves. A stay at Bailey's Wallow Lodge offers a chance to experience the island's distinct culture. Each room is decorated in what Bailey describes as "Sapelo Period" style, with furniture and memorabilia from residents of the island. Cotton chenille, a tradition on Sapelo, and quilted spreads cover the beds. ■TIP➔**The lodge has a communal kitchen. Unless you make prior arrangements for meals, you must bring your own supplies from the mainland.** ⊠*1 Main Rd., Box 34, Sapelo Island, 31327* ☎*912/485–2206* 🖷*912/485–2174* ⊕*www.gacoast.com/geecheetours* 🛏*6 rooms, 5 with bath* �*In room: no phone, no TV* ⊟*No credit cards* ⏅*EP.*

⚑**Comyam's Campground.** The name of Hog Hammock's only campground comes from the Geechee word meaning "come here." And the marsh-side view is just for backpackers coming for a more rustic taste of the island life. 🏕*Box 7, Sapelo Island, Tom's Hole, 31327* ⚊*Flush toilets, showers* 🛏*30 sites* ☎*912/485–2170* 🖷*912/485–2174* ⊕*www.gacoast.com/geecheetours* 🛆*Reservations essential* 🚐*$10 per person per day, not including ferry.*

NIGHTLIFE

It seems appropriate that the only watering hole in Hog Hammock is named the **Trough** (🏠*Box 34, 1 Main Rd.* ☎*912/485–2206*). It's a small, bare-bones, belly-up-to-the-bar establishment, but owner Julius Bailey serves his beer ice cold, and there's usually a good conversation going on. It's next to the Wallow Lodge (operated by Julius's wife, Cornelia), right "downtown."

EN ROUTE Rice, not cotton, dominated Georgia's coast in the antebellum years, and the **Hofwyl-Broadfield Plantation** is the last remaining example of a way of life that fueled an agricultural empire. The main farmhouse, in use since the 1850s when the original house burned, is now a museum with family heirlooms accrued over five generations, including extensive collections of silver and Cantonese china. A guide gives an insightful talk on rural plantation life. Though grown over, some of the original dikeworks and rice fields remain, as do some of the slave quarters. A brief film at the visitor center complements exhibits on rice technology and cultivation, and links to Sierra

Leone, from where many slaves were taken because of their expertise in growing rice. ✉ *555 U.S. 17N, 4 mi south of Darien* ☎ *912/264–7333* ⊕ *www.gastateparks.org/info/hofwyl* 💲 *$5* 🕗 *Tues.–Sat. 9–5, Sun. 2–5:30.*

ST. SIMONS ISLAND

② *22 mi south of Darien, 4 mi east of Brunswick.*

St. Simons may be the Golden Isles' most developed vacation destination: here you can swim and sun, golf, hike, fish, ride horseback, tour historic sites, and feast on local seafood at more than 50 restaurants. (It's also a great place to bike and jog, particularly on the southern end, where there's an extensive network of trails.) Despite the development, the island has managed to maintain some of the slow-paced Southern atmosphere that made it such a draw in the first place. Upscale resorts and the restaurants are here for the asking, but this island the size of Manhattan has only 20,000 year-round residents, so you can still get away from it all without a struggle. Even down in the village, the center of much of St. Simons's activity, there are unpaved roads and quiet back alleys of chalky white sand that seem like something out of the past.

In the village area, at the more developed south end of the island, you can find shops, several restaurants, pubs, and a popular public pier. For $20 a quaint **"trolley"** (☎ *912/638–8954*) takes you on a 1½-hour guided tour of the island, leaving from near the pier at 11 AM and 1 PM in high season and at 11 AM in winter.

☾ Named after St. Simons slave Neptune Small, **Neptune Park** (✉ *550 Beachview Dr.* ☎ *912/638–6803*), on the island's south end in the village, has picnic tables, a children's play park, miniature golf, and beach access. The casino swimming pool ($4 per person), is open each summer near the St. Simons Lighthouse. Bathrooms are in the library beside the visitor center.

St. Simons Lighthouse, one of only five surviving lighthouses in Georgia, has become a symbol of the island. It's been in use since 1872; a predecessor was blown up to prevent its capture by Union troops in the Civil War. The **Museum of Coastal History,** occupying two stories of the lightkeeper's cottage, has period furniture and a gallery with photo displays illustrating the significance of shipbuilding on St. Simons, the history of the lighthouse, and the life of James Gould, the first lighthouse keeper. The keeper's second-floor quarters contain a parlor, kitchen, and two bedrooms furnished with period pieces, including beds with rope mattress suspension. ✉*101 12th St.* ☎*912/638–4666* ⊕*www.saintsimonslighthouse.org* ☎*$5* ☉*Mon.–Sat. 10–5, Sun. 1:30–5.*

At the north end of the island is the **Fort Frederica National Monument,** the ruins of a fort built by English troops in the mid-1730s to protect the southern flank of the new Georgia colony against a Spanish invasion from Florida. At its peak in the 1740s, it was the most elaborate British fortification in North America. Around the fort are the foundations of homes and shops and the partial ruins of the tabby barracks and magazine. Start your visit at the National Park Service Visitors Center, which has a film and displays. ✉*Off Frederica Rd. near Christ Episcopal Church* ☎*912/638–3639* ⊕*www.nps.gov/fofr* ☎*$3* ☉*Daily 9–5.*

The white-frame, Gothic-style **Christ Episcopal Church** was built by shipwrights and consecrated in 1886 following an earlier structure's desecration by Union troops. It's surrounded by live oaks, dogwoods, and azaleas. The interior has beautiful stained-glass windows, and several of the pews were handmade by slaves. ✉*6329 Frederica Rd.* ☎*912/638–8683* ☎*Donations suggested* ☉*Weekdays 2–5.*

☾ **Maritime History Museum.** At the restored 1936 Historic Coast Guard Station, this new center is geared as much to kids as adults. It features the life of a "Coastie" in the early 1940s through personal accounts of the military history of St. Simons Island and has illustrative displays on the ecology of the islands of the coast of Georgia. ✉*East Beach Causeway* ☎*912/638–4666* ☎*$6* ☉*Mon.–Sat. 10–5, Sun. 1:30–5.*

SPORTS & THE OUTDOORS

BIKING

St. Simons has an extensive network of bicycle trails, and you can ride on the beach as well. **Ocean Motion** (✉*1300 Ocean Blvd.* ☎*912/638–5225 or 800/669–5215*) rents bikes for the entire family, from trail bikes to beach bikes to seats for infants. At **Wheel Fun** (✉*532 Ocean Blvd., just off intersection with Mallory St.* ☎*912/634–0606*) you

Where Legends Landed

CLOSE UP

In May 1803 an "Igbo" chief and his West African tribesmen became Geechee folk legends when they "walked back to Africa," drowning en masse rather than submitting to a life of slavery. Captured in what is modern-day Nigeria, the tribesmen disembarked their slave ship at **Ebo Landing** and headed straight into Dunbar Creek, chanting a hymn. Though the site is now private property, it can be seen from the road. ⊠ *From the F. J. Torras Causeway, turn left on Sea Island Rd. After Hawkins Island Dr., look left (north) just before crossing small bridge at Dunbar Creek. The landing is at bend in creek.*

can rent anything from multispeed bikes to double surreys with bimini tops that look like antique cars and carry four people.

CRABBING & FISHING

There's no simpler fun for the kids than to grab a crab basket or fishing pole and head to St. Simons Island Pier next to Neptune Park. **St. Simons Island Bait and Tackle** (⊠ *121 Mallory St.* ☎*912/634–1888*) is near the foot of the pier and is open 364½ days a year. Owners Mike and Trish Wooten have everything from crabbing and fishing gear to snacks and cold drinks. They also sell one-day, weekly, and yearly licenses.

GOLF

The top-flight golf facilities at the Lodge at Sea Island are available only to members and guests, but St. Simons has two other high-quality courses open to the general public. **The Hampton Club** (⊠ *100 Tabbystone St.* ☎*912/634–0255* ⊕*www.hamptonclub.com*), at the north end of St. Simons on the site of an 18th-century cotton, rice, and indigo plantation, is a *Golf Digest* "Places to Play" four-star winner. The par-72 course designed by Joe Lee is amid towering oaks, salt marshes, and lagoons. **Sea Palms Golf and Tennis Resort** (⊠ *5445 Frederica Rd.* ☎*912/638–3351 or 800/841–6268* ⊕*www.seapalms.com*) on a former cotton plantation, offers 27 holes of golf and a driving range.

KAYAKING & SAILING

After an instructional clinic, head off to explore the marsh creeks, coastal waters, and beaches with **Ocean Motion** (⊠*1300 Ocean Blvd.* ☎*912/638–5225 or 800/669–5215*), which has been giving kayaking tours of St. Simons for more than 20 years. If sailing is your thing, try **Barry's Beach Service** (⊠*420 Arnold Rd.* ☎*912/638–8053 or 800/669–5215*) for Hobie Cat rentals and lessons in front of the King and Prince Beach and Golf Resort on Arnold Road. Barry's also rents kayaks, boogie boards, and beach funcycles (low, reclining bikes), and conducts guided ecotours.

SCUBA DIVING

Gray's Reef, off Sapelo island, is one of only 12 National Marine Sanctuaries, home to Loggerhead turtles, and part of the northern right whale-breeding grounds, all of which make it an attractive place for diving. **Island Dive Center** (⊠*101 Marina Dr., in Golden Isles Marina on F. J. Torras Causeway* ☎*912/638–6590 or 800/940–3483*) is the place to go for scuba and snorkeling instruction, equipment rental, and charter trips. They also have Jet Skis for rent. ■TIP→ If underwater photography is your thing, this is the place for underwater classes.

WHERE TO STAY & EAT

$$$–$$$$ ✕**CARGO Portside Grill.** This superb bistro beside the port in
★ Brunswick has a menu that reads like a foodie's wish list, with succulent coastal fare from many ports. Chef Kate Buchanan puts a creative spin on Southern fare, whether it's sesame catfish, or pasta with grilled chicken in a chipotle cream sauce, or pork chops in a sauce flavored with Jack Daniels. Save room for the Georgia peach pound cake. ⊠*1423 Newcastle St., Brunswick, 31520* ☎*912/267–7330* ▭*AE, MC, V* ⊘*Closed Sun. and Mon. No lunch.*

$$$–$$$$ ✕**Christie's.** A young husband and wife team has poured their hearts into this trendy restaurant. Chef Jayson Riddinger is intent on whimsical innovation, be it in his original dishes or contemporary takes on classics like oysters Rockefellers, which he finishes off on the grill. The Grand Marnier–glazed salmon works beautifully (some of his other creations don't). The house-made green tea ice cream and apple cider panna cotta are superlative. Pricing is fair, particularly for the exceptional lunch menu. ⊠*1618 Newcastle St., Brunswick, 31520* ☎*912/262–0699* ▭*AE, MC, V* ⊘*Closed Sun. No lunch Sat.*

$$$-$$$$ ✕**Halyards.** This elegant restaurant with a laid-back attitude
★   makes everything except the ketchup right on the premises.
Chef-owner Dave Snyder's devotion to quality has earned
a faithful following of discerning locals. Slide into a cozy,
tufted booth or sit at the sophisticated bar lined photos of
yachts. Headliners include the seared, sushi-grade tuna with
a plum wine reduction and the Asian-style diver scallops. A
tasting menu with five courses is paired with wines selected
from the restaurant's impressive cellar. The signature cof-
fee hits the mark with the coconut/lime panna cotta with a
dark rum gelée layer. ✉ *55 Cinema Lane* ☎ *912/638–9100*
⌂ *Reservations essential* ▭ *AE, D, MC, V* ☉ *Closed Sun.*
No lunch.

$$$-$$$$ ✕**Tramici.** This is the new baby of David Snyder, owner
of the more refined Halyard. Tramici is billed as a neigh-
borhood restaurant, although it's in a shopping center. It
certainly is kid-friendly, with spaghetti and meatballs and
pizzas piled with favorite toppings. There's a remarkable
antipasto with prosciutto and asparagus and a superb take
on veal marsala over pasta, with sun-dried tomatoes as the
mystery ingredient. ✉ *75 Cinema Lane* ☎ *912/634–2202*
▭ *AE, D, MC, V.*

$-$$$$ ✕**Bennie's Red Barn.** The steaks are cut fresh daily and
cooked over an oak fire in this barn of a restaurant that has
been serving St. Simons for 50 years. Though there's room
for 200 people, it feels just like family with the checkered
tablecloths and the big open fireplace. There's also fresh
local seafood. The pies are homemade. And there's music
next door at Ziggy Mahoney's Thursday through Saturday
until 2 AM. ✉ *5514 Frederica Rd.* ☎ *912/638–2844* ▭ *AE,*
D, MC, V ☉ *No lunch.*

$-$$$ ✕**Gnat's Landing.** There's more than a little bit of Margari-
taville in this Key West–style bungalow catering to the
flip-flop crowd. Seafood is their specialty with a gumbo
that's outta sight. Besides being the strangest item on the
menu, the fried dill pickle is also the most popular. Sandwiches and salads are also offered. And, of course, there's
the "$8,000 margarita," which is about how much owner
Robert Bostock spent in travel and ingredients coming up
with the recipe. There's live music most Sunday nights and
once a year there's "Gnatfest," a party blowout with live
bands for all those pesky regulars. ✉ *310 Redfern Village*
☎ *912/638–7378* ▭ *AE, D, MC, V.*

2

$–$$$ ✕**Mullet Bay.** After 9 PM the older beach bar crowd has this place hopping, and at weekends the bar and wraparound porches can be standing-room only until the wee hours. By day, however, this spacious and casual restaurant is great for families, serving a good selection of burgers, pastas, and salads. The kids' menu starts at $1.95. ■TIP→**The platters of fried popcorn shrimp are delicious and perfect for sharing.** ⌧*512 Ocean Blvd.* ☎*912/638–0703* ⊟*AE, D, MC, V.*

$–$$ ✕**The Beachcomber BBQ and Grill.** No shoes, no shirt, no problem in this small, rustic eatery where the walls are covered with reed mats and the barbecue smokes away on a cooker right beside the front door. Despite the name, it doesn't boast a beachfront location. However, it's one of the best barbecue joints on the island, offering everything from sandwiches to pulled pork, ribs, and brisket by the pound. ■TIP→**The freshly squeezed lemonade is to die for.** ⌧*319 Arnold Rd.* ☎*912/634–5699* ⊟*AE, MC, V.*

★ **Fodor's**Choice ✕**Rafters.** If you're looking for cheap, delicious
¢–$ food and a raucous good time, this is the place. Revelers sit together at long tables and partake of the offerings from the prodigious bar and the equally generous kitchen. The restaurant serves ocean fare such as "u-shuck-'em" oysters, baked mussels, and a shrimp quesadilla with caramelized papaya, lime, and molasses. Rafters is open late and presents live entertainment Wednesday through Saturday. ⌧*315½ Mallery St.* ☎*912/634–9755* ⊟*AE, D, MC, V* ⊙*Closed Sun.*

$$$$ ⌷**The Lodge at Sea Island Golf Club.** Simply put, this small
★ resort overlooking the sea is one of the top golf and spa destinations in the country. It has the feel of an elegant English-country manor, with exposed ceiling beams, walls covered with tapestries, hardwood floors softened by oriental rugs, and your own private butler, on call 24 hours a day. Dashingly decorated rooms and suites have water or golf-course views. The lodge serves as the clubhouse for the Sea Island Golf Club (though the name is misleading—all of the facilities are on St. Simons Island). Seaside, the first of three courses built here, was inspired by St. Andrews in Scotland and has breathtaking panoramas of coastal Georgia. Only guests can visit the restaurants or bars. ⌧*St. Simons Island, 31522* ☎*912/638–3611 or 866/465–3563* ⊕*www.seaisland.com* ⇝*40 rooms, 2 suites* ⌂*In-room: refrigerator, DVD, VCR, dial-up. In-hotel: restaurant, bar,*

3 golf courses, tennis court, pool, spa, children's programs (ages 3–19) ⊟*AE, D, DC, MC, V* ⏀*EP.*

$$–$$$$ ⚂**King and Prince Beach and Golf Resort.** This resort is a cushy retreat with spacious guest rooms and luxurious two- and three-bedroom villas. Guests get golf privileges at the Hampton Club at the Hampton Plantation on St. Simons, as well as access to many outdoor activities such as sailing and tennis. The villas are all privately owned, so the total number available for rent varies from time to time. ■TIP➔ **The historic main building has been refurbished to include a Starbucks.** ✉*201 Arnold Rd., 31522* ☎*912/638–3631 or 800/342–0212* ℻*912/634–1720* ⊕*www.kingandprince.com* ↪*145 rooms, 2 suites, 41 villas* ⚲*In-hotel: restaurants, bar, tennis courts, pools, bicycles, bar, public Wi-Fi* ⊟*AE, D, MC, V* ⏀*EP.*

$$–$$$ ⚂**Sea Palms Golf and Tennis Resort.** If you're looking for an active getaway, this contemporary complex could be the place for you—it has golf, tennis, a fitness center loaded with state-of-the-art equipment, a beach club, sand-pit volleyball, horseshoes, and bicycling. The guest rooms, touted to be the largest standard rooms in the Golden Isles, have balconies with views of the Marshes of Glynn and the golf course; the furnishings are somewhat unimaginative. Guests have beach club privileges. ✉*5445 Frederica Rd., 31522* ☎*912/638–3351 or 800/841–6268* ℻*912/634–8029* ⊕*www.seapalms.com* ↪*112 rooms, 23 suites, 11 villas* ⚲*In-hotel: restaurants, golf course, tennis courts, pools, gym, bicycles* ⊟*AE, DC, MC, V* ⏀*EP.*

$$–$$$ ⚂**The Village Inn & Pub.** The black-and-white photographs hanging of the wall are the only clue that this inn was once a cinder-block beach house. In the heart of the village, this lodging has won awards for design as well as for preserving the mossy live oaks. The guest rooms resemble standard-issue motel rooms, although the best of them have king-size beds and double half-moon balconies. All are named after various Georgia celebrities like author Eugenia Price, whose books line one shelf. Breakfast may include make-your-own Belgian waffles.

✉*500 Mallery St., 31522* ☎*912/634–6056 or 888/635–6111* ℻*912/634–1464* ⊕*www.villageinnandpub.com* ↪*28 rooms* ⚲*In-hotel: restaurant, bar, pool, public Wi-Fi* ⊟*AE, D, DC, MC, V* ⏀*BP.*

$$ 🖼**St. Simons Inn.** This Spanish-style inn sits in a prime spot by the lighthouse, only minutes by foot from the village and the beaches. Rooms are basic but clean and comfortable. Suites have whirlpools, and apartments are fully equipped. There's a two-night minimum during high season. Discounts are available for longer stays. ✉609 Beachview Dr., 31522 ☎912/638–1101 ☒912/638–0943 ⊕www.stsimonsinn.com ↩34 rooms, 6 suites ♿In-room: refrigerator. In-hotel: pool, public Wi-Fi ⊟AE, D, DC, MC, V ⊺⊙BP.

$ 🖼**Holiday Inn Express.** With brightly decorated rooms at great prices, this no-smoking facility is an attractive option in this price category. The executive rooms have sofas and desks. ✉Plantation Village, 299 Main St., 31522 ☎912/634–2175 or 888/465–4329 ☒912/634–2174 ⊕www.hiexpress.com/stsimonsga ↩60 rooms ♿In-hotel: pool, bicycles, laundry service ⊟AE, D, MC, V ⊺⊙BP.

LITTLE ST. SIMONS ISLAND

❸ 10–15 min by ferry from Hampton River Club Marina on St. Simons Island.

Little St. Simons is 15 minutes by boat from St. Simons, but in character it's a world apart. The entire island is a privately owned resort; there are no telephones and no televisions in the only habitations, which are a rustic, former hunting lodge on the riverfront, two upscale cottages, and three river houses. This compound is so at one with its surroundings that the deer graze in the open. "Luxury" on Little St. Simons means having the time and space to get in tune with the rhythms of nature.

The island's forests and marshes are inhabited by deer, armadillos, raccoons, gators, otters, and more than 200 species of birds. As a guest at the resort, you can take part in guided activities, including tours, horseback rides, canoe trips, and fly-fishing lessons, all for no additional charge. You're also free to walk the 7 mi of undisturbed beaches, swim in the mild surf, fish from the dock, and seine for shrimp and crab in the marshes.

From June through September, up to 10 nonguests per day may visit the island for a fee of $100, which includes the ferry to the island, a tour by truck, lunch at the lodge, and a beach walk. Contact the Lodge on Little St. Simons Island for more information.

WHERE TO STAY

$$$$ ☆ **Lodge on Little St. Simons Island.** Privacy and simplicity are
★ the star attractions on this 10,000 acre island with its rustic island 1917 lodge and four cottages, with a capacity
of only 30 guests. The newer Cedar House and Helen's
Cottage are the better accommodations. A stay here is all-
inclusive: you get three meals a day, use of all equipment
and facilities, and drinks at cocktail hour. The friendly,
attentive staff includes three full-time naturalists who lead
nature talks and tours. Meals, taken family style, feature
platters heaped with fresh fish and homemade breads and
pies. Transportation from St. Simons Island is also part of
the package. ⌂*Box 21078, 31522* ☎*912/638-7472 or
888/733-5774* ☐*912/634-1811* ⊕*www.littlestsimonsis-
land.com* ⤢*14 rooms, 1 suite* ⌂*In-room: no phone, no
TV. In-hotel: restaurant, pool, beachfront, water sports,
bicycles* ⊟*AE, D, MC, V* ⊙*FAP.*

SEA ISLAND

❹ *5 mi northeast of St. Simons Island.*

Tiny Sea Island—with a full-time population of less than
200—is one of the nation's wealthiest communities. Established by Howard Coffin, the wealthy Detroit auto pio-
neer who also owned Sapelo Island, Sea Island has been the
domain of the well-heeled since 1928. The hub of activity is
the very swanky Cloister, whose recent renovations made it
even more exclusive (and expensive). Now a gated community, Sea Island is accessible only to registered guests and
Sea Island Club members.

★ **Fodor'sChoice** ☆ **The Cloister.** One of the region's grand dames
$$$$ has had a face-lift. Well, a little more than that. The legendary hotel had begun to look like tattered aristocracy, so
the owners tore it down, saving only some of the facades.
The result is a Mediterranean-style resort complemented
by semitropical landscaping. There are all the luxuries you
would expect, such as a sprawling two-story spa, as well as
those that are a wonderful surprise, like the bi-level water
garden. The Beach Club is the last of the buildings being
razed, making way for a set of beachfront suites. If you
can't afford to stay here, reserve a table at the award-winning Georgian Room. ⌂*Sea Island, 31522* ☎*912/638-
3611 or 866/465-3563* ⊕*www.seaisland.com* ⤢*153
rooms, 3 suites* ⌂*In-room: safe, dial-up, in-room Wi-Fi. In*

hotel: 4 restaurants, bars, golf courses, tennis courts, pools, beachfront, water sports, children's programs (ages 3–19) ⊟*AE, D, DC, MC, V* ⦿*EP.*

EN ROUTE Heading south toward Jekyll Island on U.S. 17, you cross over the longest spanning bridge in the state, the soaring **Sidney Lanier Bridge**, which rises 185 feet into the air. It's fittingly named for the Macon native and poet who penned "The Marshes of Glynn," a masterpiece of 19th-century American poetry. It was inspired by the breathtaking vistas of the salt marshes surrounding Brunswick, St. Simons, and Jekyll islands.

JEKYLL ISLAND

❺ 18 mi south of St. Simons Island, 90 mi south of Savannah.

For 56 winters, between 1886 and 1942, America's rich and famous faithfully came south to Jekyll Island. Through the Gilded Age, World War I, the Roaring '20s, and the Great Depression, Vanderbilts and Rockefellers, Morgans and Astors, Macys, Pulitzers, and Goodyears shuttered their 5th Avenue castles and retreated to elegant "cottages" on their wild coastal island. It's been said that when the island's distinguished winter residents were all "in," a sixth of the world's wealth was represented. Early in World War II the millionaires departed for the last time. In 1947 the state of Georgia purchased the entire island for the bargain price of $675,000.

Jekyll Island is still a 7½-mi playground, but it's no longer restricted to the rich and famous. A water park, picnic grounds, and facilities for golf, tennis, fishing, biking, and jogging are all open to the public. One side of the island is lined by nearly 10 mi of hard-packed Atlantic beaches; the other by the Intracoastal Waterway and picturesque salt marshes. Deer and wild turkeys inhabit interior forests of pine, magnolia, and moss-veiled live oaks. Egrets, pelicans, herons, and sandpipers skim the gentle surf. Jekyll Island's clean, mostly uncommercialized public beaches are free and open year-round. Bathhouses with restrooms, changing areas, and showers are open at regular intervals along the beach. Beachwear, suntan lotion, rafts, snacks, and drinks are available at the Jekyll Shopping Center, facing the beach at Beachview Drive. Visitors must pay a fee of $3, which is used to support conservation of the island's natural and cultural resources. At this writing, the Georgia Sea Turtle Center, in a converted 1903 power plant, was set to open. The center will teach people about endangered loggerhead turtles, many of which lay their eggs along Jekyll Island beaches from May through August.

The **Jekyll Island History Center** gives tram tours of the Jekyll Island National Historic Landmark District. Tours originate at the museum's visitor center on Stable Road four times a day. Tours at 11 and 2 include two millionaires' residences in the 240-acre historic district. Faith Chapel, illuminated by stained-glass windows, including one Tiffany original, is open daily 2 to 4. ✉*100 Stable Rd., I–95, Exit 29* ☎*912/635–4036* 🖷*912/635–4004* ⊕*www. jekyllisland.com* 💲*$10–$17.50* ⊘*Daily 9–5; tours daily, 10, 11, 2, and 4.*

OFF THE BEATEN PATH **Driftwood Beach. If you've ever wondered about the effects of erosion on barrier islands, head at low tide to this oceanfront boneyard on North Beach, where live oaks and pines are being consumed by the sea at an alarming rate. The snarl of trunks and limbs and the dramatic, massive root systems of upturned trees are an eerie and intriguing tableau of nature's slow and steady power. It's been estimated that nearly 1,000 feet of Jekyll's beach have been lost since the early 1900s.** ■TIP➔**Bring your camera; the photo opportunities are terrific and this is the best place to shoot St. Simons Lighthouse.** ✉*Head to far north of Jekyll on Beachview Dr. to large curve where road turns inland. When ocean is visible through forest to your left, pull over and take one of many trails through trees to beach.*

SPORTS & THE OUTDOORS

CYCLING

The best way to see Jekyll is by bicycle: a long, paved trail running right along the beach, and there's an extensive network of paths throughout the island. **Jekyll Island Mini Golf and Bike Rentals** (✉*N. Beachview Dr. at Shell Rd.* ☎*912/635–2648*) has a wide selection, from the surrey pedal cars, which can hold four people, to lay-down cycles, to the more traditional bikes. **Wheel Fun** (✉*60 S. Oceanview Dr.* ☎*912/635–9801*) sits right in front of the Days Inn and is easy to get to Jekyll's southern beachfront.

FISHING

With 40 years of experience in local waters, Captain Vernon Reynolds of **Coastal Expeditions** (⊠*Jekyll Harbor Marina* ☎*912/265–0392* ⊕*www.coastalcharterfishing. com*) provides half-day and full-day trips in-shore and off-shore for fishing, dolphin-watching, and sightseeing. Aside from his ample angling skills, Larry Crews of **Offshore Charters** (⊠*Jekyll Island Marina* ☎*912/270–7474 or 912/265–7529* ⊕*www.offshore-charters.com*) also offers his services as captain to tie the knot for anyone who's already landed the big one.

GOLF

The **Jekyll Island Golf Club** (⊠*322 Capt. Wylly Rd.* ☎*912/635–2368*) has 63 holes, including three 18-hole, par-72 courses, and a clubhouse. Green fees are $40, good all day, and carts are $17 per person per course. The nine-hole, par-36 **Oceanside Nine** (⊠*N. Beachview Dr.* ☎*912/635–2170*) is where Jekyll Island millionaires used to play. Green fees are $22, and carts are $7.25 for every nine holes.

HORSEBACK RIDING

Take a sunset ride through the Maritime forest along the North Beach with **Victoria's Carriages and Trail Rides** (⊠*100 Stable Rd., in stables at Jekyll Island History Center* ☎*912/635–9500*). Morning and afternoon rides include visits to the salt marsh and Driftwood Beach, a boneyard of live oaks and pine trees being reclaimed by the sea. Rides leave from the Clam Creek picnic area across from the Jekyll Island Campground.

NATURE CENTER

ᘓ The **Tidelands Nature Center,** a 4H program sponsored by the University of Georgia, has summer classes for kids and adults on everything from loggerhead sea turtles to live oaks to beach ecology. You can learn how the maritime forest evolves or get a lesson in seining and netting. There are guided nature walks, kayak tours, and canoe and paddle-boat rentals. The center also has touch tanks and exhibits on coastal ecology. ⊠*100 Riverview Dr.* ☎*912/635–5032* ⊕*www.tidelands4h.org* ᘓ*$1 for exhibit* ⊙*Mar.–Oct., Mon.–Sat. 9–4, Sun 10–2; Nov.–Feb., weekdays 9–4, Sat. 10–2.*

TENNIS

The **Jekyll Island Tennis Center** (✉*400 Capt. Wylly Rd.* ☎*912/635–3154* ⊕*www.gate.net/~jitc*) has 13 clay courts, with seven lighted for nighttime play. The facility hosts six USTA-sanctioned tournaments throughout the year and provides lessons and summer camps for juniors. Courts cost $18 per hour daily 9 AM to 10 PM. Reservations for lighted courts are required and must be made prior to 6 PM the day of play.

WATER PARK

☺ **Summer Waves** is an 11-acre park using more than a million gallons of water in its 18,000-square-foot wave pool, water slides, children's activity pool with two slides, and circular river for tubing and rafting. Inner tubes and life vests are provided at no extra charge. ✉*210 S. Riverview Dr.* ☎*912/635–2074* ⊕*www.summerwaves.com* 🎫*$16.95* ☉*Late May–early Sept., Sun.–Thurs. 10–6, Sat. 10–8; hrs vary at beginning and end of season.*

WHERE TO STAY & EAT

$$$$ ✗**Courtyard at Crane.** When it was built in 1917, Crane Cottage—actually an elegant Italianate villa—was the most expensive winter home on Jekyll Island. Now, as part of the Jekyll Island Club Hotel, the Courtyard at Crane offers casual alfresco dining. The menu has a Mediterranean flair with plenty of salads at lunch and more substantial dishes into the evening such as marinated grilled rib eye, and a vegetable strudel. ✉*375 Riverview Dr., Jekyll Island Club Hotel* ☎*912/635–2600* 🚫*AE, D, DC, MC, V* ☉*No dinner Fri. and Sat.*

$$$$ ✗**Grand Dining Room.** The colonnaded Grand Dining Room
★ of the Jekyll Island Club maintains a tradition of fine dining first established in the 19th century. The huge fireplace, views of the pool, and sparkling silver and crystal all contribute to the sense of old-style elegance. Signature dishes are the pistachio-crusted rack of lamb, grouper flamed with hazelnut liqueur, and the filet mignon. The menu also includes local seafood and regional dishes such as Southern fried quail salad. The wine cellar has its own label cabernet, merlot, white zinfandel, and chardonnay, made by Round Hill Vineyards. ✉*371 Riverview Dr.* ☎*912/635–2600* 🍴*Reservations essential* Jacket required 🚫*AE, D, DC, MC, V.*

2

$$–$$$$ ✕**Latitude 31.** Right on the Jekyll Island Club Wharf, in the middle of the historic district, Latitude 31 wins the prize for best location. The menu has everything from Oysters Rockefeller to seafood crepes to bourbon peach- and pecan-glazed pork tenderloin. There's also a kids' menu. ⊠*Jekyll Island Club Wharf* ☎*912/635–3800* ⊟*D, MC, V* ⊙*Closed Mon.*

$–$$$ ✕**The Rah Bar.** A tiny swamp shack right on the end of the ★ Jekyll Island Club Wharf (connected to Latitude 31), the Rah Bar is the place for a hands-on experience. It's elbow-to-elbow dining (unless you eat at the tables outside on the wharf) with "rah" oysters, "crawdaddies," and "u peel 'em" shrimp. As you eat, you look out on the shrimp boats and the beautiful salt marsh sunsets. ⊠*Jekyll Island Club Wharf* ☎*912/635–3800* ⊟*D, MC, V* ⊙*Closed Mon.*

$$ ✕**SeaJay's Waterfront Café & Pub.** A casual tavern overlooking the Jekyll Harbor Marina, SeaJay's serves delicious, inexpensive seafood, including a crab chowder that locals love. This is also the home of the wildly popular Lowcountry boil buffet: an all-you-can-eat feast of local shrimp, corn on the cob, smoked sausage, and new potatoes. There's live music Thursday through Saturday night. ■TIP➔**Bring the kids, their special menus run from $3.95.** ⊠*1 Harbor Point Rd., Jekyll Harbor Marina* ☎*912/635–3200* ⊟*AE, D, MC, V.*

$$–$$$$ ⊞**Beachview Club.** Grand old oak trees shade the grounds ★ of this luxury, all-suites lodging. Rooms are either on the oceanfront or have a partial ocean view; some rooms are equipped with hot tubs and gas fireplaces. Efficiencies have one king-size or two double beds, a desk, and a kitchenette. The interior design reflects an understated island theme, and the unique meeting room in the Bell Tower accommodates up to 35 people for business events. Higher-end suites have full kitchens. ⊠*721 N. Beachview Dr., 31527* ☎*912/635–2256 or 800/299–2228* ⊟*912/635–3770* ⊕*www.beachviewclub.com* ⊅*38 rooms, 6 suites* ⚬*In-room: some kitchens. In-hotel: bar, pool, bicycles, public Wi-Fi* ⊟*AE, D, DC, MC, V* ⊙*EP.*

$$–$$$$ ⊞**Jekyll Island Club Hotel.** This sprawling 1886 resort was ★ once described as "the richest, the most exclusive, the most inaccessible club in the world." Not so today. The resort's focal point is a four-story clubhouse, with its wraparound verandas and Queen Anne–style towers and turrets. Rooms, suites, apartments, and cottages are decorated with

mahogany beds, armoires, and plush sofas and chairs. Two beautifully restored former "millionaires' cottages"—the Crane and the Cherokee—add 23 elegant guest rooms to this gracefully groomed compound. The B&B packages are a great deal. ✉ *371 Riverview Dr., 31527* ☎ *912/635–2600 or 800/535–9547* 🖷 *912/635–2818* ⊕ *www.jekyllclub.com* ⤵ *138 rooms, 19 suites* ♿ *In-room: VCR, dial-up. In-hotel: restaurant, bar, pool, bicycles, public Wi-Fi* ▭ *AE, D, DC, MC, V* †◎† *EP.*

$$–$$$ 🏨 **Buccaneer Beach Resort.** If you want to be far from the crowds of the historic district, try this resort where most of the 200-plus rooms and suites have private balconies overlooking the ocean on Jekyll Island's southern shore. Accommodations include one-, two- and three-bedroom suites. Golf and honeymoon packages are available. ✉ *85 S. Beachview Dr., 31527* ☎ *912/635–2261* 🖷 *912/635–3230* ⊕ *www.buccaneerbeachresort.com* ⤵ *200 rooms, 6 suites* ♿ *In-hotel: restaurant, bar, tennis court, pool, bicycles* ▭ *AE, D, DC, MC, V* †◎† *EP.*

$$–$$$ 🏨 **Jekyll Oceanfront Resort & Spa.** At the largest oceanfront resort hotel on the island, the buildings are spread across 15 verdant acres. Popular with families, the inn accommodates children under 17 free when they stay with parents or grandparents. Packages include summer family-focused arrangements and romantic getaways. The restaurant offers basic, hearty fare, including an all-you-can-eat Saturday night seafood buffet. ✉ *975 N. Beachview Dr., 31527* ☎ *912/635–2531 or 800/736–1046* 🖷 *912/635–2332* ⊕ *www.jekyllinn.com* ⤵ *259 rooms, 71 villas* ♿ *In-room: refrigerator. In-hotel: restaurant, bars, pool, spa, children's programs (ages 5–12)* ▭ *AE, D, DC, MC, V* †◎† *EP.*

🛆 **Jekyll Island Campground.** At the northern end of Jekyll across from the entrance to the fishing pier, this campground lies on 18 wooded acres with more than 200 sites that can accommodate everything from backpackers looking for primitive sites to RVs needing full hookups. Pets are welcome but there's a $2 fee. ♿ *Flush toilets, dump station, guest laundry, showers, electricity, public telephone* ✉ *1197 Riverview Dr., 31527* ☎ *912/635–3021 or 866/658–3021* ⊕ *www.jekyllisland.com* ▭ *AE, MC, V* 🛏 *$30–$42.*

CUMBERLAND ISLAND

★ **Fodor's**Choice *47 mi south of Jekyll Island; 115 mi south*
⑥ *of Savannah to St. Marys via I–95; 45-min by ferry from*
St. Marys.

Cumberland, the largest of Georgia's coastal isles, is a national treasure. The 18-mi spit of land off the coast of St. Marys is a nearly unspoiled sanctuary of marshes, dunes, beaches, forests, lakes, and ponds. And although it has a long history of human habitation, it remains much as nature created it: a dense, lacework canopy of live oak shades sand roads and foot trails through thick undergrowths of palmetto. Wild horses roam freely on pristine beaches. Waterways are homes for gators, sea turtles, otters, snowy egrets, great blue herons, ibises, wood storks, and more than 300 other species of birds. In the forests are armadillos, wild horses, deer, raccoons, and an assortment of reptiles.

In the 16th century, the Spanish established a mission and a garrison, San Pedro de Mocama, on the southern end of the island. But development didn't begin in earnest until the wake of the American Revolution, with timbering operations for shipbuilding, particularly construction of warships for the early U.S.–naval fleet. Cotton, rice, and indigo plantations were also established. In 1818, Revolutionary War hero Gen. "Lighthorse" Harry Lee, father of Robert E. Lee, died and was buried near the Dungeness estate of General Nathaniel Greene. Though his body was later moved to Virginia to be interred beside his son, the gravestone remains. During the 1880s the family of Thomas Carnegie (brother of industrialist Andrew) built several lavish homes here. In the 1950s the National Park Service named Cumberland Island and Cape Cod as the most significant natural areas on the Atlantic and Gulf coasts. And in 1972, in response to attempts to develop the island by Hilton Head–developer Charles Fraser, Congress passed a bill establishing the island as a national seashore. Today most of the island is part of the national-park system.

Though the **Cumberland Island National Seashore** is open to the public, the only public access to the island is via the *Cumberland Queen,* a reservations-only, 146-passenger ferry based near the National Park Service Information Center at St. Marys. Ferry bookings are heavy in summer. Cancellations and no-shows often make last-minute space

CLOSE UP

Georgia's Black Republic

After capturing Savannah in December 1864, General William Tecumseh Sherman read the Emancipation Proclamation at the Second African Baptist Church and issued his now famous Field Order No. 15, giving freed slaves 40 acres and a mule. The field order set aside a swath of land reaching 30 mi inland from Charleston to northern Florida (roughly the area east of Interstate 95), including the coastal islands, for an independent state of freed slaves.

Under the administration of General Rufus Saxton and his assistant, Tunis G. Campbell, a black New Jersey native who represented McIntosh County as a state senator, a black republic was established with St. Catherines Island as its capital. Hundreds of former slaves were relocated to St. Catherines and Sapelo islands,

where they set about cultivating the land. In 1865 Campbell established himself as virtual king, controlling a legislature, a court, and a 275-man army. Whites called Campbell "the most feared man in Georgia."

Congress repealed Sherman's directive and replaced General Saxton with General Davis Tillison, who was sympathetic to the interests of former plantation owners, and in 1867 Federal troops drove Campbell off St. Catherines and into McIntosh County, where he continued to exert his power. In 1876 he was convicted of falsely imprisoning a white citizen and sentenced, at the age of 63, to work on a chain gang. After being freed, he left Georgia for good and settled in Boston, where he died in 1891. Every year on the fourth Saturday in June, the town of Darien holds a festival in Campbell's honor.

available, but don't rely on it. You can make reservations up to six months in advance. ■TIP→ **Note that the ferry does not transport pets, bicycles, kayaks, or cars.**

From the park-service docks at the island's south end, you can follow wooded nature trails, swim and sun on 18 mi of undeveloped beaches, go fishing and bird-watching, and view the ruins of Thomas Carnegie's great estate, **Dungeoness.** You can also join history and nature walks led by park-service rangers. Bear in mind that summers are hot and humid and that you must bring everything you need, including your own food, soft drinks, sunscreen, and insect repellent. There's no public transportation on the island. ✐ *Cumberland Island National Seashore, Box*

*806, St. Marys, 31558 ☎912/882–4335 or 888/817–3421
📠912/673–7747 ⊕www.nps.gov/cuis ⌖Round-trip ferry
$15, day pass $4 ⊙Mar.–Sept., ferry departure from St.
Marys daily 9 AM and 11:45 AM; from Cumberland, Sun.–
Tues. 10:15 AM and 4:45 PM, Wed.–Sat. 10:15 AM, 2:45 PM,
4:45 PM. Oct. and Nov., ferry departure from St. Marys
daily 9 AM and 11:45 AM; from Cumberland 10:15 AM and
4:45 PM. Dec.–Feb., Thurs.–Sun., ferry departure from St.
Marys 9 AM and 11:45 AM, from Cumberland 10:15 AM
and 4:45 PM.*

OFF THE BEATEN PATH The First African Baptist Church. This small,
one-room church on the north end of Cumberland Island is
where John F. Kennedy Jr. and Carolyn Bessette were married
on September 21, 1996. Constructed of whitewashed logs, it's
simply adorned with a cross made of sticks tied together with
string and 11 handmade pews seating 40 people. It was built in
1937 to replace a cruder 1893 structure used by former slaves
from the High Point–Half Moon Bluff community. The Kennedy–
Bessette wedding party stayed at the Greyfield Inn, built on the
south end of the island in 1900 by the Carnegie family. ⊠*North
end of Cumberland near Half Moon Bluff.*

SPORTS & THE OUTDOORS

KAYAKING
Whether you're a novice or skilled paddler, **Up The Creek
Xpeditions** (⊠*111 Osborne St., St. Marys* ☎*912/882–0911*)
can guide you on kayak tours through some of Georgia
and Florida's most scenic waters. Classes include navigation, tides and currents, and kayak surfing and racing.
Trips include Yulee, the St. Marys River, and the Cumberland Sound. The sunset dinner paddle includes a meal at
Borrell Creek Restaurant overlooking the marsh.

WATER PARK
☺ If the heat has you and the kids are itching to get wet, head
to the **St. Marys Aquatic Center** (⊠*301 Herb Bauer Dr., St.
Marys* ☎*912/673–8118* ⊕*www.ci.st-marys.ga.us/aquatic.
htm*), a full-service water park where you can get an inner
tube and relax floating down the Continuous River, hurtle
down Splash Mountain, or corkscrew yourself silly sliding
down the Orange Crush.

WHERE TO STAY & EAT

ON THE ISLAND

$$$$ ×⊡ **Greyfield Inn.** Once described as a "Tara by the sea,"
★ this turn-of-the-last-century Carnegie family home is
Cumberland Island's only accommodation. Built in 1900
for Lucy Ricketson, Thomas and Lucy Carnegie's daughter, the inn is filled with period antiques, family portraits,
and original furniture that evoke the country elegance of
a bygone era. And with a 1,000-acre private compound, it
offers a solitude that also seems a thing of the past. Prices
include all meals, transportation, tours led by a naturalist, and bikes. Nonguests can dine at the restaurant ($$$$)
on delicious dishes that changes daily. The catch of the
day might produce a homemade carrot and thyme spatzel
with baked halibut, sautéed local chanterelles, and asparagus in a pearl-onion cream sauce. Dining is family style.
🏠 8 N. 2nd St., Box 900, Fernandina Beach, FL 32035-
0900 ☎904/261–6408 or 866/410–8051 🖷904/321–0666
⊕www.greyfieldinn.com ⮫16 rooms, 4 suites ⚅In-room:
no phone, no TV. In-hotel: restaurant, bar, bicycles ⊟D,
MC, V ⭗FAP.

⚠ **Hickory Hill, Yankee Paradise, Stafford Beach, Brickhill
Bluff, and Sea Camp.** The island has five camping sites in a
National Wilderness Area, all of which require reservations
usually at least two months in advance. Sea Camp is the
ideal spot for first-time campers. It's a half mile from the
dock and has restrooms and showers nearby. None of the
sites allow pets or fires, and stays are limited to seven days.
The other locations are primitive sites and are a 4 to 10
mi hike. ■TIP➜ Because ferry reservations are mandatory to
camp, book the boat at the same time. 🏠Cumberland Island
National Seashore, Box 806, St. Marys, 31558 ☎912/882–
4335 or 877/860–6787 🖷912/673–7747 ⊕www.nps.gov/
cuis ⮫Park access, $4 per person; backcountry sites, $2
per person per day; Sea Camp, $4 per person per day.

ON THE MAINLAND

$–$$$ × **Lang's Marina Restaurant.** Everything's made from scratch
at this popular waterside restaurant, including the des-
serts. And the seafood comes fresh from the owner's boats.
You can order shrimp, scallops, and oysters, or opt for the
Captain's Platter and get some of everything. Fish is avail-
able fried, grilled, or blackened. ✉307 W. St. Marys St.,
near waterfront park, St. Marys ☎912/882–4432 ⊟MC, V
⭗Closed Sun. and Mon. No dinner Tues. No lunch Sat.

$–$$ ✕**The Williams' Saint Marys Seafood and Steak House.** Don't let the tabby-and-porthole decor fool you. In a region rife with seafood restaurants, this one's full of locals for a reason. The food is fresh, well prepared, and plentiful, and the price rarely gets so right. The menu includes frogs' legs and alligator tail for more adventurous eaters. ✉*1837 Osborne Rd., St. Marys* ☎*912/882–6875* ▭*MC, V.*

$$–$$$ ☖**Spencer House Inn.** At this pink Victorian inn, built in 1872, some rooms have expansive balconies (with obligatory rockers), which overlook the neatly tended grounds, and some have antique claw-foot bathtubs. Innkeepers Mike and Mary Neff will prepare picnic lunches if you ask. The inn is listed in the National Register of Historic Places, and is a perfect base for touring the St. Marys and Cumberland Island area. ✉*200 Osborne St., St. Marys, 31558* ☎*912/882–1872 or 888/840–1872* 📠*912/882–9427* ⊕*www.spencerhouseinn.com* ⇨*13 rooms, 1 suite* ♿*In-hotel: public Wi-Fi* ▭*AE, D, MC, V* ⧆*BP.*

¢–$$ ☖**Cumberland Island Inn and Suites.** Children under 18 stay free at this modern, moderately priced hotel on Osborne Road, 3 mi from the St. Marys waterfront. The spacious suites have complete kitchens, large refrigerators, sleeper sofas, executive work desks with ergonomic chairs, and free high-speed Internet access. Some suites feature Jacuzzis. ✉*2710 Osborne Rd., St. Marys, 31558* ☎*912/882–6250 or 800/768–6250* 📠*912/882–4471* ⊕*www.cumberland-islandinn.com* ⇨*79 rooms, 39 suites* ♿*In-room: refrigerator, dial-up. In-hotel: restaurants, bar, pool, laundry facilities* ▭*AE, D, MC, V* ⧆*BP.*

¢ ☖**Riverview Hotel.** A giant step back in time, this 1916 hotel looks straight out of the Old West. The lobby resembles a museum, with old cameras in a glass case and high-backed typewriters on display. A Tiffany lamp—the real thing—hangs over the reception desk. Guest rooms with river views have ornate iron beds and antique furniture from the owner's family. The popular Seagles's Waterfront Café features steaks and seafood, including delicious rock shrimp. Picnic lunches can be packed for your Cumberland Island excursion. ✉*105 Osborne St., St. Marys, 31558* ☎*912/882–3242* ⊕*www.riverviewhotelstmarys.com* ⇨*18 rooms* ♿*In-room: no phones. In-hotel: restaurant, bar* ▭*AE, D, DC, MC, V* ⧆*BP.*

NIGHTLIFE

The closer you get to borders, the more pronounced allegiances become. A case in point is **Seagle's Saloon and Patio Bar** (⌂*105 Osborne St., St. Marys* ☎*912/882–1807*), a smoky watering hole not far from the Florida state line that's festooned with University of Georgia memorabilia. Bawdy bartender Cindy Deen is a local legend, so expect some southern sass.

EN ROUTE On your way back from Cumberland Island, stop in at the St. Marys Submarine Museum (⌂*102 W. St. Marys St., across from Cumberland Island Ferry office* ☎*912/882-2782* ⊕*http:// stmaryssubmuseum.com*). This small, fascinating museum is a natural in a town that owes much of its existence to the nearby Kings Bay Naval Base, home of the Atlantic Trident fleet. The museum has an extensive collection of photos and artifacts, including uniforms, flags, scale models, designs, sonar consoles, hatches, working steering positions, and a working periscope.

THE COASTAL ISLES ESSENTIALS

TRANSPORTATION

BY AIR

The coastal isles are served by the Brunswick Golden Isles Airport, 6 mi north of Brunswick, and the McKinnon St. Simons Airport on St. Simons Island. McKinnon accommodates light aircraft and private planes.

Contacts **Atlantic Southeast Airlines** (☎*800/282-3424, 800/221-1212, or 912/267-1325*). **The Brunswick Golden Isles Airport** (⌂*500 Connole St.* ☎*912/265-2070* ⊕*www.glynncountyairports. com*). **McKinnon St. Simons Island Airport** (⌂*Off Demere Rd.* ☎*912/628-8617*).

BY BOAT & FERRY

Cumberland Island, Sapelo Island, and Little St. Simons are accessible only by ferry or private launch. The *Cumberland Queen* serves Cumberland Island and the *Anne Marie* serves Sapelo Island. The Lodge on Little St. Simons Island operates a private launch that is available only to overnight or day-trip guests by prior arrangement.

Contacts Anne Marie (⌂*Sapelo Island Visitors Center, Rte. 1, Box 1500, Darien, 31305* ☎*912/437-3224* ⊕*www.sapelonerr.org*).

Cumberland Queen (☞ *Cumberland Island National Seashore* ⌂ *Box 806, 101 Wheeler St., St. Marys, 31558* ☎ *912/882–4336 or 877/860–6787* 🖷 *912/673–7747* ⊕ *www.nps.gov/cuis*). **The Lodge on Little St. Simons Island** (⌂ *Box 21078, Little St. Simons Island, 31522* ☎ *912/638–7472 or 888/733–5774* 🖷 *912/634–1811* ⊕ *www. littlestsimonsisland.com*).

BY CAR

From Brunswick take the Jekyll Island Causeway ($3 per car) to Jekyll Island and the Torras Causeway to St. Simons and Sea Island. You can get by without a car on Jekyll Island and Sea Island, but you'll need one on St. Simons. You cannot bring a car to Cumberland Island, Little St. Simons, or Sapelo.

BY TAXI

Courtesy Cab provides taxi service from Brunswick to and from the islands for a set rate that ranges from $15 to $25 to St. Simons and from $25 to Jekyll Island with a $2 per person surcharge to a maximum of seven persons. Island Cab Service can shuttle you around St. Simons for fares that range between $7 and $15 depending on your destination.

Contacts Courtesy Cab (✉ *4262B Norwich Exit, Brunswick* ☎ *912/264–3760*). **Island Cab Service** (✉ *708 E. Island Square Dr., St. Simons, 31522* ☎ *912/634–0113*).

CONTACTS & RESOURCES

BANKS & EXCHANGE SERVICES

Brunswick has several major bank branch offices. Bank of America is open weekdays 9 to 6 (the Atama Connector location also opens until 1 PM on Saturday). Sun Trust Bank is open Monday through Thursday 9 to 4, and 9 to 5 on Friday. The drive-in opens at 8 AM.

Contacts Bank of America (✉ *777 Gloucester St., Brunswick, 31520* ☎ *912/267–4901* ✉ *167 Altama Connector, Brunswick, 31520* ☎ *912/264–0972*). **Sun Trust Bank** (✉ *2203 Demere Rd., St. Simons, 31522* ☎ *912/638–3349*).

INTERNET, MAIL & SHIPPING

Although most hotels have Internet or Wi-Fi access, if you're touring and just want to check e-mail, your best bet is the free service provided to visitors at the Visitor Welcome Centre on St. Simons. Bits, Bytes N Buns, a nifty café-cum-bakery in Brunswick, offers free Wi-Fi access with a $3 purchase and has computer stations to let you blast through a Word document or spreadsheet. It's open 6:30 AM to 6 PM, weekdays. U.S. Postal Services are also available.

Contacts **Bits, Bytes N Buns** (⊠*1178 Chapel Crossing Rd., Brunswick* ☎*912/265-2737*). **Brunswick Golden Isles Visitor Center** (⊠*530 Beachview Dr., St. Simons* ☎*912/638-9014*). **U.S. Postal Service**(⊠*18 S. Beachview Dr., Jekyll Island* ☎*912/635-2625* ⊠*620 Beachview Dr., St. Simons* ☎*912/635-2625* ⊠*1501 N. Way, Darien* ☎*912/437-4318*).

TOUR OPTIONS

St. Simons Transit Company offers year-round bus, boat, and trolley tours from St. Simons Island and Jekyll Island that explore the surrounding marshes and rivers and get you up close and personal with dolphins, manatees, and other marine life. Kayaks and canoes are also a great way to explore the creeks. Tour operators include Southeast Adventure Outfitters, St. Simons Island, and Brunswick.

Contacts **St. Simons Transit Company** (⊠*105 Marina Dr., St. Simons, 31522* ☎*912/638-5678* ⊕*www.saintsimonstransit.com*). **Southeast Adventure Outfitters** (⊠*313 Mallory St., St. Simons, 31522* ☎*912/638-6372* ⊕*www.southeastadventure.com*).

VISITOR INFORMATION

The Brunswick and the Golden Isles Visitors Center provides helpful information on all of the Golden Isles. For camping, tour, ferry and other information and reservations contact the Georgia State Parks Department.

Contacts **Brunswick and the Golden Isles Visitors Center**(⊠*4 Glynn Ave., Brunswick, 31520* ☎*912/265-6620* ⊠*530 Beachview Dr., St. Simons, 31522* ☎*912/638-9014* ☎*800/809-1790* ⊕*www. bgicvb.com*). **Georgia State Parks** (☎*800/864-7275 for reservations, 770/398-7275 within metro Atlanta, 404/656-3530 for general park information* ⊕*www.gastateparks.org*). **Jekyll Island Welcome Center** (⊠*1 Downing Musgrove Causeway, Jekyll Island* ☎*912/635-3636* ⊕*www.jekyllisland.com*). **St. Simons Visitors Center** (⊠*St. Simons, F.J. Torras, Causeway at U.S. 17, St. Simons Island, 31522* ☎*912/265-6620* ⊕*www.bgicvb.com*).

Charleston

WORD OF MOUTH

"I hope you plan to stay in the historic district. A walking map is all you need. Go to the [Old City Market] for fun flea market shopping. Slip into an old church for a rest. Be cheesy . . . take a carriage ride. Eat shrimp and grits. Read some Pat Conroy before you go."

—twigsbuddy

Updated
by Eileen
Robinson
Smith

WANDERING THROUGH THE CITY'S historic district, you would swear it was a movie set. The spires and steeples of more than 180 churches punctuate the low skyline, and the horse-drawn carriages pass centuries-old mansions and carefully tended gardens overflowing with heirloom plants. It's known for its quiet charm, and has been called the most mannerly city in the country.

Immigrants settled here in 1670. They flocked here initially for religious freedom and later for prosperity (compliments of the rice, indigo, and cotton plantations). Preserved through the poverty following the Civil War, and natural disasters like fires, earthquakes, and hurricanes, many of Charleston's earliest public and private buildings still stand. And thanks to a rigorous preservation movement and strict Board of Architectural Review, the city's new structures blend with the old ones. In many cases, recycling is the name of the game—antique handmade bricks literally lay the foundation for new homes. But although locals do live—on some literal levels—in the past, the city is very much a town of today.

Take the internationally heralded Spoleto Festival, for instance. For two weeks every summer, arts patrons from around the world come to enjoy local and international concerts, dance performances, operas, improv shows, and plays at venues citywide. Day in and out, diners can feast at upscale Southern restaurants, shoppers can look for museum-quality paintings and antiques, and outdoor adventurers can explore all Charleston's outlying beaches, parks, and marshes. But as cosmopolitan as the city has become, it's still the South, and just outside the city limits are farm stands cooking up boiled peanuts, recently named the state's official snack.

EXPLORING CHARLESTON

The heart of the city is on a peninsula, sometimes just called "downtown" by the nearly 60,000 residents who populate the area. Walking Charleston's peninsula is the best way to get to know the city. The main downtown historic district is roughly bounded by Lockwood Boulevard to the west, Calhoun Street to the north, the Cooper River to the east, and the Battery to the south. Nearly 2,000 historic homes and buildings occupy this fairly compact area divided into South of Broad (Street) and North of Broad.

King Street, the main shopping street in town, cuts through Broad Street, and the most trafficked tourist area ends a few blocks south of the Crosstown, where U.S. 17 cuts across Upper King. Downtown is best explored by foot. Otherwise, there are bikes, pedicabs, and trolleys. Street parking is irksome, as meter readers are among the city's most efficient public servants. Parking garages, both privately and publicly owned, charge around $1.50 an hour.

Beyond downtown, the Ashley River hugs the west side of the peninsula, and the region on the far shore is called West Ashley. The Cooper River runs along the east side of the peninsula, with Mount Pleasant on the opposite side and the Charleston Harbor in between. Last, there are outlying sea islands—James' Island with its Folly Beach, John's Island, Kiawah and Seabrook Islands, Isle of Palms, and Sullivan's Island—with their own appealing attractions. Everything that entails crossing the bridges is best explored by car or bus.

NORTH OF BROAD

Large tracts of available land made the area North of Broad ideal for suburban plantations during the early 1800s. A century later, the peninsula had been built out, and today the area is a vibrant mix of residential neighborhoods and commercial clusters, with verdant parks scattered throughout. Though there are a number of majestic homes and prerevolutionary buildings in this area (including the oldest public building in the city, the Old Powder Magazine), the main draw is the area's collection of stores, museums, restaurants, and historic churches.

As you explore, note that the farther north you travel (up King Street in particular), the newer and more commercial development becomes. Although pretty much anywhere on the peninsula is considered prime real estate these days, the farther south you go, the more expensive the homes become. In times past, Broad Street was considered the cutoff point for the most coveted addresses. Those living in the area Slightly North of Broad were called mere "SNOBs," and their neighbors South of Broad were nicknamed "SOBs."

Numbers in the margins correspond to numbers on the Charleston map.

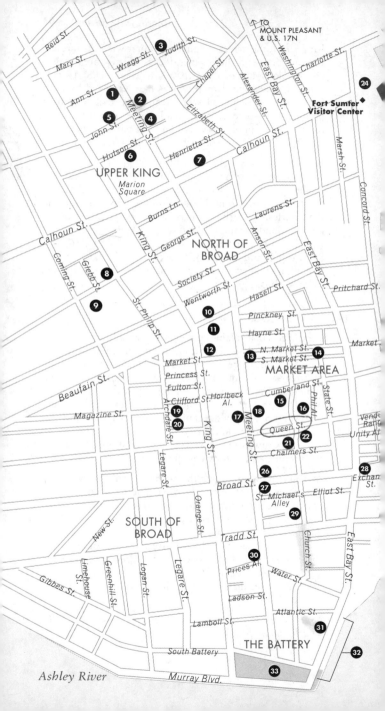

**Charleston
Maritime Center**

Downtown
Charleston

Cooper River

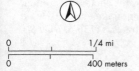

82 Queen St Restaurant

Aiken-Rhett House, **3**

Avery Research Center, **9**

The Battery, **32**

Charleston Museum, **2**

Charleston Place, **12**

Charleston Visitor Center, **1**

Children's Museum of the Lowcountry, **5**

Circular Congregational Church, **18**

City Hall, **26**

College of Charleston, **8**

Dock Street Theatre, **21**

Edmondston-Alston House, **31**

Emanuel African Methodist Episcopal Church, **7**

Fort Sumter, **25**

French Protestant (Huguenot) Church, **22**

Gibbes Museum of Art, **17**

Heyward-Washington House, **29**

Joseph Manigault House, **4**

Kahal Kadosh Beth Elohim, **10**

Market Hall, **13**

Nathaniel Russell House, **30**

Old Citadel, **6**

Old City Market, **14**

Old Exchange Building /Provos Dungeon, **28**

Old Powder Magazine, **15**

St. John's, **19**

St. Mary's, **11**

St. Michael's, **27**

St. Philip's, **16**

South Carolina Aquarium, **24**

Unitarian Church, **20**

Waterfront Park, **23**

White Point Gardens, **33**

0 —— 1/4 mi

0 —— 400 meters

CHARLESTON TOP 5

Dining Out: Charleston has become a culinary destination, with talented chefs who offer innovative twists on the city's traditional cuisine. Bob Waggoner at the Charleston Grill is one outstanding example.

Viewing Art: The city is home to more than 133 galleries, so you'll never run out of places to see world-class art. The Charleston Museum and dozens of others add to the mix.

Spoleto Festival USA: If you're lucky enough to visit in May or June you can find a city under siege: Spoleto's flood of indoor and outdoor performances (opera, music, dance, and theater) is impossible to miss and almost as difficult not to enjoy.

The Battery: The views from the point—both natural and man-made—are the loveliest in the city. Look west to see the harbor; to the east you can find elegant Charleston mansions.

Historic Homes: Charleston's preserved 19th-century houses, including the Nathaniel Russel House, are highlights; outside the city, plantations like Middleton Place, with its extensive garden and grounds, make scenic excursions.

MAIN ATTRACTIONS

❷ Charleston Museum. Founded in 1773, the country's oldest museum is housed in a contemporary complex. The museum's decorative-arts holdings and its permanent Civil War exhibit are extraordinary. There are more than 500,000 items in the collection, including silver, toys, and snuffboxes. There are also fascinating exhibits on natural history, archaeology, and ornithology. ■TIP→**Combination tickets that give you admission to the Joseph Manigault House and the Heyward-Washington House are a bargain at $22.** ✉*360 Meeting St., Upper King* ☎*843/722–2996* ⊕*www.charlestonmuseum.org* 🎫*$10* ⏰*Mon.–Sat. 9–5, Sun. 1–5.*

❿ Charleston Place. The city's most renowned hotel is flanked by upscale boutiques and specialty shops. Stop by for afternoon tea at the classy Thoroughbred Club. The city's finest public rest rooms are downstairs by the shoe-shine station. Entrances for the garage and reception area are on Hasell Street between Meeting and King streets. ✉*130 Market St., Market area* ☎*843/722–4900.*

❶ Charleston Visitors Center. The center's 20-minute film *Forever Charleston* is a fine introduction to the city. ■TIP→Tip: **The first 30 minutes are free at the parking lot, making it a real bargain.** ✉*375 Meeting St., Upper King* ☎*843/853–8000 or 800/868–8118* ⊕*www.charlestoncvb.com* ✑*Free* ⊙*Apr.– Oct., daily 8:30–5:30; Nov.–March 31., daily 8:30–5.*

❺ Children's Museum of the Lowcountry. Hands-on exhibits at this top-notch museum keep kids up to 12 occupied for hours. They can climb on a replica of a local shrimp boat, play in exhibits that show how water evaporates, and wander the inner workings of a medieval castle. ✉*25 Ann St., Upper King* ☎*843/853–8962* ⊕*www.explorecml.org* ✑*$7* ⊙*Tues.–Sat. 10–5, Sun. 1–5.*

NEED A BREAK?Take a break with an icy treat at **Paolo's Gelato Italiano** (✉*41 John St., Upper King* ☎*843/577– 0099*). Flavors include various fruits and florals, as well as traditional flavors like pistachio. It also serves crepes covered with delicious sauces.

⓮ Circular Congregational Church. The first church building erected on this site in the 1680s gave bustling Meeting Street its name. The present-day Romanesque structure, dating from 1890, is configured on a Greek-cross plan and has a breathtaking vaulted ceiling. Explore the graveyard, the oldest in the city, with records dating to 1696. ✉*150 Meeting St., Market area* ☎*843/577–6400* ⊕*www. circularchurch.org.*

❽ College of Charleston. Randolph Hall—an 1828 building designed by Philadelphia architect William Strickland— anchors the central Cistern area of the college. Majestic oaks envelop the Cistern's lush green quad, where graduation ceremonies and concerts take place. The college was founded in 1770. Scenes from *Cold Mountain* were filmed here. ✉*St. Philip and George sts., College of Charleston Campus* ⊕*www.cofc.edu.*

㉑ Dock Street Theatre. Incorporating the remains of the Old Planter's Hotel (circa 1809), this theater is draped in red-velvet curtains and has wonderful woodwork. At this writing it was slated to close for two years of much-needed renovations. ✉*135 Church St., Market area* ☎*843/720– 3968* ⊕*www.charlestonstage.com.*

㉕ Fort Sumter National Monument. The first shot of the Civil War was fired at Fort Sumter on April 12, 1861. After a

34-hour battle, Union forces surrendered the fort, which became a symbol of Southern resistance. The Confederacy held it, despite almost continual bombardment, from August of 1863 to February of 1865. When it was finally evacuated, the fort was a heap of rubble. Today, the National Park Service oversees it. The **Fort Sumter Liberty Square Visitor Center**, next to the South Carolina Aquarium, contains exhibits on the Civil War. This is a departure point for ferries headed to the island where you can find Fort Sumter itself. ⊠*340 Concord St., Upper King* ☎*843/577–0242* ⊆*Free* ☉*Daily 8:30–5*. Rangers conduct guided tours of the restored **Fort Sumter**. To reach the fort, you have to take a ferry; boats depart from Liberty Square Visitor Center and from Patriot's Point in Mount Pleasant. There are six crossings daily between mid-March and mid-August. The schedule is abbreviated the rest of the year, so call ahead for details. ⊠*Charleston Harbor* ☎*843/577–0242* ⊕*www.nps.gov/fosu* ⊆*Fort free; ferry $14* ☉*Apr.–early Sept., daily 10–5:30; early Sept.–Mar., daily 10–4.*

② **French Protestant (Huguenot) Church.** The tiny Gothic-style church is the only one in the country still using the original Huguenot liturgy. English-language services are held Sunday at 10:30. ⊠*136 Church St., Market area* ☎*843/722–4385* ⊕*www.frenchhuguenotchurch.org* ☉*Mid-Mar.–mid-June and mid-Sept.–mid-Nov., Mon.–Thurs. 10–4, Fri. 10–1.*

⑰ **Gibbes Museum of Art.** Housed in a beautiful beaux arts building, this museum boasts a collection of 10,000 works, principally American with a local connection. Each year there are a dozen special exhibitions, often of contemporary art. The museum shop is exceptional, with artsy, Charlestonian gifts. ⊠*135 Meeting St., Market area* ☎*843/722–2706* ⊕*www.gibbesmuseum.org* ⊆*$9* ☉*Tues.–Sat. 10–5, Sun. 1–5.*

❹ **Joseph Manigault House.** An outstanding example of federal architecture, this home was designed by Charleston architect Gabriel Manigault in 1803. It's noted for its carved-wood mantels, elaborate plasterwork, and garden "folly." The pieces of rare tricolor Wedgwood are noteworthy. ⊠*350 Meeting St., Upper King* ☎*843/722–2996* ⊕*www.charlestonmuseum.org* ⊆*$10* ☉*Mon.–Sat. 10–5, Sun. 1–5.*

❻ **Old Citadel Building.** A fortresslike building on Marion Square was the first home of the Carolina Military College and once housed troops and arms. The present-day Citadel

is in Hampton Park on the Ashley River. ⊠*341 Meeting
St., Upper King* ☎*843/723–6900*.

🆔 **Old City Market.** This area is often called the Slave Market
☙ because it's where house slaves once shopped for produce
and fish. Today stalls are lined with restaurants and shops
selling children's toys, leather goods, and regional souvenirs. Local "basket ladies" weave and sell sweetgrass, pine-
straw, and palmetto-leaf baskets—a craft passed down
through generations from their West African ancestors.
⊠*North and South Market sts. between Meeting and E.
Bay sts., Market area* ☉*Daily 9–dusk.*

🆔 **St. Philip's (Episcopal) Church.** The namesake of Church
Street, this graceful late-Georgian building is the second
on its site: the congregation's first building burned down
in 1835 and was rebuilt in 1838. During the Civil War,
the steeple was a target for shelling; one Sunday a shell
exploded in the churchyard. The minister bravely continued his sermon. Afterward, the congregation gathered elsewhere for the duration of the war. Notable Charlestonians
like John C. Calhoun are buried in the graveyard. ⊠*146
Church St., Market area* ☎*843/722–7734* ⊕*www.stphilip-
schurchsc.org* ☉*Church weekdays 9–11 and 1–4; cemetery
daily 9–4.*

🆔 **South Carolina Aquarium.** The 380,000-gallon Great Ocean
☙ Tank has the tallest aquarium window in North America.
★ Exhibits display more than 10,000 creatures, representing
more than 500 species. You travel through the five major
regions of the Southeast Appalachian Watershed: the Blue
Ridge Mountains, the Piedmont, the coastal plain, the
coast, and the ocean. Little ones can pet stingrays at one
touch tank and horseshoe crabs and conchs at another.
⊠*100 Aquarium Wharf, Upper King* ☎*843/720–1990
or 800/722–6455* ⊕*www.scaquarium.org* ☞*$16* ☉*Mid-
Apr.–mid-Aug., Mon.–Sat. 9–5, Sun. noon–5; mid-Aug.–
mid-Apr., Mon.–Sat. 9–4, Sun. noon–4.*

HISTORY LESSON A ferry ride to Fort Sumter is a great way to sneak
in a history lesson for the kids. For about the same price as a
standard harbor cruise you get a narrated journey that points out
the historic sites and explains how the Civil War began.

🆔 **Unitarian Church.** Completed in 1787, this church was
remodeled in the mid-19th century using plans inspired by
the Chapel of Henry VII in Westminster Abbey. The Gothic

fan-tracery ceiling was added during that renovation. An entrance to the church grounds is at 161½–163 King Street and leads to a secluded, overgrown Victorian-style graveyard that invites contemplation. Sunday service is at 11 AM. ✉*8 Archdale St., Market area* ☎*843/723–4617* ⌖*Free* ⊙*Church Fri. and Sat. 10–1, graveyard daily 9–5.*

㉓ **Waterfront Park.** Enjoy the fishing pier's porch-style swings,
★ stroll along the waterside path, or relax in the gardens overlooking Charleston Harbor. You can even jump into the fountain nicknamed "the pineapple" to get refreshed on hot summer days. The park is at the foot of Vendue Range, along the east side of Charleston Harbor and Cooper River. ✉*Prioleau St., Market area* ☎*843/724–7321* ⌖*Free* ⊙*Daily 6* AM*–midnight.*

ON THE CHEAP A $39.95 Charleston Heritage Passport, sold at the Charleston Visitors Center, gets you into the Gibbes Museum of Art, the Nathaniel Russell House, the Edmondston-Alston House, the Aiken-Rhett House, Drayton Hall, and Middleton Place. It's good for two days.

ALSO WORTH SEEING

❸ **Aiken-Rhett House.** This stately 1818 mansion still has its original wallpaper, paint schemes, and even some of its furnishings. The kitchen, slave quarters, and work yard are much as they were when the original occupants lived here, making this one of the most complete examples of urban slave life. Confederate general P. G. T. Beauregard made his headquarters here in 1864. ✉*48 Elizabeth St., Upper King* ☎*843/723–1159* ⊕*www.historiccharleston.org* ⌖*$10; $16 with admission to Nathaniel Russell House* ⊙*Mon.– Sat. 10–5, Sun. 2–5.*

❾ **Avery Research Center for African-American History and Culture.** This center, part museum and part archive, was once a school for freed slaves. Collections include slavery artifacts like badges, manacles, and bills of sale. A riveting mural chronicles the Middle Passage—the journey slaves made from Africa to Charleston's shores. The free tours include a brief film. ✉*125 Bull St., College of Charleston Campus* ☎*843/953–7609* ⊕*www.cofc.edu* ⌖*Free* ⊙*Weekdays noon–5, mornings by appointment.*

❼ **Emanuel African Methodist Episcopal Church.** Home of the South's oldest African Methodist Episcopal congregation, the church had its beginnings in 1818. Authorities closed it in 1822 when they suspected freedman Denmark Vesey used the sanctuary to plan a massive slave uprising. The church reopened on the present site after the Civil War ended. ✉ *110 Calhoun St., Upper King* ☎ *843/722–2561* 💲 *Donations accepted* 🕐 *Daily 9–4.*

🔟 **Kahal Kadosh Beth Elohim Reform Temple.** Considered one of the nation's finest examples of Greek-revival architecture, this temple was built in 1840 to replace an earlier one. The original was the birthplace of American Reform Judaism in 1824. Tours are conducted Sunday to Friday. ✉ *90 Hasell St., Market area* ☎ *843/723–1090* 🌐 *www.kkbe.org* 💲 *Free* 🕐 *Weekdays 10–noon, Sun. 12:30–3:45.*

🔞 **Market Hall.** Built in 1841, this imposing landmark was modeled after the Temple of Nike in Athens. The hall contains the **Confederate Museum,** in which the United Daughters of the Confederacy displays flags, uniforms, swords, and other Civil War memorabilia. ✉ *188 Meeting St., Market area* ☎ *843/723–1541* 💲 *$5* 🕐 *Tues.–Sat. 11–3:30.*

🔵 **Old Powder Magazine.** Built in 1713, the oldest public building in South Carolina is the only one that remains from the time of the Lords Proprietors. The city's volatile—and precious—gunpowder was kept here during the Revolutionary War. The building was designed to explode if detonated (and thus save Charleston). ✉ *79 Cumberland St., Market area* 💲 *$2* 🕐 *Tues.–Sat. 11–3:30.*

🔟 **St. John's Lutheran Church.** This Greek-revival church with delicate wrought-iron gates was completed in 1817 for a congregation that was established in 1742. Its most noteworthy leader, Dr. John Bachman, served as preacher 1815–74 and was known for ministering to local African-Americans and for collaborating on two books with his friend, naturalist John James Audubon. ✉ *5 Clifford St., Market area* ☎ *843/723–2426* 🌐 *www.stjohnscharleston.org.*

🔟 **St. Mary's Catholic Church.** Beautiful stained glass, wall paintings, and an interesting cemetery tucked between stone walls are highlights of the earliest Roman Catholic church in the Carolinas and Georgia. The white-pillar structure was constructed in 1839. ✉ *95 Hasell St., Market area* ☎ *843/722–7696* 🕐 *By appointment.*

BUILDING BOOM Charleston boomed with the plantation economy in the years before the Civil War. South Carolina's rice, indigo, and cotton crops produced an extraordinary concentration of wealth. Seeking a social and cultural lifestyle to match its financial success, the plantocracy entertained itself in style. The city was also renowned for its talented goldsmiths, silversmiths, gunsmiths, tobacconists, brewers, and cabinetmakers. More than 200 private residences were built during this period, and the city was one of the top shopping places in North America.

THE BATTERY & SOUTH OF BROAD

Locals have long joked that just off the Battery (at Battery Street and Murray Boulevard), the Ashley and Cooper rivers join to form the Atlantic Ocean. Such a lofty proclamation speaks volumes about the area's rakish flair. To observe their pride and joy, head to the point of the downtown peninsula. Here, handsome mansions surrounded by elaborate gardens greet incoming boats and passersby. The look is reminiscent of the West Indies with good reason: before coming to the Carolinas in the late 17th century, many early British colonists had first settled on Barbados and other Caribbean isles where homes with high ceilings and broad porches caught the sea breezes.

The heavily residential area south of Broad Street and west of the Battery brims with beautiful private homes, most of which bear plaques with a short written description of the property's history. Mind your manners, but feel free to peek through iron gates and fences at the verdant displays in elaborate gardens. Although an open gate once signified that guests were welcome to venture inside, that time has mostly passed—residents tell stories of how they came home to find tourists sitting in their front porch rockers. But you never know when an invitation to look around from a friendly owner-gardener might come your way. Several of the city's lavish house museums call this famously affluent neighborhood home.

Numbers in the margins correspond to numbers on the Charleston map.

MAIN ATTRACTIONS

★ Fodor'sChoice **Battery.** From the intersection of Water Street
❸❷ and East Battery you can look east toward the city's most photographed mansions; look west for views of Charleston Harbor and Fort Sumter. Walk south along East Battery to White Point Gardens, where the street curves and

becomes Murray Boulevard. ⊠*East Bay St. and Murray Blvd., South of Broad.*

㉙ Heyward-Washington House. The area where rice planter Daniel Heyward built his home in 1772 is believed to have been the inspiration for the folk opera *Porgy and Bess*. President George Washington stayed in the house during his 1791 visit. The period furnishings include the Holmes Bookcase, one of the finest remaining American furniture pieces of the late 18th century. Pay attention to the restored kitchen, the only one like it in Charleston open to the public. ⊠*87 Church St., South of Broad* ☎*843/722–2996* ⊕*www.charlestonmuseum.org* ⊡*$8* ⊙*Mon.–Sat. 10–5, Sun. 1–5.*

3

IF THE SHOE FITS Wear good walking shoes, because the sidewalks, brick streets, and even Battery Promenade are very uneven. Take a bottle of water, or take a break to sip from the fountains in White Point Gardens, as there are practically no shops south of Broad Street.

㉚ Nathaniel Russell House. One of the nation's finest examples of Adam-style architecture, the Nathaniel Russell House was built in 1808. The interior is distinguished by its ornate detailing, its lavish period furnishings, and the "free flying" staircase that spirals three stories with no visible support. The garden is well worth a stroll. ⊠*51 Meeting St., South of Broad* ☎*843/724–8481* ⊕*www. historiccharleston.org* ⊡*$10; $16 with admission to Aiken-Rhett House* ⊙*Mon.–Sat. 10–5, Sun. 2–5.*

㉗ St. Michael's Episcopal Church. The first cornerstone of St. Michael's was set in place in 1752, making it Charleston's oldest surviving church. Through the years other elements were added: the steeple clock and bells (1764); the organ (1768); the font (1771); and the altar (1892). The pulpit—original to the church—was designed to maximize natural acoustics. ⊠*14 St. Michael's Alley, South of Broad* ☎*843/723–0603* ⊕*www.stmichaelschurch.net* ⊙*Weekdays 9–4:30, Sat. 9–noon.*

㉝ White Point Gardens. Pirates once hung from gallows here; now it's a serene park with Charleston benches—small wood-slat benches with cast-iron sides—and views of the harbor and Fort Sumter. Children love to climb on the replica cannon and pile of cannonballs. ⊠*Murray Blvd. and*

E. Battery, South of Broad ☎843/724–7327 ⊙ *Weekdays 9–5, Sat. 9–noon.*

OLD-FASHIONED WALK In spring and summer, Charleston's gardens are in full glory. In fall and winter the homes are dressed in their holiday finest. Twilight strolls are a Dickensian experience, with homes lit from within showing off one cozy scene after another.

ALSO WORTH SEEING

㉖ **City Hall.** The intersection of Meeting and Broad streets is known as the Four Corners of Law, representing the laws of nation, state, city, and church. On the northeast corner is the graceful, pale pink City Hall, dating from 1801. The second-floor council chambers double as a museum where you can find John Trumbull's 1791 satirical portrait of George Washington and Samuel F. B. Morse's likeness of James Monroe. ☒ *80 Broad St., South of Broad* ☎843/577–6970 *or* 843/724–3799 ☞*Free* ⊙ *Weekdays 8:30–5.*

㉛ **Edmondston-Alston House.** First built in 1825 in late-federal style, the Edmondston-Alston House was transformed into the imposing Greek-revival structure you see today during the 1840s. Tours of the home—furnished with antiques, portraits, silver, and fine china—are informative. ☒ *21 E. Battery, South of Broad* ☎843/722–7171 ⊕*www.middletonplace.org* ☞*$10; $41 with combination ticket for Middleton Place* ⊙ *Tues.–Sat. 10–4:30, Sun. and Mon. 1:30–4:30.*

㉘ **Old Exchange Building & Provost Dungeon.** Originally a customs house with a waterside entrance, this building was used by the British to house prisoners during the Revolutionary War. Today costumed guides bring the revolutionary era to life. ☒ *122 E. Bay St., South of Broad* ☎843/727–2165 ⊕*www.oldexchange.com* ☞*$7* ⊙*Daily 9–5.*

MOUNT PLEASANT & VICINITY

East of Charleston, across the Arthur Ravenel Jr. Bridge, the largest single-span bridge in North America, is the town of Mount Pleasant, named not for a mountain or a hill but for a plantation in England from which some of the area's settlers hailed. In its Old Village neighborhood are antebellum homes and a sleepy, old-time town center with a drugstore where patrons sidle up to the soda fountain and lunch counter for egg-salad sandwiches and floats. Along Shem Creek, where the local fishing fleet brings in the daily catch, several seafood restaurants serve the area's freshest (and most deftly fried) seafood. Other attractions in the area include military and maritime museums, plantations, and, farther north, the Cape Romain National Wildlife Refuge.

MAIN ATTRACTIONS

★ **Boone Hall Plantation and Garden.** A ½-mi drive through a live-oak alley draped in Spanish moss introduces you to the still-operating plantation, the oldest of its kind. Tours take you through the 1935 mansion, the butterfly pavilion, the heirloom rose garden, and nine antebellum-era brick slave cabins. Stroll along the winding river, tackle the fields to pick your own strawberries or pumpkins, or dine in Serena's Kitchen, which serves Southern fare. *North and South, Queen,* and Nicholas Sparks's *The Notebook* were filmed here. ■TIP➔**Plan your visit to coincide with annual events like June's Blue Grass Festival and January's Oyster Festival.** ⊠ *1235 Long Point Rd., off U.S. 17N, Mount Pleasant* ☎ *843/884–4371* ⊕ *www.boonehallplantation.com* ☜ *$14.50* ☉ *Apr.–early Sept., Mon.–Sat. 8:30–6:30, Sun. 1–5; early Sept.–Mar., Mon.–Sat. 9–5, Sun. 1–4.*

☾ **Fort Moultrie National Monument.** Here Colonel William Moultrie's South Carolinians repelled a British assault in one of the first Patriot victories of the Revolutionary War. Completed in 1809, this is the third fort on this site at **Sullivan's Island,** reached on Route 703 off U.S. 17N (10 mi southeast of Charleston). A 20-minute film tells the history of the fort. ■TIP➔**Plan to spend the day relaxing bicycling through Sullivan's Island, a cluster of early-20th-century beach houses.** ⊠ *1214 Middle St., Sullivan's Island* ☎ *843/883–3123* ⊕ *www.nps.gov* ☜ *$3* ☉ *Daily 9–5.*

☾ **Patriots Point Naval & Maritime Museum.** Ships berthed here
★ include the aircraft carrier USS *Yorktown,* the World War II submarine USS *Clamagore,* the destroyer USS *Laffey,* and the Coast Guard cutter *Ingham,* responsible for sinking a U-boat during World War II. A Vietnam exhibit showcases naval air and watercraft used in the military action. ⊠ *Foot of Ravenel Bridge, Mount Pleasant* ☎ *843/884–2727* ⊕ *www.patriotspoint.org* ☜ *$15* ☉ *Daily 9–6:30.*

BASKET LADIES Drive along U.S. 17N, through and beyond Mount Pleasant, to find the basket ladies set up at rickety roadside stands, weaving sweetgrass, pine-straw, and palmetto-leaf baskets. Baskets typically cost less on this stretch than in downtown Charleston. Each purchase supports the artisans, who are becoming fewer and fewer each year.

ALSO WORTH SEEING

Cape Romain National Wildlife Refuge. A grouping of barrier islands and salt marshes, this 60,000-acre refuge is one of the most outstanding in the country. The **Sewee Visitor & Environmental Education Center** has information and exhibits on the refuge, trails, and rescued or breeding live birds of prey and red wolves. ■TIP→ **From Cape Romain National Wildlife Refuge you can take a $30 ferry ride to Bull Island. The island is a nearly untouched wilderness; the beach here, strewn with bleached driftwood, is nicknamed Boneyard Beach.** ✉*5821 U.S. 17N, Awendaw* ☎*843/928–3368* ⊕*http://caperomain.fws.gov* ✆*Free* ⊗*Tues.–Sun. 9–5.*

Charles Pinckney National Historic Site. Across the street from Boone Hall Plantation, this is a remnant of the country estate of Charles Pinckney, drafter and signer of the Constitution. A self-guided tour focuses on African-American farm life, including the plantation owner–slave relationship. You can also tour an 1820s tidewater cottage. ✉*1254 Long Point Rd., off U.S. 17N, Mount Pleasant* ☎*843/881–5516* 🖷*843/881–7070* ⊕*www.nps.gov* ✆*Free* ⊗*Daily 9–5.*

Old Village. This neighborhood is distinguished by white-picket-fenced colonial cottages, antebellum manses, tiny neighborhood churches, and restored (or new) waterfront homes with pricetags in the millions. It's a lovely area to stroll or bike. The Blessing of the Fleet seafood festival takes place each April. ✉*South of Alhambra Park.*

☾ **Palmetto Islands County Park.** This 943-acre park has a playground, paved trails, an observation tower, and boardwalks extending over the marshes. You can rent bicycles and paddleboats, or pay an extra fee for a small water park. ✉*Long Point Rd., ½ mi past Boone Hall Plantation, Mount Pleasant* ☎*843/884–0832* ⊕*www.ccprc.com* ✆*$2* ⊗*Apr., Sept., and Oct., daily 9–6; May–Aug., daily 9–7; Nov.–Feb., daily 10–5; Mar., daily 10–6.*

WEST OF THE ASHLEY RIVER

Ashley River Road, Route 61, begins a few miles northwest of downtown Charleston, over the Ashley River Bridge. Sights are spread out along the way and those who love history, old homes, and gardens may need several days to explore places like Drayton Hall, Middleton Place, and Magnolia Plantation and Gardens. Spring is a peak time for the flowers, although the gardens are in bloom throughout the year.

MAIN ATTRACTIONS

Magnolia Plantation and Gardens. The extensive informal garden, begun in 1685, has evolved into an overflowing collection of plants that bloom year-round, including a vast array of azaleas and camellias. You can take a tram or boat to tour the grounds. Rent a canoe to paddle through the 125-acre Waterfowl Refuge, or explore the 30-acre Audubon Swamp Garden along boardwalks and bridges. You can walk or rent bikes to traverse the more than 500 acres of trails. There are also a petting zoo and a miniature-horse ranch. You can tour the 19th-century plantation house, which originally stood in Summerville. The home was taken apart, floated down the Ashley River, and reassembled here. ✉*3550 Ashley River Rd., West Ashley* ☎*843/571–1266 or 800/367–3517* ⊕*www.magnoliaplantation.com* ⌨*Grounds $14; tram $7; boat $7* ⊙*Daily 8–5:30.*

★ **Fodor'sChoice Middleton Place.** Blooms of all seasons form floral *allées* (alleys) along terraced lawns, and around ornamental lakes shaped like butterfly wings. Much of the year, the landscaped gardens, begun in 1741, are ablaze with camellia, magnolia, azalea, and rose blossoms. A large part of the mansion was destroyed during the Civil War, but the gentlemen's wing has been restored and houses impressive collections of silver, furniture, paintings, and historic documents. In the stable yard craftspeople use authentic tools to demonstrate spinning, weaving, and other skills from the plantation era. Farm animals, peacocks, and other creatures roam freely. The Middleton Place restaurant serves Lowcountry specialties for lunch and dinner. There are also a delightful gift shop that carries local arts, crafts, and souvenirs, and a garden shop that sells rare seedlings. You can sign up for kayak, bike, wagon, or horseback tours, and you can stay overnight at the inn, where floor-to-ceiling windows splendidly frame the Ashley River. ✉*4300 Ashley*

River Rd., West Ashley ☎*843/556–6020 or 800/782–3608* ⊕*www.middletonplace.org* 🖼*Grounds $25; house tour $10* ☉*Grounds daily 9–5; house tours Tues.–Sun. 10–4:30, Mon. noon–4:30.*

ALSO WORTH SEEING

☾ **Charles Towne Landing State Historic Site.** Commemorating
★ the site of the original 1670 Charleston settlement, this park has a reconstructed village and fortifications, English park gardens with bicycle trails and walkways, and a replica 17th-century vessel moored in the creek. In the animal park native species roam freely—among them alligators, bison, pumas, bears, and wolves. Bicycle rentals are available. ✉*1500 Old Towne Rd., Rte. 171, West Ashley* ☎*843/852–4200* ⊕*www.southcarolinaparks.com* 🖼*$5* ☉*Daily 8:30–5.*

Drayton Hall. Considered the nation's finest example of unspoiled Georgian–Palladian architecture, this mansion is the only plantation house on the Ashley River to have survived the Civil War. A National Trust historic site, built between 1738 and 1742, it's an invaluable lesson in history as well as in architecture. Drayton Hall has been left unfurnished to highlight the original plaster moldings, opulent hand-carved woodwork, and other ornamental details. Watch *Connections,* which details the conditions under which slaves were brought from Africa. You can also see copies of documents that recorded the buying and selling of local slaves. Tours depart on the hour; guides are known for their in-depth knowledge of the era. ✉*3380 Ashley River Rd., West Ashley* ☎*843/769–2600* ⊕*www. draytonhall.org* 🖼*$14* ☉*Mar.–Oct., daily 9:30–4; Nov.– Feb., daily 9:30–3.*

SPORTS & THE OUTDOORS

BASEBALL

The **Charleston Riverdogs** (✉*Joseph P. Riley, Jr. Stadium, 360-Fishburne St.* ☎*843/577–3647* ⊕*www.riverdogs.com*) play at "The Joe," on the banks of the Ashley River near to the Citadel. Kids love their mascot, Charlie T. Riverdog. The season runs April to October.

Charleston Preserved

It's easy to think Charleston is a neverland, sweetly arrested in pastel perfection. But look at Civil War–era images of the Battery mansions on East Bay Street, one of the most photographed areas in town today, and you see the surrounding homes disfigured with crippling battle scars. Because of the poverty that followed the Civil War, on the whole locals simply couldn't afford to build anew from the late 1860s through the latter part of the 20th century, so they put the homes they had back together. In the 1920s it was community activism that rescued the old homes from being destroyed. According to Jonathan Poston, author of *Buildings of Charleston,* the preservation movement began when an Esso gas station was slated to take the place of the Joseph Manigault House. Citizens formed the Society for the Preservation of Old Dwellings (the first such group in the nation) and saved what's now a popular house museum. By 1931 Charleston's City Council had created the Board of Architectural Review (BAR), and designated the historic district protected from unrestrained development—two more national firsts. The Historic Charleston Foundation was established in 1947, and preservation is now second nature (by law).

As you explore, look for Charleston single houses: just one room wide, these houses were built with the narrow end streetside and multistory south or southwestern porches (often called piazzas) to catch prevailing breezes. Cool air drifts across these shaded porches, entering houses through open windows.

You'll see numerous architectural vestiges along Charleston's preserved streets. Many houses have plaques detailing their history, and others have Carolopolis Awards given for fine restoration work. Old fire-insurance plaques are more rare; they denote the company that insured the home and that would extinguish the flames if a fire broke out. Notice the bolt heads and washers that dot house facades along the Battery; some are in the shape of circles or stars, and others are capped with lion heads. These could straighten sagging houses when tightened via a crank under the floorboards.

Note the iron spikes that line the tops of some residential gates, doors, walls, and windows. Serving the same purpose as razor wire atop prison fences, most of these *cheveux de frise* (French for frizzy hair) were added after a thwarted 1822 slave rebellion, to deter break-in—or escape.

BEACHES

The Charleston area's mild climate means you can swim March to October. Public beaches, run by the Charleston County Parks & Recreation Commission, generally have lifeguards in season, snack bars, rest rooms and dressing areas, outdoor showers, umbrella and chair rental, and large parking lots.

Trees, palmettos, and other natural foliage cover the interior, and there's a river that winds through **Folly Beach County Park.** The beach, 12 mi southwest of Charleston, is more than six football fields long. ⊠*1100 W. Ashley Ave., off U.S. 17, Folly Island* ☎*843/588–2426* ☎*$5 per car* ⊗*Apr., Sept., and Oct., daily 10–6; May–Aug., daily 9–7; Nov.–Mar., daily 10–5.*

Play beach volleyball or rent a raft at the 600-foot-long beach in the **Isle of Palms County Park.** ⊠*1 14th Ave., Isle of Palms, Mount Pleasant* ☎*843/886–3863 or 843/768–4386* ☎*$5 per car* ⊗*May–Aug., daily 9–7; Apr., Sept., and Oct., daily 10–6; Nov.–Mar., daily 10–5.*

The public **Kiawah Beachwalker Park,** about 28 mi southwest of Charleston, has 500 feet of deep beach. ⊠*Beachwalker Dr., Kiawah Island* ☎*843/768–2395* ☎*$5 per car* ⊗*Mar., weekends 10–5; Apr. and Oct., weekends 10–6; May–Aug., daily 10–7; Sept., daily 10–6.*

BIKING

The historic district is ideal for bicycling as long as you stay off the busier roads. Many of the city's green spaces, including Colonial Lake and Palmetto Islands County Park, have biking trails.

You can rent bikes at the **Bicycle Shoppe** (⊠*280 Meeting St., Market area* ☎*843/722–8168* ⊠*1539 Johnnie Dodds Blvd., Mount Pleasant* ☎*843/884–7433*). **Bike the Bridge Rentals** (⊠*360 Concord St., Upper King* ☎*843/853–2453*) can set you up with a seven-speed bike to ride the paths on the spectacular Ravenel Bridge. You'll get a map, a self-guided tour booklet, and free water-taxi ride back. **Carolina Beach Cruisers** (⊠*4053 Rhett Ave., North Charleston* ☎*843/747–245* ⊕*www.carolinabeachcruisers.com*) rents all kinds of bikes, including those with special seats for youngsters. It delivers to all area islands.

BOATING

Kayak through marsh rivers and to outlying islands with **Coastal Expeditions** (⊠*514B Mill St., Mount Pleasant* ☎*843/884–7684*). You can rent kayaks from **Middleton Place Plantation** (⊠*4300 Ashley River Rd., West Ashley* ☎*843/556–6020* ⊕*www.theinnatmiddletonplace.com*) and glide along the Ashley River.

To hire a sailing charter, contact **AquaSafaris** (⊠*Patriots Point Marina, Mount Pleasant* ☎*843/886–8133* ⊕*www. aqua-safaris.com*). To learn how to command your own sailboat, enlist with **Ocean Sailing Academy** (⊠*24 Patriots Point Rd., Mount Pleasant* ☎*843/971–0700* ⊕*sasailing. com*).

FISHING

Anglers can rent gear ($8 to $10) and cast a line at the 1,000-foot fishing pier at **Folly Beach County Park** (⊠*101 E. Arctic Ave., Folly Beach* ☎*843/795–3474*). Baby sharks are commonly on the end of your line.

Fly-fishing guides generally charge between $300 and $400 for two people for a half-day. Fly-fishers looking for a native guide do best by calling **Captain Richard Stuhr** (⊠*547 Sanders Farm Lane, North Charleston* ☎*843/881–3179* ⊕*www.captstuhr.com*); he'll haul his boat to you.

Deep-sea fishing charters cost about $1,400 for 12 hours for a boatload of anglers. March through October is the time to go for yellowfin tuna aboard the 54-foot boat run by **Aut-top-Sea Charters** (⊠*Shem Creek docks, Mount Pleasant* ☎*843/454–0312*). **Palmetto Charters** (⊠*224 Patriots Point Rd., Mount Pleasant* ☎*843/849–6004* ⊕*www. palmettocharters.com*) has guided trips that take you out in the ocean or stay close to shore. **Bohicket Yacht Charters** (⊠*1880 Andell Bluff Blvd., Seabrook Island* ☎*843/768–7294* ⊕*www.bohicketboat.com*) has half- and full-day charters on 24- to 48-foot boats. It also offers dolphin-watching and dinner cruises.

GOLF

With fewer golfers than in Hilton Head, the courses around Charleston have more choice starting times available. Nonguests can play at private island resorts, such as Kiawah Island, Seabrook Island, and Wild Dunes. To find out about golf vacation packages in the area, contact the **Charleston Area Golf Guide** (☎*800/774–4444* ⊕*www. charlestongolfinc.com*).

Tom Fazio designed the Links and the Harbor courses at **Wild Dunes Resort** (✉*10001 Back Bay Dr., Isle of Palms* ☎*843/886–2180* ✉*5881 Palmetto Dr., Isle of Palms* ☎*843/886–2301*). **Seabrook Island Resort** (✉*Seabrook Island Rd., Seabrook Island* ☎*843/768–2529*) has two championship courses: Crooked Oaks, by Robert Trent Jones Sr., and Ocean Winds, by Willard Byrd. The prestigious **Ocean Course** (✉*1000 Ocean Course Dr., Kiawah Island* ☎*843/768–7272*), designed by Pete Dye, was the site of the 1991 Ryder Cup. Of the three championship courses at **Kiawah Island Resort** (✉*12 Kiawah Beach Dr., Kiawah Island*), Gary Player designed Marsh Point; Tom Fazio designed Osprey Point; and Jack Nicklaus designed Turtle Point.

The public **Charleston Municipal Golf Course** (✉*2110 Maybank Hwy., James Island* ☎*843/795–6517*) is a walker-friendly course. **Patriots Point** (✉*1 Patriots Point Rd., Mount Pleasant* ☎*843/881–0042*) has a partly covered driving range and spectacular harbor views. **Shadowmoss Golf Club** (✉*20 Dunvegan Dr., West Ashley* ☎*843/556–8251*) is a well-marked, forgiving course with one of the best finishing holes in the area.

Charleston National Country Club (✉*1360 National Dr., Mount Pleasant* ☎*843/884–7799*) is well maintained and tends to be quiet on weekdays. The **Dunes West Golf Club** (✉*3535 Wando Plantation Way, Mount Pleasant* ☎*843/856–9000*) has great marshland views and lots of modulation on the greens. **Links at Stono Ferry** (✉*4812 Stono Links Dr., Hollywood* ☎*843/763–1817*) is a popular public course with reasonable rates.

HORSEBACK RIDING

★ **Seabrook Island Equestrian Center** (✉*Seabrook Island Rd., Seabrook Island* ☎*843/768–7541*) is open to the public. The center, 24 mi southwest of Charleston, has trail rides on the beach and through maritime forests. There are also pony rides for kids About 7 mi south of Charleston, **Stono River Stables & Farms** (✉*3000 River Rd., John's Island* ☎*843/559–0773* ⊕*www.stonoriverstable.com*) offers trail rides through maritime forests

SCUBA DIVING

Experienced divers can explore the Cooper River Underwater Heritage Diving Trail, upriver from Charleston. The 2-mi-long trail has six submerged sites, including ships that date to the Revolutionary War. Charters will run you out to the starting point.

Charleston Scuba (✉*335 Savannah Hwy., West Ashley* ☎*843/763–3483* ⊕*www.charlestonscuba.com*) has maps, equipment rentals, and charters trips to the Cooper River Trail.

SOCCER

Charleston Battery (✉*Blackbaud Stadium, 1990 Daniel Island Dr., Daniel Island* ☎*843/971–4627* ⊕*www.charlestonbattery.com*) plays from April to September. After the games, fans retreat to the clubby English pub.

SPAS

Charleston Place Spa (✉*130 Market St., Market Area* ☎*843/722–4900* ⊕*www.charlestonplacespa.com*), a truly deluxe day spa, has nine treatment rooms and a wet room where seaweed body wraps and other treatments are administered. Four-handed massages for couples are a popular option. Locker rooms for men and women have showers and saunas; men also have a steam room. Adjacent is a fitness room, an indoor pool with skylights, and a spacious hot tub.

In a historic home, **Stella Nova** (✉*78 Society St., Ansonborogh* ☎*843/723–0909* ⊕*www.stella-nova.com*) lets you enjoy refreshments on the breezy verandas. This boutique spa is serious about all of its treatments, from waxings to salt scrubs. For couples there are aromatherapy massages.

TENNIS

You can play for free at neighborhood courts, including several near Colonial Lake and at the Isle of Palms Recreation Center. **Charleston Tennis Center** (✉*19 Farmfield Ave., West Ashley* ☎*843/724–7402*) is a city facility with lots of courts and locker rooms. **Maybank Tennis Center** (✉*1880 Houghton Dr., James Island* ☎*843/406–8814*) has lights on its six courts. The women's tennis Family Circle Cup is hosted each April at the **Family Circle Tennis Center** (✉*161 Seven Farms Dr., Daniel Island* ☎*843/856–7900* ⊕*www.familycirclecup.com*). The 17 lighted courts (13 clay, four hard) are open to the public.

WATER SPORTS

The pros at **McKevlin's Surf Shop** (⊠ *8 Center St., Folly Beach* ☎*843/588–2247*) can teach you what you need to know about surfing at Folly Beach County Park.

WHERE TO EAT

Eating is a serious pastime in Charleston. You can dine at nationally renowned restaurants serving the best of Southern nouveau, or if you prefer, a waterfront shack with some of the best fried seafood south of the Mason-Dixon line. Big-name chefs, including Bob Waggoner of the Charleston Grill, Robert Carter of the Peninsula Grill, Ken Vedrinkski of Sienna, Frank Lee of Slightly North of Broad, Mike Lata of FIG, and Craig Deihl of Cypress, have earned reputations for preparing Lowcountry cuisine with a contemporary flair. Incredible young talents include Tarver King of the Woodlands, Jason Schloz of High Cotton, and Ciaran Duffy of Tristan's. Sean Brock of McCrady's and David Szlam and Corey Elliott of Cordavi are putting a new spin on things.

Reservations are a good idea for dinner year-round, especially on weekends, as there is almost no off-season for tourism. Tables are especially hard to come by during the Southeastern Wildlife Expo (President's Day weekend in February) and the Spoleto Festival (late May to mid-June). The overall dress code is fairly relaxed: casual khakis and an oxford or polo shirt for men, casual slacks (or a skirt), top, and sandals for women work for any place you might pull up a chair.

PRICES

A gastro-tour can be expensive. You might try several of the small plates that many establishments offer as an option to keep costs down. In general, prices in restaurants over the bridges and on the islands, are considerably lower.

WHAT IT COSTS				
AT DINNER				
$$$$	$$$	$$	$	¢
over $22	$17–$22	$12–$16	$7–$11	under $7

Restaurant prices are for a main course at dinner.

AMERICAN–CASUAL

¢ ✕**Jack's.** There *is* a Jack, and he personally greets regulars and newcomers alike. Juicy burgers and just-right fries attract locals to this no-frills diner. Try the cheese-steak subs or the fat Reubens for lunch, or the made-from-scratch biscuits for breakfast. The restaurant is one block off King Street's busiest shopping area. ✉*41 George St., College of Charleston Campus* ☎*843/723–5237* ▭*MC, V* ◷*Closed weekends. No dinner.*

CONTEMPORARY

$$$$ ✕**Circa 1886.** If you're celebrating, come to this formal,
★ conducive-to-conversation dining room in a carriage house behind the Wentworth Mansion. There's a formality here, and the waitstaff has both skill and decorum. Chef Marc Collins has created dishes that are real originals; don't resist the Vidalia onion cream soup or the foie gras with crushed almonds. Crab is the central ingredient in his signature soufflé. The coffee-rubbed strip loin with corn pudding, asparagus, and truffles is remarkable. After all that beef, you may experience a chemical need for dessert—try the chocolate tasting with wonders like chocolate-chunk-brownie gelato. ✉*149 Wentworth St., Market area* ☎*843/853–7828* ≗*Reservations essential* ▭*AE, D, DC, MC, V* ◷*No lunch.*

$$$$ ✕**Cordavi.** This pair of Californians, David Szlan and Corey Elliott, won a major culinary award when they took over this restaurant in 2006. They strive to be culinary trendsetters. Alas, that goal sometimes overshadows one rule: food should taste good. At times, they are more concerned with presentation than they are serving dishes at the right temperature. Some items are close to perfection, like the complex glazed oysters with melted leeks and caviar. Prices are high, but a way to get around that is to order the three-course tasting menu. That tactic doesn't work if you want specialties like the divine foie gras served over French toast with sauterne sorbet. The wine list, which is equally as pricey, starts with just a couple bottles at $28 and then soars to $200. You'll applaud the flamenco guitarist on Tuesday evenings. ✉*14 N. Market St., Market area* ☎*843/ 577–0090* ▭*AE, D, DC, MC, V* ◷*Closed Monday. No lunch.*

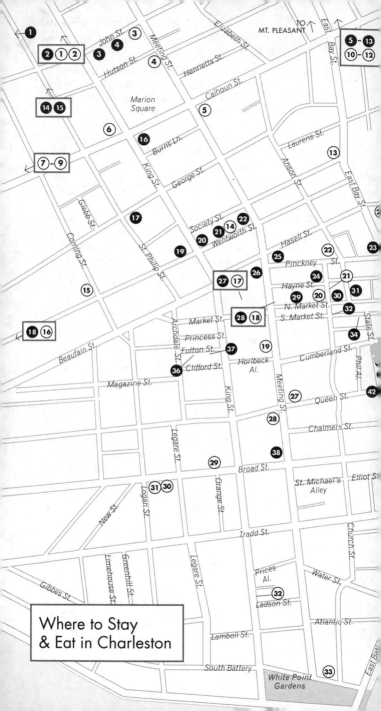

Where to Stay & Eat in Charleston

Restaurants

Andolini's Pizza, **19**
Anson, **31**
Blossom, **40**
Boathouse Restaurant, **10, 13**
Boulevard Diner, **9**
Bubba Gump, **34**
Carolina's, **46**
Charleston Crab House, **32**
Charleston Grill, **27**
Circa 1886, **18**
Coast, **4**
Coco's, **8**
Cordavi, **33**
Cru Café, **23**
Cypress, **41**
FIG, **25**
Five Loaves Cafe, **16**
Fulton Five, **36**
Gaulart & Maliclet Café, **38**
Grill 225, **35**
Gullah Cuisine, **5**
Hank's Seafood, **24**
High Cotton, **39**
Hominy Grill, **1**
Il Cortile del Re, **37**
J. Bistro, **6**
Jack's, **17**
Jestine's Kitchen, **22**
Juanita Greenberg's Nacho Royale, **14**
La Fourchette, **2**
Magnolias, **42**
McCrady's, **45**
Mercato, **29**
Oak Steakhouse, **47**
Old Village Post House, **11**
Peninsula Grill, **28**
Pita King, **15**
Robert's of Charleston, **44**
Sermet's Corner, **20**
Sienna, **12**
Slightly North of Broad, **43**
Sticky Fingers, **26**
39 Rue de Jean, **3**
Tristan, **30**
Wentworth Grill, **21**

The Wreck of the Richard and Charlene, **7**

Hotels

Andrew Pinckney Inn, **22**
Ansonborough Inn, **23**
Broad Street Guesthouse, **31**
Cannonboro Inn and Ashley Inn, **1**
Charleston Harbor Resort & Marina, **10**
Charleston Marriott, **9**
Charleston Place, **17**
Doubletree Guest Suites Historic Charleston, **20**
1837 Bed and Breakfast and Tea Room, **15**
Elliott House Inn, **27**
Embassy Suites Historic Charleston, **4**
Francis Marion Hotel, **6**
French Quarter Inn, **21**
Governors House Inn, **30**
Hampton Inn— Historic District, **3**
HarbourView Inn, **25**
Hayne House, **32**
Holiday Inn Historic District, **5**
John Rutledge House Inn, **29**
Kiawah Island Golf Resort, **7**
Market Pavilion Hotel, **24**
Meeting Street Inn, **19**
Mills House Hotel, **28**
Not So Hostel, **2**
Old Village Post House, **12**
Phoebe Pember House, **13**
Planters Inn, **18**
Renaissance Charleston Hotel Historic District, **14**
Seabrook Island Resort, **8**
Two Meeting Street, **33**
Vendue Inn, **26**
Wentworth Mansion, **16**
Wild Dunes, **11**

$$$$ ✕**McCrady's.** Sean Brock is passionate about his profession, and spends his nights coming up with innovative pairings, most of which work, though a few are too far out there. Try the slow-cooked lobster tail with parsnips, leeks, and citrus, or the seared tuna with a chorizo sausage puree. The cold soft chocolate with a crème anglais filling is one of the impressive desserts. The bar area has a centuries-old tavern feel. The encyclopedia-size wine list gave rise to the adjoining McCrady's Wine Bar, a more casual establishment. ⊠2 *Unity Alley, Market area* ☎843/577–0025 ⚑*Reservations essential* ⊟*AE, MC, V* ⊘*No lunch.*

$$$$ ✕**Robert's of Charleston.** Owner Robert Dickson is both a classically trained chef and an effusive baritone who belts out show tunes in the intimate dining room. The set menu changes, but might include scallop mousse with lobster sauce, duck with Asian barbecue sauce, and chateaubriand with a red wine sauce. Manager Joseph Raya picks the best wines to pair with each course. The restaurant is a family-run affair, which puts a warm spin on the experience. Robert's daughter, Maria-Elena, now reigns in the kitchen. ⊠*182 E. Bay St., Market area* ☎843/577–7565 ⚑*Reservations essential* ⊟*D, MC, V* ⊘*Closed Sun.–Wed. No lunch.*

$$$–$$$$ ✕**Cypress.** From the owners of Magnolias and Blossom comes a renovated 1834 brick-wall building with an urbane contemporary decor. Rust-color leather booths, a ceiling with light sculptures that change color, and a "wine wall" of 5,000 bottles keeps things interesting. The cuisine is classic American, with fresh local ingredients accented with exotic flavors, notably from the Pacific Rim. Try fabulous salads, like the hearts of palm and baby greens with local goat cheese topped with a walnut vingarette. The duck is a good entrée choice, as is the fillet cooked over hickory wood and topped with a Madeira wine sauce. Executive chef Craig Deihl consistently creates simple yet elegant fare, and you can do the same with his new cookbook called, of course, *Cypress.* ⊠*167 E. Bay St., Market area* ☎843/727–0111 ⚑*Reservations essential* ⊟*AE, DC, MC, V* ⊘*No lunch.*

$$$–$$$$ ✕**Peninsula Grill.** Eighteenth century–style portraits hang
★ on walls covered in olive-green velvet in this dining room. You sit beneath black-iron chandeliers feasting on longtime executive chef Robert Carter's imaginative entrées, including rack of lamb with a sesame-seed crust and a coco-

nut-mint pesto. The bourbon-grilled jumbo shrimp with lobster-basil hush puppies is scrumptious. The signature dessert is the three-way chocolate that comes with a shot of ice-cold milk. The servers, who work in tandem, are pros; the personable sommelier makes wine selections that truly complement your meal. The atmosphere is animated and convivial. ✉*Planters Inn, 112 N. Market St., Market area* ☎*843/723–0700* ✍*Reservations essential* Jacket required ▭*AE, D, DC, MC, V* ☉*No lunch.*

3

$$$–$$$$ ✕**Tristan.** Within the French Quarter Inn, this fine din-
★ ing room has a sleek, contemporary style with lots of metal, glass, and fresh flowers. Chef Ciaran Duffy purposely tailored the menu to complement the decor; it's ultrachic, innovative, and always evolving. The prix-fixe lunch, consisting of three courses from the dinner menu, is an astounding $15—less than that chicken wings place down the block. Imagine sitting down to a lunch of oyster chowder, then lamb ribs with a chocolate barbecue sauce, and moving on to molten black forest cake. After dark, the prices escalate—it's a status place, but always worth the money. Locals love the complimentary amuse bouche and digestif. On Sunday there's a fab brunch with a jazz trio. ✉*French Quarter Inn, 55 S. Market St., Market area* ☎*843/534–2155* ▭*AE, D, MC, V.*

$$–$$$$ ✕**Wentworth Grill.** A Continental flair prevails in this dining room with ceiling-to-floor windows, a handsome fireplace, and a mesmerizing pattern in the mosaic-tile floor. The cuisine begins in France with dishes like escargot and leeks sautéed in Pernod and stuffed in a puff pastry, then travels around the Mediterranean with offerings such as grouper with pancetta, arugula, and white beans. It returns to the Lowcountry with the bourbon–mustard barbecued scallops and pecan-dressed mustard greens. On Sunday there's a popular jazz brunch. ✉*Renaissance Charleston Hotel, 68 Wentworth St., Ansonborough* ☎*843/534–0300* ▭*AE, DC, MC, V.*

$$$ ✕**FIG.** Acronyms are popular here; the name, for instance, stands for Food Is Good. Chef Michael Lata's mantra is KIS, a reminder for him to Keep It Simple. Spend an evening here for fresh-off-the-farm ingredients cooked with unfussy, flavorful finesse. The menu changes frequently, but the family-style vegetables might be young beets in sherry vinegar placed in a plain white bowl. But his dishes do get more complex: there's the pureed cauliflower soup with

pancetta, incredible veal sweetbreads with smoked bacon and escarole, and grouper with a perfect golden crust accompanied by braised artichokes. The bar scene is lively, especially on Tuesday when there's smokin' live jazz. ⊠*232 Meeting St., Market area* ☎*843/805–5900* ▭*AE, D, DC, MC, V* ⊙*No lunch.*

$$–$$$ ✕**Cru Café.** One reason people come to this 18th-century house is to have lunch on the sunny wraparound porch. But the inventive menu keeps them coming back. Fried chicken breasts are topped with poblano peppers and mozzarella, and the duck confit is served with caramelized pecans and goat cheese, topped with fried shoestring onions, and dressed with port-wine vinaigrette. Chef John Zucker likes to go heavy on the starches, and his flavorful whipped potatoes are made with heavy cream. Meat dishes come with sauces made with green peppercorns, port wine, pear sherry, chipotle peppers, and horseradish cream. ⊠*18 Pinckney St., Market area* ☎*843/534–2434* ▭*AE, D, DC, MC, V* ⊙*Closed Sun. and Mon.*

$$–$$$ ✕**Old Village Post House.** If you've been on the road too long, this circa-1888 inn will provide warmth and sustenance. Many residents of this tree-lined village consider this their neighborhood tavern. The second, smaller dining room is cozy, and the outdoor space under the market umbrellas is open and airy. Expect contemporary takes on Southern favorites. Frank Sinatra serenades as you sample the fried eggplant Napoléon, the sautéed sea bass with fried green tomatoes, and the city's best succotash. In season, plump soft-shell crabs are deftly fried. And you'll love thyme ice cream! ⊠*101 Pitt St., Mount Pleasant* ☎*843/388–8935* ▭*AE, MC, V.*

$$ ✕**Five Loaves Cafe.** At this café tucked in the back of Millennium Music, the food is as fresh as that sold at the farmers' market in nearby Marion Square. Each day there are five new soups—if you're lucky, one of them will be pureed eggplant. A favorite is the spinach salad with grilled polenta croutons, fresh mozzarella, and toasted almonds. The mix-and-match lunch options are ideal, particularly for small appetites. For $7.50 you can choose a cup of soup or a small salad and half a sandwich. Everything is super healthful (if you can forgo the sinful desserts). ⊠*372 King St., Upper King* ☎*843/805–7977* ⊠*Blvd., Mount Pleasant* ☎*843/937–1043* ▭*AE, DC, MC, V.*

$-$$ ×**Sermet's Corner.** Bold artwork by Chef Sermet Aslan decorates the walls of this lively eatery. The dining room's plate-glass windows look out onto the King Street shopping district. Sermet gets artistic in the kitchen, which means the Mediterranean menu is speckled with innovations. The poached pear and salmon salad is a favorite, as is the sautéed calamari with fennel and oranges. The atmosphere is bohemian, and the bar is filled with colorful locals. ⊠276 *King St., Market area* ☎843/853–7775 ⊟AE, MC, V.

3

FRENCH

$$–$$$$ ×**La Fourchette.** French owner Perig Goulet moves agilely through the petite dining room of this unpretentious bistro. With back-to-back chairs making things cozy (and noisy), this place could be in Paris. Kevin Kelly chooses the wines—predominately French and esoteric, but befitting the authentic fare. Perig boasts of his country pâté, from a recipe handed down from his *grand-mère*. Other favorites include duck salad, scallops sautéed in cognac, and shrimp in a leek sauce. Dieters may be shocked by the golden *frites* fried in duck fat and served with aioli, but they keep putting their hungry hands in the basket. Check the blackboard for fish straight off the boats. ⊠432 *King St., Upper King* ☎843/722–6261 ⊟AE, MC, V ⊙*Closed Sun. No lunch Aug.–Mar.*

$$–$$$ ×**39 Rue de Jean.** In classic French-bistro style—gleaming
★ wood, cozy booths, and white-papered tables—Charleston's trendy set wines and dines until late on such favorites as steamed mussels in a half-dozen preparations. Order them with *pomme frites,* as the French do. Each night of the week there's a special, such as the bouillabaisse on Sunday. Rabbit with a whole-grain mustard sauce was so popular it jumped to the nightly menu. If you're seeking quiet, ask for a table in the dining room on the right. It's noisy—but so much fun—at the bar, especially since it has the city's best bartenders. ⊠39 *John St., Upper King* ☎843/722–8881 ≜*Reservations essential* ⊟AE, D, DC, MC, V.

$$ ×**Coco's Cafe.** A nondescript strip mall hosts this gem of a bistro. Make the trip over the bridge to Mount Pleasant for freshly made duck pâté, escargot in garlic butter, rabbit in a red wine and mushroom sauce, and panfried flounder in brown butter. Prices are less inflated here than downtown. The $10.95 prix-fixe lunch includes soup or salad, a main course, *and* a glass of wine. ⊠863 *Houston*

Northcutt Blvd., Mount Pleasant ☎843/881–4949 ⊟*AE, MC, V* ⊘*Closed Sun.*

$–$$ ✕**Gaulart and Maliclet Café.** Sharing high, family-style tables for breakfast, lunch, or dinner leads to camraderie at this bistro. Thursday brings a crowd for fondue. The cheese fondue can be disappointing, but the seafood, which you cook yourself in broth, is better. The bucheron cheese salad is wonderful. Nightly specials, such as bouillabaisse or couscous, are reasonably priced and come with a petite glass of wine. The service is often imperfect, but fun. The subtly sweet chocolate mousse cake is the best. ⊠*98 Broad St., South of Broad* ☎843/577–9797 ⊟*AE, D, MC, V* ⊘*Closed Sun. No dinner Mon.*

ITALIAN

$$$–$$$$ ✕**Fulton Five.** In the antique district, this romantic restaurant has chartreuse walls and antique brass accents. In warm weather you can opt for a seat on the second-floor terrace. Either way, the northern Italian specialties are worth savoring. Mushroom risotto with sweet corn accompanies the beef with porcini mushrooms. There's pappardelle with rabbit, and crabmeat and tarragon-laced butter flavor the spinach gnocchi. ⊠*5 Fulton St., Lower King St.* ☎843/853–5555 ⚑*Reservations essential* ⊟*AE, DC, MC, V* ⊘*Closed Sun. and late Aug.–early Sept. No lunch.*

$$–$$$$ ✕**Mercato.** Mercato is the new darling of those who like to see and be seen. Placed throughout the two floors are 18th-century antiques and Venetian lighting fixtures juxtaposed with contemporary artworks hung on elaborately plastered walls. Reserve a banquette under the 24-foot-long oil painting inspired by an early Italian circus banner. Music six nights a week, like the incredible gypsy band, is kept low key until after the normal dinner hour. (There's a late-night menu, too.) After that the volume goes up, adding fuel to the firey bar scene. Kudos go to the house-made pastas, like the gnocchi in a parmesan-reggiano cream sauce and the veal-cheek ravioli with wild mushrooms. The veal ossobuco will make any chilly night as warm as Tuscany in the summer. Desserts like the panna cotta and the warm chocolate cake with vanilla gelato are most agreeable with a small glass of limoncello. ⊠*102 N. Market St., Market area* ☎843/722–6393 ⊟*AE, D, DC, MC, V* ⊘*No lunch.*

$$–$$$$ ✕**Sienna.** Sumptuous meals here have all the flavor and
★ flair befitting a celebrity chef—but without the pomp. Ken
Vedrinkski has earned rave reviews for this laid-back eat-
ery. You may taste things here that you have never heard
of before, such as his "deconstructed" tiramisu that sepa-
rates the cake, the gelato, and the pana cotta. Four- and
seven-course tasting menus are the way to dine. Well worth
the drive over the bridges, it's the best of downtown din-
ing, minus the crowding, price markups, and paid park-
ing. ⊠*901 Island Park Dr., Daniel Island* ☎*843/881–9211*
🖃*AE, MC, V* ☉*Closed Sun. No lunch weekends.*

$$–$$$ ✕**Il Cortile del Re.** Hearty soups and pastas, fresh cheeses
and breads, and great wines make this a slice of Tus-
cany. This trattoria has an Italian-born chef whose dishes
couldn't be more authentic: braised lamb shank, porcini-
mushroom ravioli, baby arugula salad. An expansion to
this charming old building, which has lots of character,
added streetfront views. The animated bar is popular with
locals. ⊠*193A King St., Lower King St.* ☎*843/853–1888*
🖃*MC, V* ☉*Closed Sun. No lunch Sun.–Wed.*

KOSHER

$–$$$$ ✕**Pita King.** The renderings of typical Middle Eastern
dishes—falafel, hummus, and *shawarma* (a type of gyro)—
are uncommonly good at the city's only fully glatt kosher
establishment. The baba ghanoush is excellent, as is the
Israeli salad. ⊠*437 King St., Upper King* ☎*843/722–1977
or 843/224–5100* 🖃*AE, D, MC, V* ☉*Closed Sat. and Jew-
ish holidays. No dinner Fri.*

LOWCOUNTRY & SOUTHERN

★ Fodor'sChoice ✕**Charleston Grill.** Bob Waggoner's ground-
$$$$ breaking New South cuisine is now served in a dining
room highlighted by pale wood floors, flowing drapes, and
elegant Queen Anne chairs. A jazz ensemble adds a hip,
yet unobtrusive, element. The "new" Grill is more relaxed
than its previous incarnation, so as to attract a younger and
more vibrant clientele. The affable and highly talented chef
raised the culinary bar in this town, and continues to pro-
vide what many think of as its highest gastronomic experi-
ence. He employs only the best produce, like the organic
vegetables used in the golden beet salad. The menu is now
in four quadrants: simple, lush (foie gras and other delica-

cies), cosmopolitan, and southern. A nightly tasting menu is a way to taste it all. Master pastry chef Vinzenze Ascabacher sends out divine creations like praline parfait. Sommelier Rick Rubel has 1,300 wines in his cellar, with 25 of them served by the glass. ⊠*Charleston Place Hotel, 224 King St., Market area* ☎843/577–4522 ⌖*Reservations essential* ═AE, D, DC, MC, V ⊘*No lunch*.

$$$–$$$$ ✕**Anson.** Nearly a dozen windows afford views of the passing horse-drawn carriages. The softly lighted, gilt-trim dining room is romantic. Some locals prefer the more casual scene downstairs. The cuisine is traditional Lowcountry, like shrimp with grits and oysters fried in cornmeal (both served as appetizers). The she-crab soup is one of the best around. The chef takes liberty with some classics, like the crispy flounder in apricot sauce and the roasted red snapper with succotash and shrimp. Gooey, molten chocolate cake with house-made peanut butter ice cream is a favorite. ⊠*12 Anson St., Market area* ☎843/577–0551 ═AE, D, DC, MC, V ⊘*No lunch*.

$$$–$$$$ ✕**Carolina's.** On a quiet side street between East Bay Street and Waterfront Park, this longtime favorite occupies a former wharf building. The smartened-up decor includes romantic banquettes. The evolving menu by Chef Jeremiah Bacon has a strong emphasis on healthful ingredients. (Owner Richard Stoney has Kensington Plantation, where most of the produce is grown.) Lowcountry favorites stand next to original dishes like scallops with roasted cauliflower. Local grouper works amazingly well with a port-wine broth. Ask about the special prix-fixe dinners, including ones with beer pairings. Sunday and Monday the price of bottles of wine is cut in half. The free valet parking is appreciated. ⊠*10 Exchange St., South of Broad* ☎843/724–3800 ⌖*Reservations essential* ═D, MC, V ⊘*No lunch*.

$$$–$$$$ ✕**High Cotton.** Lazily spinning paddle fans, palm trees, and
★ brick walls create a plantation ambience. Chef Jason Scholz combines wonderful flavors and flawless presentation for memorable meals. His take on foie gras, for example, is a terrine with port-wine cherry chutney. You can feast on bourbon-glazed pork and white-cheddar grits. The chocolate soufflé with blackberry sauce and the praline soufflé are both remarkable. Sunday brunch is accompanied by musicians who sweeten the scene. At night the bar is enlivened with jazz. ⊠*199 E. Bay St., Market area* ☎843/724–

CLOSE UP

Lowcountry Cuisine

Colonial settlers to Charles Towne found maritime forests, winding rivers, and vast marshes along a flat coastal plain, which came to be called the Lowcountry. This expansive backyard provided a cornucopia of sustenance—seafood, game, and produce—and the recipes French and English settlers brought from their homeland were altered to match the ingredients found here. After slaves were brought in from the West Indies and West Africa to work the rice fields, the Gullah language—a rollicking creole of English with African words and accents—and culture developed. Because blacks and whites were in such close proximity (slaves outnumbered whites for generations), languages, accents, and cuisines melded. The mix of continental recipes and African flavors, made by using the harvest of the region, became known as Lowcountry cooking.

Rice, rice, and more rice is ever-present in Lowcountry dishes, including *pilau*, also spelled *purlieu* (both pronounced pur-*low*), which is a pilaf—rice cooked in meat or vegetable broth. Salty-sweet shrimp and grits are on menus of every price category in Charleston. You can buy creamy she-crab soup in restaurants and stores. Other essential dishes are Hoppin' John (rice and beans), and Frogmore Stew (with shrimp, sausage, and corn). Okra, eggplant, *hominy* (cooked grits), tomatoes, butterbeans, benne seeds, ham, shrimp, fish, and game are all part of the regional cuisine. Southern favorites like fried green tomatoes, fried fish and oysters, bacon-wrapped shad roe, and stuffed quail are popular here, too. But Charleston cuisine is not all about things past; true to the spirit of Lowcountry cooking, "city" chefs continue to innovate and create using the local harvest of farm-fresh heirloom vegetables and seafood caught daily just offshore.

3

3815 ✍Reservations essential ▤*AE, D, DC, MC, V* ⊘*No lunch weekdays.*

$$$–$$$$ ✕**Slightly North of Broad.** This former warehouse with brick-
★   and-stucco walls has a chef's table that looks directly into the open kitchen. It's a great place to perch, as chef Frank Lee, who wears a baseball cap instead of a toque, is one of the city's culinary characters. Known for his talent in preparing game, his venison is exceptional. Many of the items come as small plates, which make them perfect for

sharing. The braised lamb shank with a ragout of white beans, arugula and a red demi-glace is divine. Lunch can be as inexpensive as $7.95 for something as memorable as mussels with spinach, grape tomatoes, and smoked bacon. ✉ *192 E. Bay St., Market area* ☎ *843/723–3424* ⊟ *AE, D, DC, MC, V* ⊘ *No lunch weekends.*

$$–$$$$ ✕ **Magnolias.** The theme here is evident in the vivid paintings of creamy white blossoms that adorn the walls. A visit from Oprah Winfrey revived the reputation of "Mags," a pioneer of innovative Lowcountry cuisine. (Many locals, particularly the younger ones, prefer its more youthful siblings, Cypress and Blossom.) Executive chef Don Drake refreshes classic dishes like fried green tomatoes with white cheddar grits, carmelized onions, and country ham. Sunday brunch is a more affordable way to sample the fare; the free parking helps defray the cost. ✉ *185 E. Bay St., Market area* ☎ *843/577–7771* ⚒ *Reservations essential* ⊟ *AE, DC, MC, V.*

$$–$$$ ✕ **Blossom.** Exposed white rafters and linenless tables make this place casual and yet upscale. The terrace with a view of St. Philip's majestic spire, the dining room, and the bar are heavily populated with young professionals. The open, exhibition kitchen adds to the high-energy atmosphere. Lowcountry seafood is a specialty, and the pastas are made on the premises. ✉ *171 E. Bay St., Market area* ☎ *843/722–9200* ⊟ *AE, DC, MC, V.*

$–$$$ ✕ **Gullah Cuisine.** Charlotte Jenkins cooks up a mean lunch
★ buffet stocked with fried chicken, collard greens with ham, crispy okra, and macaroni pie. But it's the Gullah dishes— with roots in African cuisines—that make her place unique. The Gullah rice—with chicken, sausage, shrimp, and vegetables—and the fried alligator tails are both delightful lessons in regional flavors. Dinner options have expanded to include lobster. ✉ *1717 U.S. 17N, Mount Pleasant* ☎ *843/881–9076* ⊟ *AE, MC, V* ⊘ *Closed Sun.*

$–$$$ ✕ **Hominy Grill.** The wooden barber poles from the last century still frame the door of this small, homespun café. Chalkboard specials are often the way to go here, be it breakfast, lunch, or dinner. Chef Robert Stehling is a Carolina boy who lived in New York; that dichotomy shows in his "uptown" comfort food. Have the perfect soft-shell crab sandwich with homemade fries, but leave room for the tangy buttermilk pie or the chocolate peanut butter pie. The young servers are sometimes frantic. ✉ *207 Rutledge*

Ave., Canonboro ☎843/937–0930 ⊟*AE, MC, V* ⊗*No dinner Sun.*

$–$$$ ✕**J. Bistro.** Funky steel cutouts liven up outside and inside walls, and quirky lights hang low over tables. A varied list of appetizers and small plates makes this a great place to graze. Main dishes include pistachio-encrusted duck breast with a cassis glaze or loin of lamb with lingonberry port-wine sauce. Sunday Brunch has heavenly choices like crab cakes Benedict. ✉*819 Coleman Blvd., Mount Pleasant* ☎*843/971–7778* ⌂*Reservations essential* ⊟*AE, MC, V* ⊗*Closed Mon. No lunch Tues.–Sat.*

$–$$$ ✕**Sticky Fingers.** The sound of blues and the aroma of ribs reaches the street—where you may have to wait to get seated. This family-oriented local chain was founded by three Charleston buddies who admired Memphis barbecue. The pulled pork is popular, but the ribs are *it*. You have your choice of five different sauces, including some made with honey or bourbon. ✉*235 Meeting St., Market area* ☎*843/853–7427* ✉*341 Johnnie Dodds Blvd., Mount Pleasant* ☎*843/856–9840* ✉*1200 N. Main St., Summerville* ☎*843/875–7969* ⊟*AE, DC, MC, V.*

$–$$ ✕**Jestine's Kitchen.** Enjoy dishes made from passed-down family recipes—like sweet chicken with limas—at the last of the true down-home, blue-plate Southern restaurants in the historic district. This casual eatery is known for its fried everything: chicken, okra, shrimp, pork chops, and green tomatoes. The cola cake and coconut-cream pie are divine. ✉*251 Meeting St., Upper King* ☎*843/722–7224* ⊟*MC, V* ⊗*Closed Mon.*

¢–$$ ✕**Boulevard Diner.** This former Dairy Queen is now a no-frills counter-and-booth diner. The service is attentive, but the waitresses don't call you hon. The food, soulfully prepared, includes a fried eggplant-and-blue-cheese sandwich, Cajun-style meat loaf, and chili served in a sundae glass with sour cream and a cherry tomato on top. ✉*409 W. Coleman Blvd., Mount Pleasant* ☎*843/216–2611* ⊟*MC, V* ⊗*Closed Sun.*

PIZZA

$ ✕**Andolini's Pizza.** A cheap-date spot, Andolini's caters to college students who hide out in tall booths or on the rear patio. The dough and sauce are made daily, and the cheese is freshly grated. Toppings include the expected, plus banana peppers, feta, jalapeños, and extra-tasty Italian sausage. Call in advance for takeout. ⊠*82 Wentworth St., College of Charleston Campus* ☎*843/722–7437* ═*AE, D, MC, V.*

SEAFOOD

$$–$$$$ ×**Boathouse Restaurant.** Large portions of fresh seafood at doable prices make both Charleston-area locations wildly popular. The shrimp hush puppies with spicy mayonnaise and lightly battered fried shrimp and oysters are irresistible. Entrées come with mashed potatoes, grits, collard greens, or blue-cheese coleslaw. The original Isle of Palms location is right on the water, so tables are hard to come by. At the Upper King branch, the architecture is strikingly contemporary, with a fisherman's boat hoisted at the bar. Brunch is popular on Sunday. ⊠*101 Palm Blvd., Isle of Palms* ☎*843/886–8000* ⊠*549 E. Bay St., Upper King* ☎*843/577–7171* ⌖*Reservations essential* ═*AE, DC, MC, V* ⊙*No lunch Mon.–Sat.*

$$–$$$$ ×**Coast Bar & Grill.** Tucked off a little alley in a restored warehouse, Coast has pared-down trappings like exposed brick-and-wood floors. Fried fare and heavy sauces are staples, but lighter dishes such as the fish tacos and ceviche make it a standout. The best choices include oak-grilled fish and lobster served with pineapple-chili salsa, white-wine-and-lemon sauce, or garlic butter. ⊠*39D John St., Upper King* ☎*843/722–8838* ═*AE, D, DC, MC, V* ⊙*No lunch.*

$$–$$$$ ×**Hank's Seafood.** A lively spot with a popular bar and community dining area flanked by paper-topped private tables, Hank's is an upscale fish house. Seafood platters come with sweet-potato fries and coleslaw. That location off the Old Market, and the fact it's sister restaurant to the fancy-pants Peninsula Grill, makes the place noteworthy. ⊠*Church and Hayne sts., Market area* ☎*843/723–3474* ═*AE, D, DC, MC, V* ⊙*Closed Mon. No lunch.*

$$–$$$ ×**Charleston Crab House.** When you cross over the Wapoo Creek Bridge to James Island, you catch a glimpse of this tiered restaurant. Its decks are splashed by the waters of the Intracoastal Waterway. Boaters tie up and mingle with the fun crowd. Crab is the specialty, of course, with she-crab soup a perennial award winner. There's also good crab cakes and baked oysters. ⊠*125A Wapoo Creek Dr., James*

3

Island ☎843/795–1963 ✉1101 Stockade Lane, Mount
Pleasant ☎843/884–1617 ✉41 S. Market St., Market area
☎843/853–2900 ⊟AE, DC, MC, V.

$$–$$$ ✕**The Wreck of the Richard and Charlene.** At first glance you
★ think the name might refer to the waterfront restaurant—a
shabby, screened-in porch. In actuality, the *Richard and
Charlene* was a trawler that slammed into the building
during a hurricane in 1989. The kitchen serves up Southern tradition on a plate: boiled peanuts, fried shrimp, and
stone crab claws. The best deal is the most expensive: the
$18 platter with fried flounder, shrimp, oysters, and scal-
lops. ✉106 Haddrell St., Mount Pleasant ☎843/884–
0052 ⌕Reservations not accepted ⊟No credit cards
⊘No lunch.

$–$$$ ✕**Bubba Gump.** If you loved Forrest, Jenny, Lieutenant Dan,
and the others from *Forrest Gump,* then head to this chain
eatery. The food, particularly the shrimp with mango-
pineapple salsa, is surprisingly good. You won't be able
to resist the chocolate-chip-cookie sundae. Children who
weren't even born when the movie came out in 1994 adore
the Gumpisms scrawled on the dining room tables. ✉96
S. Market St., Market area ☎843/723–5665 ⊟AE, DC,
MC, V.

STEAK

$$$$ ✕**Grill 225.** Expect hefty portions and upscale renderings
of steak-house favorites, accompanied by silver pitchers of
special barbecue sauces. Blue-crab chowder and the seared
tuna tower are superior starters. The veal chop stuffed with
prosciutto and provolone is a revered house specialty. The
pastry chef shines; the banana-bread pudding with caramel
ice cream and the molten chocolate cake with raspberry
couli are the best sweet flings. Wood floors, white linens,
and red-velvet upholstery add to the elegance. ✉Market
Pavilion Hotel, 225 E. Bay St., Market area ☎843/266–
4222 ⊟AE, D, DC, MC, V.

$$$–$$$$ ✕**Oak Steakhouse.** In a 150-year-old bank building, this
dining room juxtaposes antique crystal chandeliers with
contemporary art. Reserve a table on the third floor for
the full effect and the best vistas. It's pricey, but the filet
mignon with a foie-gras-black-truffle butter is excellent,
and the side dishes, such as creamed spinach, are perfectly
executed. Favorite appetizers include beef carpaccio and

gorgonzola fondue. Service is professional and cordial. ✉*17 Broad St., Market area* ☎*843/722–4220* ⊟*AE, MC, V* ⊘*Closed Sun. No lunch.*

TEX-MEX

¢ ✕**Juanita Greenberg's Nacho Royale.** Fast and fresh are the priorities here. Order a brick-size burrito, or try the tasty quesadillas. Wash down the Royale Nachos (steak, salsa, black beans, black olives, jalapeños, and cheese) with a Mexican soda or a foamy draft beer. ✉*439 King St., Upper King* ☎*843/723–6224* ⊟*AE, D, MC, V.*

WHERE TO STAY

In a city known for its old mansions, atmospheric bed-and-breakfasts are found in the residential blocks of the historic district. Upscale hotels are in the heart of downtown. Unique, boutique hotels provide a one-of-a-kind experience. Chain hotels line the busy, car-trafficked areas (like Meeting Street). In addition, there are chain properties in the nearby areas of West Ashley, Mount Pleasant, and North Charleston.

PRICES

Charleston's downtown lodgings have three seasons: high season (spring, March to May and fall, September to November); mid-season (summer, June to August); and low season (late November to February). Prices drop significantly during the short low season, except during holidays and special events; high season is summer at the island resorts; rates drop for weekly stays and during off-season. ■TIP➔**If you're on a budget, lodgings outside the city limits tend to be less expensive. Also try booking online, where you can often find good deals.**

WHAT IT COSTS				
HOTELS				
$$$$	$$$	$$	$	¢
over $220	$161–$220	$111–$160	$70–$110	under $70

Prices are for two people in a standard double room in high season.

HOTELS & MOTELS

$$$$ ☎ **Charleston Place.** Even casual passersby enjoy gazing up at
★ the handblown Moreno glass chandelier in the hotel's open
lobby, clicking across the Italian marble floors, and admir-
ing the antiques from Sotheby's. A gallery of upscale shops
completes the ground-floor offerings. Rooms are furnished
with period reproductions. The impeccable service is what
you would expect from an Orient-Express property, particularly on the Club Level, where rooms carry a $100 sur-
charge that gets you a breakfast spread, afternoon tea, and
cocktails in the evening and pastries. A truly deluxe day
spa, with an adjacent fitness room, has an inviting indoor
pool illuminated by skylights. ■TIP➔ **Even if you aren't staying here, stop by for afternoon tea at the equestrian-theme
Thoroughbred Club.** ✉ *130 Market St., Market area, 29401*
☎*843/722–4900 or 800/611–5545* 📠*843/724–7215*
⊕*www.charlestonplacehotel.com* ⇱*400 rooms, 42 suites*
⌂*In-room: refrigerator, Ethernet. In-hotel: 2 restaurants,
bar, pool, gym, spa, bar, concierge, no-smoking rooms*
▭*AE, D, DC, MC, V* ◎*EP.*

$$$$ ☎ **French Quarter Inn.** The first architectural detail you'll
★ notice is a circular staircase with a wrought-iron bannister
embellished with iron leaves. This award-winning property is known for its chic French style. Guests appreciate
the lavish breakfasts, the afternoon wine and cheese, and
evening cookies and milk. The pillow menu is a luxury;
you can order whatever kind you desire, including big
body pillows. Some rooms have fireplaces, others balconies. Among the best are No. 220, a business suite with
a corner office niche overlooking the courtyard, and No.
104, with a spacious L-shape design. ✉ *166 Church·St.,
Market area, 29401* ☎*843/722–1900 or 866/812–1900*
📠*843/722–5682* ⊕*www.fqicharleston.com* ⇱*46 rooms, 4
suites* ⌂*In-room: Ethernet. In-hotel: restaurant, bar, public
Wi-Fi, concierge, no-smoking rooms* ▭*AE, MC, V* ◎*BP.*

$$$$ ☎ **Market Pavilion Hotel.** The melee of one of the busiest corners in the city vanishes as soon as the uniformed bellman
opens the lobby door to dark, wood-panel walls, antique
furniture, and chandeliers hung from high ceilings. It
resembles a grand hotel from the 19th century, and you feel
like visiting royalty. Get used to being pampered—smartly
attired bellmen and butlers are quick at hand. Rooms are
decadent with French-style chaises and magnificent marble
baths. One of Charleston's most prestigious fine-dining

spots, Grill 225, is here. ■**TIP**→ **Join sophisticated Charlestonians who** *do* **cocktails and apps at the rooftop Pavilion Bar.**
✉*225 E. Bay St., Market area, 29401* ☎*843/723–0500 or
877/440–2250* 🖷*843/723–4320* ⊕*www.marketpavilion.
com* 🛏*61 rooms, 9 suites* ౿*In-room: Ethernet. In-hotel:
restaurant, bar, pool, concierge, public Internet, no-smoking rooms* ⊟*AE, D, DC, MC, V* ⵏ◯*EP.*

$$$$ 🖼**Renaissance Charleston Hotel Historic District.** A sense of
history prevails in this hotel, one of Charleston's newest upscale properties. Legend has it that British Admiral
George Anson won this neighborhood, dubbed Ansonborough, in a card game in 1726. (This is why his image
is on the playing cards in the library lounge.) The hotel
has a delightful courtyard where you can enjoy cocktails.
Guest rooms are smallish but have nice touches like period-
style bonnet beds. The Wentworth Grill serves a mix of
French and Lowcountry specialties. ✉*68 Wentworth St.,
Ansonborough, 29401* ☎*843/534–0300* 🖷*843/534–0700*
⊕*www.renaissancecharlestonhotel.com* 🛏*163 rooms, 3
suites* ౿*In-room: dial-up. In-hotel: restaurant, bar, pool,
public Wi-Fi, concierge, no-smoking rooms* ⊟*AE, D, DC,
MC, V* ⵏ◯*EP.*

$$$–$$$$ 🖼**Charleston Harbor Resort & Marina.** Mount Pleasant's fin-
est hotel sits on Charleston Harbor, so you can gaze at the
city's skyline. If you'd rather be there, a water taxi will
get you across in 10 minutes. A lot goes on here, from
splashy boat shows at the marina to wedding celebrations
on the white sand. Ask for one of the renovated rooms
with fireplaces and plasma TVs. Children can jump into
the mini-mariners' program, while parents are navigat-
ing a sailboat. ✉*20 Patriots Point Rd., Mount Pleasant,
29464* ☎*843/856–0028 or 888/856–0028* 🖷*843/856–
8333* ⊕*www.charlestonharborresort.com* 🛏*160 rooms,
6 suites* ౿*In-room: Wi-Fi. In-hotel: restaurant, bar, pool,
water sports, children's programs (ages 7–12)* ⊟*AE, DC,
MC, V* ⵏ◯*BP.*

$$$–$$$$ 🖼**Charleston Marriott.** Residents watched to see how the
construction crews would transform this riverview hotel,
which had been on a downhill slide for years. In some ways
this reincarnation is far better, such as the glamorous glass
addition with a cascading waterfall that houses the con-
cierge desk. The sunset views only get better on the sec-
ond floor, especially on the outdoor terrace where drinks
and tapas are served. The reconstructed pool area is grand,

3

with an plenty of palms and a gazebo. The aromas from the brick oven in Saffires are intoxicating, as are the myriad flatbreads it produces. The cuisine is laudable—contemporary dishes with refreshingly flavorful low calorie options. ⊠170 Lockwood Dr., Charleston, 29403 ☎843/ 723–3000 ⊕www. marriott.com ➦337 rooms, 3 suites ⏃In-room: dial-up. In-hotel: restaurant, bar, pool, public Wi-Fi ⊟AE, DC, MC, V ⏃⏃EP.

$$$–$$$$ ☒**Doubletree Guest Suites Historic Charleston.** This one-time bank wears a restored entrance portico from 1874. Fountains bubble in the three interior garden courtyards. This is not a glamorous property, but it has clean, spacious suites with nice touches like antique reproductions and canopy beds. The efficient and friendly staff dotes on families, even giving out chocolate-chip cookies. ⊠181 Church St., Market area, 29401 ☎843/577–2644 or 877/408–8733 ☎843/577–2697 ⊕www.doubletree.com ➦47 rooms, 165 suites ⏃In-room: refrigerator, Ethernet. In-hotel: bar, laundry facilities, no-smoking rooms ⊟AE, D, DC, MC, V ⏃⏃EP.

$$$–$$$$ ☒**Embassy Suites Historic Charleston.** A courtyard where cadets once marched is now an atrium with skylights, palm trees, and a fountain. The restored brick walls of the breakfast room and some guest rooms in this contemporary hotel contain original gun ports, reminders that the 1822 building was the Old Citadel. Handsome teak and mahogany furniture and sisal rugs in the common areas recall the British-colonial era. Guest rooms are not nearly as chic, but are clean and serviceable. ⊠337 Meeting St., Upper King, 29403 ☎843/723–6900 or 800/362–2779 ☎843/723–6938 ⊕www.embassysuites.com ➦153 suites ⏃In-room: refrigerator, dial-up. In-hotel: restaurant, pool, gym, laundry facilities, no-smoking rooms ⊟AE, D, DC, MC, V ⏃⏃BP.

$$$–$$$$ ☒**HarbourView Inn.** Ask for a room facing the harbor and you can gaze down at the landmark pineapple fountain of Waterfront Park. Calming earth tones and rattan soothe and relax; four-poster beds and sea-grass rugs complete the Lowcountry look. Some of the rooms are in a former 19th-century shipping warehouse with exposed brick walls, plantation shutters, and whirlpool tubs. Afternoon wine and cheese and evening milk and cookies are included. ⊠2 Vendue Range, Market area, 29401 ☎843/853–8439 or 888/853–8439 ☎843/853–4034 ⊕www.harbourview-

charleston.com ↻*52 rooms* ☆*In-room: refrigerator, Wi-Fi. In-hotel: concierge, public Internet, no-smoking rooms* ☰*AE, D, DC, MC, V* ⎮○⎮*BP.*

$$$–$$$$ ⊞**Mills House.** A favorite local landmark, the Mills House is reconstruction of an 1853 hotel where Robert E. Lee waved from the wrought-iron balcony. All of the guest rooms have been completely refurbished and have nice touches like antique reproductions. There are some additions to the original design, such as a fitness center and a delightful pool deck. Lowcountry specialties are served in the Barbados Room, which opens onto the terrace courtyard. ✉*115 Meeting St., Market area, 29401* ☎*843/577–2400 or 800/874–9600* ☎*843/722–0623* ⊕*www.millshouse. com* ↻*199 rooms, 16 suites* ☆*In-room: dial-up. In-hotel: Restaurant, bar, pool, gym, no-smoking rooms* ☰*AE, D, DC, MC, V* ⎮○⎮*EP.*

$$$ ⊞**Francis Marion Hotel.** Wrought-iron railings, crown moldings, and decorative plasterwork speak of the elegance of 1924, when the Francis Marion was the largest hotel in the Carolinas. Bountiful throw pillows and billowy curtains add flair to the guest rooms, many of which have views of Marion Square. Some are small, however. Flavorful Lowcountry cuisine is served at the Swamp Fox. ✉*387 King St., Upper King, 29403* ☎*843/722–0600 or 877/756–2121* ☎*843/723–4633* ⊕*www.francismarioncharleston.com* ↻*193 rooms, 34 suites* ☆*In-room: dial-up. In-hotel: restaurant, gym, spa, public Internet, public Wi-Fi, no-smoking rooms* ☰*AE, D, DC, MC, V* ⎮○⎮*EP.*

$$$ ⊞**Hampton Inn–Historic District.** Hardwood floors and a fireplace in the lobby of what was once an 1800s warehouse help elevate this chain hotel a bit above the rest. Spindle posts on the headboards give guest rooms a little personality. Rooms are not large but have little perks like coffeemakers. The location is perfect for exploring downtown. ✉*373 Meeting St., Upper King, 29403* ☎*843/723–4000 or 800/426–7866* ☎*843/722–3725* ⊕*www.hamptoninn.com* ↻*166 rooms, 5 suites* ☆*In-room: refrigerator, dial-up. In-hotel: pool, babysitting, laundry facilities, concierge, public Internet, no-smoking rooms* ☰*AE, D, DC, MC, V* ⎮○⎮*BP.*

$$$ ⊞**Holiday Inn Historic District.** Thanks to its staff, this hotel has an outstanding track record for guest satisfaction. And then there's the great location—across from Marion Square and a block from Gaillard Auditorium. Rooms are traditional, with wood armoires, headboards, and side tables.

✉125 Calhoun St., Upper King, 29401 ☎843/805–7900 or 877/805–7900 🖷843/805–7700 🌐www.charleston-hotel.com ⇨122 rooms, 4 suites ♿In-room: dial-up. In-hotel: restaurant, bar, pool, bar, concierge, public Internet, no-smoking rooms ▭AE, D, DC, MC, V 🍽BP.

DOGGY DAY CARE If you have brought your dog along, but don't want to leave him in your room all day, call Charlie Freeman at Dog Daze (*✉307 Mill St., Mount Pleasant ☎843/884-7387 or 843/324-6945*). His services are $20 a day. With advance notice he'll even pick up Rover at your hotel for an additional $10.

3

INNS, B&BS & GUESTHOUSES

To find rooms in homes, cottages, and carriage houses, contact **Historic Charleston Bed and Breakfast** (*✉60 Broad St., South of Broad ☎843/722–6606 🌐www.historiccharlestonbedandbreakfast.com*).

$$$$ ★ **Governors House Inn.** This quintessential Charleston lodging radiates 18th-century elegance. Its stately architecture typifies the grandeur, romance, and civility of the city's bountiful colonial era. A National Historic Landmark, it's filled with family antiques and period reproductions in the public rooms and the high-ceiling guest rooms. The best room is the Rutledge Suite, a legacy to the original owner, Governor Edward Rutledge. Nice touches include a proper afternoon tea. *✉117 Broad S., South of Broad, 29401 ☎843/720–2070 or 800/720–9812 🖷843/805–6549 🌐www.governorshouse.com ⇨7 rooms, 4 suites ♿In-hotel: concierge, no-smoking rooms ▭AE, MC, V 🍽BP.*

$$$$ **Hayne House.** Vintage furnishings combine with a fresh, light spirit at Hayne House. Colonial brickwork, working fireplaces, and a narrow cypress stairway are characteristic of the mid-1700s, when the original wings were built. Ceilings in the guest rooms are low, and the bathrooms are small and need some work. A full Southern breakfast is served on English porcelain. The price is a bit high for what you get. *✉30 King St., South of Broad, 29401 ☎843/577–2633 🖷843/577–5906 🌐www.haynehouse.com ⇨4 rooms ♿In-room: no phone, no TV, refrigerator. In-hotel: no-smoking rooms ▭MC, V 🍽BP.*

$$$$ ★ **John Rutledge House Inn.** In 1791 George Washington visited this elegant mansion, residence of one of South Carolina's most influential politicians, John Rutledge. This

National Historic Landmark has spacious accommodations within the lovingly restored main house (Nos. 6, 8, and 11 are the most appealing). Solid painted walls—in forest green and buttercream yellow—complement the billowy fabrics on the four-poster beds. Parquet floors sit beneath 14-foot ceilings adorned with plaster moldings. Families gravitate to the privacy of the two carriage houses overlooking the shaded brick courtyard. Afternoon tea or port is served in the lounge. ⊠ *116 Broad St., South of Broad, 29401* ☎*843/723–7999 or 800/476–9741* 📠*843/720–2615* ⊕*www.charminginns.com* ⇱*16 rooms, 3 suites* ⌂*In-room: refrigerator. In-hotel: public Wi-Fi, concierge, no-smoking rooms* ⊟*AE, D, DC, MC, V* ⊺◎⊺*BP.*

$$$$ ⊡**Planters Inn.** Part of the Relais & Châteaux group, this ★ boutique property is a stately sanctuary amid the bustle of Charleston's Market. Light streams into a front parlor with its velvets and Oriental antiques. It serves as the lobby for this exclusive inn that has both an historic side and a new building wrapped around a two-story piazza and overlooking a tranquil garden courtyard. Yet the rooms all look similar, and are beautifully maintained. Service is gentile and unobtrusive, and the hospitality feels genuine. Best choice rooms are those with fireplaces, or verandas, four-poster canopy beds, and the "piazza" suites with whirlpool baths. ⊠*112 N. Market St., Market area, 29401* ☎*843/722–2345 or 800/845–7082* 📠*843/577–2125* ⊕*www.plantersinn. com* ⇱*56 rooms, 6 suites* ⌂*In-room: safe. In-hotel: restaurant, public Wi-Fi, concierge, no-smoking floors* ⊟*AE, D, DC, MC, V* ⊺◎⊺*EP.*

$$$$ ⊡**Vendue Inn.** This lodging's rooftop restaurant and bar have sweeping views of the nearby waterfront (but rooms look out on a condo). Two 19th-century warehouses have been transformed into an inn with a variety of nooks and crannies filled with antiques. Bathrobes hang in the closet, and full buffet breakfast, afternoon wine and hors d' oeuvres, and evening milk and cookies are complimentary. ⊠*19 Vendue Range, Market area, 29401* ☎*843/577–7970 or 800/845–7900* ⊕*www.vendueinn.com* ⇱*31 rooms, 35 suites* ⌂*In-room: safe. In-hotel: restaurant, bar, public Wi-Fi, no-smoking rooms* ⊟*AE, D, DC, MC, V* ⊺◎⊺*BP.*

★ **Fodor'sChoice** ⊡**Wentworth Mansion.** Charlestonian Francis $$$$ Silas Rodgers made his money in cotton, and in 1886 had built this four-story mansion with such luxuries as Austrian crystal chandeliers and hand-carved marble mantles.

3

You can admire the Second Empire antiques and reproductions, the rich fabrics, and inset wood paneling. In the colder months, the baronial, high-ceiling guest rooms have the velvet drapes drawn and the gas fireplaces lighted. The breakfast buffet and evening wine and cheese are complimentary. Circa 1886, the restaurant shares the former carriage house with a spa. ✉ *149 Wentworth St., College of Charleston Campus, 29403* ☎ *843/853–1886 or 888/466–1886* ☏ *843/720–5290* ⊕ *www.wentworthmansion.com* ⤶ *21 rooms* � *In-room: dial-up. In-hotel: restaurant, spa, concierge, no-smoking rooms* ☰ *AE, D, DC, MC, V* ⌷ *BP.*

$$$-$$$$ ⊞ **Ansonborough Inn.** A shipping warehouse dating from the early 1900s, this building's architectural details have been emphasized by leaving brick walls exposed and designing around the grand, heart-pine beams and wood ceilings. Oil paintings of hunting dogs hang above clubby leather chairs and sofas. You can enjoy evening wine and cheese on a rooftop terrace while you watch the ships sail past. ✉ *21 Hasell St., Market area, 29401* ☎ *843/723–1655 or 800/522–2073* ☏ *843/577–6888* ⊕ *www.ansonborough-inn.com* ⤶ *37 suites* ⚫ *In-room: safe, refrigerator, dial-up. In-hotel: bar, public Wi-Fi, no-smoking rooms* ☰ *AE, MC, V* ⌷ *BP.*

$$$-$$$$ ⊞ **Cannonboro Inn and Ashley Inn.** These sister B&Bs on the edge of the historic district have a lot in common. At both inns expect a full breakfast served on a wide porch overlooking a garden, tea in the afternoon, and free use of bicycles. Rooms have antiques from the 19th century, when they were built. The pinkish Ashley Inn has a two-bedroom carriage house with kitchen, while the gray Cannonboro has one suite with a kitchen. ✉ *Cannonboro Inn, 184 Ashley Ave., Medical University of South Carolina, 29403* ☎ *843/723–8572 or 800/235–8039* ☏ *843/723–8007* ⊕ *www.charleston-sc-inns.com* ⤶ *7 rooms, 1 suite* ⚫ *Dining room, cable TV, bicycles, business services, free parking; no kids under 10, no smoking* ☰ *AE, D, DC, MC, V* ⌷ *BP* ✉ *Ashley Inn, 201 Ashley Ave., Medical University of South Carolina, 29403* ☎ *843/723–1848 or 800/581–6658* ☏ *843/579–9080* ⊕ *www.charleston-sc-inns.com* ⤶ *6 rooms, 1 suite, 1 house* ⚫ *In-room, no phone, kitchen. In-hotel: bicycles, no kids under 10, no-smoking rooms* ☰ *AE, D, DC, MC, V* ⌷ *BP.*

$$$–$$$$ ☐**Phoebe Pember House.** The 1807 property is split between a carriage house with two guest rooms and a coach house with three guest rooms. The decor is tastefully done, and each room has nice touches like lace-covered canopy beds. The vibrant artwork is by Charleston artists. Enjoy breakfast in the walled garden shaded by an arbor. ⊠*26 Society St., Ansonborough, 29401* ☎*843/722–4186* ⎙*843/722–0557* ⊕*www.phoebepemberhouse.com* ⤳*5 rooms* ⌂*In-room: dial-up. In-hotel: no-smoking rooms* ☐*MC, V* ⍟*BP.*

$$$–$$$$ ☐**Two Meeting Street.** As pretty as a wedding cake, this
★   Queen Anne mansion has overhanging bays, colonnades, balustrades, and a turret. While rocking on the front porch you can look through soaring arches to White Point Gardens and the Ashley River. Tiffany windows, carved-oak paneling, and a crystal chandelier dress up the public spaces. Two guest rooms have balconies and working fireplaces. Expect to be treated to afternoon high tea as well as a delightful, creative southern breakfast. ⊠*2 Meeting St., South of Broad, 29401* ☎*843/723–7322* ⊕*www.twomeetingstreet.com* ⤳*9 rooms* ⌂*In-room: no phone, no TV. In-hotel: no kids under 12, no-smoking rooms* ☐*No credit cards* ⍟*BP.*

$$–$$$ ☐**Andrew Pinckney Inn.** The lobby of this boutique inn has a homey ambience that blends South Carolina and the West Indies. The two-story town-house suites, which sleep four, are ideal for longer stays. A heavenly breakfast with fresh-baked pastries and biscuits with sausage gravy is taken on its rooftop, which overlooks the church spires. It's in the bustling market area, so ask for an interior room. ⊠*40 Pinckney St., Market area, 29401* ☎*843/937–8800 or 800/505–8983* ⎙*843/937–8810* ⊕*www.andrewpinckney-inn.com* ⤳*41 rooms, 3 town houses, 1 suite* ⌂*In-room: refrigerator (some), dial-up. In-hotel: laundry service, concierge, public Internet, public Wi-Fi, no-smoking rooms* ☐*AE, MC, V* ⍟*BP.*

$$–$$$ ☐**Broad Street Guesthouse.** Hadassah Rothenberg, an accomplished cook and baker, has realized her dream of opening the city's first kosher B&B. She completely transformed this 1880s frame house, artfully decorating it with a mix of Victorian furnishings, religious art, and vintage family photos. Friday evening guests can join in traditional prayers and partake in a multicourse Shabbat dinner. Rothenberg's glatt kosher dishes are lovely and fresh, the

baked goods delectable. The wholesome breakfast is even better when taken on the terrace. ⊠*133 Broad St., South of Broad, 29401* ☏*843/577–5965* 🖷*843/202–8601* ⊕*www. charlestonkosherbedandbreakfast.com* ⮂*2 suites, 1 cottage* ⚭*In-room: no phone, no TV, kitchen. In-hotel: public Wi-Fi, no-smoking rooms* ⊟*AE, D, MC, V* ⊚*BP.*

$$-$$$ 🖳**1837 Bed and Breakfast and Tea Room.** A hospitable staff helps you get a sense of what it would be like to live in one of Charleston's grand old homes. Antique lace-canopy beds fill much of the guest rooms, which are in the main house and in the carriage house. A delicious breakfast includes homemade breads and hot entrées such as sausage pie or ham frittatas. ⊠*126 Wentworth St., Market area, 29401* ☏*843/723–7166 or 877/723–1837* 🖷*843/722–7179* ⊕*www.1837bb.com* ⮂*8 rooms, 1 suite* ⚭*In-room: no phone, refrigerator* ⊟*AE, DC, MC, V* ⊚*BP.*

$$-$$$ 🖳**Elliott House Inn.** Listen to the chimes of St. Michael's Episcopal Church as you sip wine in the courtyard of this lovely inn in the heart of the historic district. You can then retreat to a cozy room with period furniture, including canopied four-posters and Oriental carpets. Some previous loyal guests complain that it has lost some of its personal, homey ambience since it was taken over by a corporate management company; others seem quite pleased with the change. ⊠*78 Queen St., Market area, 29401* ☏*843/723–1855 or 800/729–1855* 🖷*843/722–1567* ⊕*www.elliotthouseinn. com* ⮂*24 rooms* ⚭*In-hotel: bicycles, no kids, no-smoking rooms* ⊟*AE, D, MC, V* ⊚*BP.*

$$-$$$ 🖳**Meeting Street Inn.** This 1874 house with second- and third-story porches originally had a tavern on the ground floor. Rooms overlook a lovely courtyard with fountains and a garden; many have hardwood floors and handwoven rugs. Four-poster or canopy beds, chair rails, and patterned wallpaper create a period feel. Despite its good downtown location, the inn has managed to keeps its prices affordable. ⊠*173 Meeting St., Market area, 29401* ☏*843/723–1882 or 800/842–8022* 🖷*843/577–0851* ⊕*www.meetingstreet-inn.com* ⮂*56 rooms* ⚭*In-room: refrigerator. In-hotel: bar, public Wi-Fi* ⊟*AE, D, DC, MC, V* ⊚*BP.*

$$-$$$ 🖳**Old Village Post House.** This white wooden building anchoring Mount Pleasant's historic district is a cozy inn, an excellent restaurant, and a neighborly tavern. Up the high staircase, rooms have hardwood floors and reproduction furnishings that will remind you of Cape Cod. The dark-

wood furnishings feel right at home in a building with roots in the 1880s. The food is wonderful, from the pastries at breakfast to the entrées at dinner. Staying on this charming tree-lined village, you're within walking distance to Charleston Harbor. ⊠*101 Pitt St., Mount Pleasant, 29464* ☎*843/388–8935* ᐸ*843/388–8937* ⊕*www.oldvillageposthouse.com* ⟿*6 rooms* ⌂*In-hotel: restaurant, bar, no-smoking rooms* ⊟*AE, D, DC, MC, V* ⍾❘*BP.*

¢ ▣**Not So Hostel.** Several 1840s-era buildings were combined to make this hostel. Pancakes and waffles for breakfast, a garden where you can pick vegetables, and prices that put the rest of the city's lodgings to shame make this place a great place to stay. Of course, you need to be able to handle a little peeling paint, a bit of clutter, and a less gentile neighborhood. Linens, a locker, and Internet access are free. ⊠*156 Spring St., Medical University of South Carolina, 29403* ☎*843/722–8383* ⊕*www.notsohostel.com* ⟿*14 dorm beds, 7 rooms with communal baths* ⌂*In-room: no phone, no TV. In-hotel: bicycles, laundry facilities, public Internet room, no-smoking rooms* ⊟*AE, D, DC, MC, V* ⍾❘*BP.*

SOMETHING EXTRA When you book your room, ask about special packages. Extras that are often available include romantic carriage rides, dinners, interesting guided tours, and champagne or other goodies delivered to your room.

RESORTS

For condo and house rentals on Kiawah Island, Seabrook Island, Sullivan's Island, the Isle of Palms, and Wild Dunes, call **Resort Quest** (⊠*1517 Palm Blvd., Isle of Palms, 29451* ☎*800/344–5105* ⊕*www.resortquest.com*).

$$$$ ▣**Wild Dunes Resort.** This 1,600-acre island resort has as
★ its focal point the plantation-style Boardwalk Inn. It sits among a cluster of villas that have been painted in pastels to resemble Charleston's Rainbow Row. The guest rooms and suites on the fourth and fifth floors have balconies that overlook the ocean. You can also choose one- to six-bedroom villas that sit near the sea or the marshes. You have a long list of recreational options here including Tom Fazio golf courses and nationally ranked tennis programs; packages are available. Nearby is a yacht harbor on the Intracoastal Waterway. Chef Enzo Steffenelli reigns

over the highly-rated Sea Island Grill. ⊠*Palm Blvd. at 41st Ave., Isle of Palms* ⒹBox 20575, Charleston, 29413 ☎843/886–6000 or 888/845–8926 ⎙843/886–2916 ⊕*www.wilddunes.com* ⇌*430 units, 93 rooms* ⎈*In-hotel: 3 restaurants, golf courses, tennis courts, pools, gym, water sports, bicycles, public Internet, public Wi-Fi, children's programs (ages 3–12), concierge, no-smoking rooms* ⊟*AE, D, DC, MC, V* ⦿*EP.*

★ **Fodor's**Choice ⛺**Kiawah Island Golf Resort.** Choose from one-to four-bedroom villas and three- to seven-bedroom private homes in two upscale resort villages on 10,000 wooded and oceanfront acres. Or opt to stay at the Sanctuary at Kiawah Island, an amazing 255-room luxury waterfront hotel and spa. The vast lobby is stunning, with walnut floors covered with handwoven rugs and a wonderful collection of artworks. The West-Indies theme is evident in the guest rooms; bedposts are carved with impressionistic pineapple patterns, and plantation-style ceilings with exposed planks are painted white. Along with the 10 mi of island beaches, recreational options include kayak and surfboard rental, nature tours, and arts-and-crafts classes. ⊠*12 Kiawah Beach Dr., Kiawah Island, 29455* ☎843/768–2121 or 800/654–2924 ⎙843/768–6099 ⊕*www.kiawahresort. com* ⇌*255 rooms, 600 villas and homes* ⎈*In-room: safe (some), refrigerator, VCR, Ethernet, Wi-Fi. In-hotel: 10 restaurants, golf courses, tennis courts, pools, gym, spa, beachfront, water sports, children's programs (ages 3–12), concierge, public Internet, no-smoking rooms* ⊟*AE, D, DC, MC, V* ⦿*EP.*

$$–$$$$

$–$$$$ ⛺**Seabrook Island.** The most private of the area's island resorts, Seabrook is endowed with true Lowcountry beauty. Wildlife sightings are common: look for white-tailed deer and even bobcats. Going to the beach is as popular as playing golf or tennis, but erosion has whisked away a lot of the sand. About 200 fully equipped one- to six-bedroom homes are available. The Beach Club and Island House are centers for dining and leisure activities. ⊠*3772 Seabrook Island Rd., Seabrook Island, 29455* ☎843/768–1000 or 800/845–2233 ⎙843/768–2361 ⊕*www.seabrook.com* ⇌*200 units* ⎈*In-room: kitchen, VCR. In-hotel: 3 restaurants, bar, golf courses, tennis courts, pools, gym, beachfront, water sports, bicycles, children's programs (ages 4–17), no-smoking rooms* ⊟*AE, D, DC, MC, V* ⦿*EP.*

NIGHTLIFE & THE ARTS

THE ARTS

CONCERTS

The **Charleston Symphony Orchestra** (☎843/723–7528 ⊕*www.charlestonsymphony.com*) season runs from October through April, with pops series, chamber series, family-oriented series, and holiday concerts.

DANCE

The **Charleston Ballet Theatre** (✉*477 King St., Upper King* ☎*843/723–7334* ⊕*www.charlestonballet.com*) performs everything from classical to contemporary dance. The **Robert Ivey Ballet Company** (☎*843/556–1343* ⊕*www.cofc. edu*), a semiprofessional company that includes College of Charleston students, puts on a fall and spring program of jazz, classical, and modern dance at the Sottile Theater.

FILM

The **IMAX Theater** (✉*360 Concord St., Upper King* ☎*843/725–4629*) is next to the South Carolina Aquarium.

THEATER

Charleston Stage Company (✉*135 Church St., Market area* ☎*843/965–4032* ⊕*www.charlestonstage.com*) performs at the Dock Street Theatre. The **Footlight Players** (✉*20 Queen St., Market area* ☎*843/722–4487* ⊕*www.footlightplayers. net*) regularly perform fun plays and musicals.

VENUES

Bluegrass, blues, and country musicians grace the stage at **Charleston Music Hall** (✉*37 John St., Upper King* ☎*843/853–2252* ⊕*www.charlestonmusichall.com*).

Gaillard Municipal Auditorium (✉*77 Calhoun St., Upper King* ☎*843/577–7400*) hosts symphony and ballet companies, as well as numerous festival events. The box office is open weekdays from 10 to 6.

Dance, symphony, and theater productions are among those staged at the **North Charleston Performing Art Center** (✉*5001 Coliseum Dr., North Charleston* ☎*843/529–5050* ⊕*www.coliseumpac.com*).

Performances by the College of Charleston's theater department and musical recitals are presented during the school year at the **Simons Center for the Arts** (✉*54 St. Phillips St., College of Charleston Campus* ☎*843/953–5604*).

NIGHTLIFE

A new city ordinance mandates that bars close no later than 2 AM.

BARS & BREWERIES

More than 20 on-tap beers make **Charleston Beer Works** (⊠*468 King St., Upper King* ☎*843/577–5885*) a student hangout. **Club Habana** (⊠*177 Meeting St., Market area* ☎*843/853–5900*) is a chic martini bar with a cigar shop downstairs. Adjacent rooms of dark hardwood are dimly lighted, furnished with couches and have an intimate ambience. Cheap "mystery beers" make **Cumberland's** (⊠*301 King St., Market area* ☎*843/577–9469*) the favorite of laid-back locals.

A list of 100 bottled brews make **King Street Grille** (⊠*304 King St., Upper King* ☎*843/723–5464*) a hard-core sports bar for those who like the game loud and the beer cold. **Mad River Bar & Grille** (⊠*32 N. Market St., Market area* ☎*843/723–0032*) attracts a young, high-energy crowd. It's in the atmospheric Old Seamen's Chapel.

Southend Brewery (⊠*161 E. Bay St., Market area* ☎*843/853–4677*) has a lively bar serving beer brewed on the premises; try the wood-oven pizzas and the smokehouse barbecue. Thursday is salsa night, Friday showcases a bluegrass band, and Saturday night a guitarist. **Vickery's Bar & Grill** (⊠*139 Calhoun St., Market area* ☎*843/577–5300*) is a festive nightspot with an outdoor patio and good late-night food.

DANCE CLUBS

The throbbing dance beat of DJ Amos draws the crowds at **213 Top of the Bay** (⊠*213C E. Bay St., Market area* ☎*843/722–1311*), a lively and lighthearted part of downtown's single scene. There's a see-and-be-seen crowd at the **City Bar** (⊠*5 Faber St., Market area* ☎*843/577–7383*). Dance to the music Wednesday through Saturday at **Trio Club** (⊠*139 Calhoun St., Upper King* ☎*843/965–5333*), where funky '70s and '80s sounds are perennially popular.

DINNER CRUISES

Cruise the harbor on the *Charleston Belle* (☎*843/344–4483* ⊕*www.charlestonharbortours.com*). Dine and dance the night away aboard the luxury yacht *Spirit of Carolina* (☎*843/881-7337* ⊕*www.spiritlinecruises.com*). ■TIP➔**Remember that reservations for all evening cruises are essential.**

Celebrating Charleston

Spoleto USA is only the beginning—there are dozens of festivals held throughout the city each year. Some focus on food and wine, whereas others are concerned with gardens and architecture. Charleston is one of the few American cities that can claim a distinctive regional cuisine. The **BB&T Charleston Food + Wine Festival** (☎843/763-0280 or 866/369-3378 ⊕www.charlestonfoodandwine.com) allows the city to "strut its stuff" at an annual festival. Some of the most sought-after events, such as the Restaurant Dine-Around with celebrity chefs, Blues & Brew, the Lowcountry Gospel Brunch with entertainment by local gospel choirs, and the Saturday Night Celebration where guests can interact with hip winemakers, sell out early. Reserve well in advance.

The **Fall Candlelight Tours of Homes and Gardens** (☎843/722-4630 ⊕www.preservationsociety.org), sponsored by the Preservation Society of Charleston in September and October, provides an inside look at Charleston's private buildings and gardens.

More than 100 private homes, gardens, and historic churches are open to the public for tours during the **Festival of Houses and Gardens** (☎843/722-3405 ⊕www.

historiccharleston.org), held during March and April each year. There are also symphony galas in stately drawing rooms, plantation oyster roasts, and candlelight tours.

The **MOJA Arts Festival** (☎843/724-7305 ⊕www.mojafestival.com), which takes place during the last week of September and first week of October, celebrates African heritage and Caribbean influences on African-American culture. It includes theater, dance, and music performances, art shows, films, lectures, and tours of the historic district.

Piccolo Spoleto (☎843/724-7305 ⊕www.piccolospoleto.org) is the spirited companion festival of Spoleto Festival USA, showcasing the best in local and regional talent from every artistic discipline. There are hundreds of events—from jazz performances to puppet shows and expansive art shows in Marion Square—from mid-May through early June, and many of the performances are free.

The **Southeastern Wildlife Exposition** (☎843/723-1748 or 800/221-5273 ⊕www.sewe.com) in mid-February is one of Charleston's biggest annual events, with fine art by renowned wildlife artists, live animals, an oyster roast, and a gala.

JAZZ CLUBS

★ The elegant **Charleston Grill** (✉*Charleston Pl., 224 King St., Market area* ☎*843/577–4522*) has live jazz and dinner nightly. Make a reservation. There are 40 types of martinis at **Cintra** (✉*16 N. Market St., Market area* ☎*843/377–1090*), where you can hear live jazz on Thursday, Friday, and Sunday. At **Mistral** (✉*99 S. Market St., Market area* ☎*843/722–5709*) live blues and jazz make patrons feel good on Monday, Tuesday, Thursday, and Saturday nights. On Wednesday, two French musicians sing their renditions of pop and folk songs. On Friday, a Dixieland band really stirs things up.

LIVE MUSIC

Best Friend Lounge (✉*Mills House Hotel, 115 Meeting St., Market area* ☎*843/577–2400*) has a guitarist playing on weekends. The cavernous **Music Farm** (✉*32 Ann St., Upper King* ☎*843/853–3276*), in a renovated train station, showcases live local and national rock and alternative bands. Listen to authentic Irish music at **Tommy Condon's** (✉*15 Beaufain St., Market area* ☎*843/577–5300*).

JB Pivot's Beach Club (✉*1662 Savannah Hwy., West Ashley* ☎*843/571–3668*) is a no-frills place, with live beach music and shag or swing dancing lessons Tuesday to Thursday. **Bert's Bar** (✉*2209 Middle St., Sullivan's Island* ☎*843/883–3924*), a true beach-bum hangout, has live music on weekends. The **Windjammer** (✉*1000 Ocean Blvd., Isle of Palms* ☎*843/886–8596*) is an oceanfront bar with local and national rock bands playing Thursday through Sunday.

SHOPPING

SHOPPING DISTRICTS

The Market area is a cluster of shops and restaurants centered around the **Old City Market** (✉*E. Bay and Market sts., Market area*). Sweetgrass basket weavers work here, and you can buy the resulting wares. **King Street** is the major shopping street in town. Lower King (from Broad to Market streets) is lined with high-end antiques dealers. Middle King (from Market to Calhoun streets) is a mix of national chains like Banana Republic and Pottery Barn. Upper King (from Calhoun Street to Cannon street) is the up-and-coming area where fashionistas like the alternative shops such as Putumayo.

Spoleto Festival USA

For 17 glorious days in late May and early June, Charleston gets a dose of culture from the Spoleto Festival USA (☎ 843/722–2764 ⊕ www.spoletousa.org). This internationally acclaimed performing-arts festival features a mix of distinguished artists and emerging talent from around the world. Performances take place in magical settings, such as beneath a canopy of ancient oaks or inside a centuries-old cathedral. Everywhere you turn, the city's music halls, auditoriums, theaters, and outdoor spaces (including the Cistern at the College of Charleston) are filled with the world's best in opera, music, dance, and theater.

The 140 events, costing between $25 and $50, include everything from improv to Shakespeare, from rap to chamber music, from ballet to salsa. A mix of formal concerts and casual performances is what Pulitzer Prize–winning composer Gian Carlo Minotti had in mind when, in 1977, he initiated the festival as a complement to his opera-heavy Italian festival. He chose Charleston because of its European looks, and because its residents love the arts—and any cause for celebration. He wanted the festival to be a "fertile ground for the young" and a "dignified home for the masters."

The finale is a must, particularly for the younger crowd. Staged outdoors at Middleton Place, the plantation house and lush landscaped gardens provide a dramatic backdrop. The inexpensive seating is unreserved and unlimited. The lawn is covered with blankets and chairs, and many cooks prepare lavish spreads. After the Spoleto Festival Orchestra plays a spirited concert of contemporary and classic pieces, spectacular fireworks explode over the Ashley River.

Because events sell out quickly, insiders say you should buy your tickets several months in advance. (Tickets to midweek performances are a bit easier to secure.) Hotels fill up quickly, so book a room at the same time. While you're at it, reserve your tables for our trendy downtown restaurants. You won't be able to get in the door if you wait until the last minute.

The Italian word *piccolo* means "little," but this hardly applies to **Piccolo Spoleto** (☎ 843/724–7305 ⊕ www.piccolospoleto.com). The only thing small about this younger sibling of the Spoleto Festival USA is the ticket prices.

ANTIQUES

Birlant & Co. (⊠*191 King St., Lower King* ☎*843/722–3842*) mostly carries 18th- and 19th-century English antiques, but keep your eye out for a Charleston Battery bench. **Livingstons' Antiques** (⊠*163 King St., Lower King* ☎*843/723–9697*) deals in 18th- and 19th-century English and Continental furnishings, clocks, and bric-a-brac. **Period Antiques** (⊠*194 King St., Lower King* ☎*843/723–2724*) carries 18th- and 19th-century pieces. **Petterson Antiques** (⊠*201 King St., Lower King* ☎*843/723–5714*) sells objets d'art, porcelain, and glass.

English Rose Antiques (⊠*436 King St., Upper King* ☎*843/722–7939*) has country-style accessories at some of the best prices on the Peninsula. The **King Street Antique Mall** (⊠*495 King St., Upper King* ☎*843/723–2211*) is part flea market, part antiques store.

On James Island, **Carolopolis Antiques** (⊠*2000 Wappoo Dr., James Island* ☎*843/795–7724*) has good bargains on country antiques. In Mount Pleasant, **Hungryneck Mall** (⊠*401 Johnnie Dodds Blvd., Mount Pleasant* ☎*843/849–1744*) has more than 60 antiques dealers hawking sterling silver, oak and mahogany furnishings, and Civil War memorabilia. **Page's Thieves Market** (⊠*1460 Ben Sawyer Blvd., Mount Pleasant* ☎*843/884–9672*) has furniture, glassware, and occasional auctions.

ART GALLERIES

The downtown neighborhood known as the French Quarter, named after the founding French Huguenots, has become a destination for art lovers. The French Quarter Gallery Association consists of roughly 30 art galleries within the original walled city. Galleries here host an art walk from 5 to 8 PM on the first Friday in March, May, October, and December.

Serious art collectors head to **Ann Long Fine Art** (⊠*12 State St., Market area* ☎*843/577–0447*) for neoclassical and modern works. The **Charleston Renaissance Gallery** (⊠*103 Church St., South of Broad* ☎*843/723–0025*) carries museum-quality Southern art. The **Corrigan Gallery** (⊠*62 Queen St., Market area* ☎*843/722–9868*) displays the paintings of owner Lese Corrigan, as well as rotating shows from other painters and photographers.

★ The **Eva Carter Gallery** (⊠*132 E. Bay St., Market area* ☎*843/722–0506*) displays the paintings of owner Eva Carter and abstract works by the late William Halsey. **Horton Hayes Fine Art** (⊠*30 State St., Market area* ☎*843/958–0014*) displays sought-after Lowcountry paintings by brothers Bernie Horton and Mark Kelvin Horton. These atmospheric originals depict coastal life. The **Martin Gallery** (⊠*18 Broad St., South of Broad* ☎*843/723–7378*) has art by nationally and internationally acclaimed artists, sculptors and photographers.

★ **Nina Liu and Friends** (⊠*24 State St., Market area* ☎*843/722–2724*) sells contemporary art, including pottery, hand-blown glass, jewelry, and photographs. **Smith-Killian Fine Art** (⊠*9 Queen St., Market area* ☎*843/853–0708*) exhibits the paintings of Betty Smith and her talented triplets, Jennifer, Shannon, and Tripp. Her son is a nature photographer specializing in black-and-white images.

BOOKS

The **Preservation Society of Charleston** (⊠*King and Queen Sts., Market area* ☎*843/722–4630*) carries books and tapes of historic and local interest, as well as sweetgrass baskets, prints, and posters. Look for out-of-print and rare books at **Boomer's Books & Collectibles** (⊠*420 King St., Upper King* ☎*843/722–2666*).

CLOTHING

Charleston's own **Ben Silver** (⊠*149 King St., Market area* ☎*843/577–4556*), premier purveyor of blazer buttons, has more than 800 designs, including college and British regimental motifs. He also sells British neckties, embroidered polo shirts, and blazers. **Bob Ellis** (⊠*332 King St., Market area* ☎*843/722–2515*) sells shoes from Dolce & Gabbana, Prada, and Manolo Blahnik. **Christian Michi** (⊠*220 King St., Market area* ☎*843/723–0575*) carries chichi women's clothing and accessories.

Shop **Copper Penny** (⊠*311 King St., Market area* ☎*843/723–2999*) for trendy dresses. **Moo Roo** (⊠*316 King St., Market area* ☎*843/724–1081*) is famous for its original handbags. **Nula** (⊠*320 King St., Market area* ☎*843/853–6566*) sells hipster wear.

Need a ballgown? **Berlins** (⌧*114 King St., South of Broad* ☏*843/723–5591*) is the place for designer outfits. **Magar Hatworks** (⌧*557 ½ King St., Upper King* ☏*843/577–7740*) sells hand-crafted headgear. **The Trunk Show** (⌧*281 Meeting St., Market area* ☏*843/722–0442*) is an upscale consignment shop selling designer dresses and vintage apparel. The back room is all about interior design.

GIFTS

ESD (⌧*314 King St., Market area* ☏*843/577–6272*) is a top local interior-design firm; its King Street shop sells coffee-table books, jewelry, and pillows. Look for cool kitchen gear at **Fred** (⌧*237 King St., Market area* ☏*843/723–5699*). **Indigo** (⌧*4 Vendue Range, Market area* ☏*843/723–2983*) stocks funky home and garden accessories.

Magnets, cards, and books are found at **Metropolitan Deluxe** (⌧*164 Market St., Market area* ☏*843/722–0436*). Artsy and hip baby gear, house-warming gifts, jewelry, books, and even office supplies make the mundane fun at **Worthwhile** (⌧*268 King St., Market area* ☏*843/723–4418*).

FOODSTUFFS

Bull Street Gourmet (⌧*60 Bull St., College of Charleston Campus* ☏*843/720–8992*) sells upscale picnic fare made fresh daily. It has great deals on wine and sponsors friendly tastings. **Charleston Candy Kitchen** (⌧*32A N. Market St., Market area* ☏*843/723–4626*) sells freshly made fudge, Charleston chews, and sesame-seed wafers. The 24-hour **Harris Teeter** (⌧*290 E. Bay St., Market area* ☏*843/722–6821*) is one of the best local supermarkets, and it carries Charleston foodstuffs.

Kennedy's Bakery and Market (⌧*60 Calhoun St., Upper King* ☏*843/723–2026*) sells wine and cheeses, as well as freshly baked breads, muffins, and scones. Make time to stop at **Market Street Sweets** (⌧*100 N. Market St., Market area* ☏*843/722–1397*) for the melt-in-your-mouth pralines and fudge. **Ted's Butcherblock** (⌧*334 East Bay St., Ansonborough* ☏*843/577–0094*) sells gourmet meals to go. Light fare includes deli sandwiches, paninis, and regional specialties from around the globe.

FURNITURE

Historic Charleston Reproductions (⊠*105 Broad St., South of Broad* ☎*843/723–8292*) has superb replicas of Charleston furniture and accessories, all authorized by the Historic Charleston Foundation. Royalties from sales contribute to restoration projects. At the **Old Charleston Joggling Board Co.** (⊠*652 King St., Upper King* ☎*843/723–4331*) these Low-country oddities (on which people bounce) are for sale. **Carolina Lanterns** (⊠*917 Houston Northcutt Blvd., Mount Pleasant* ☎*843/881–4170* ⊕*www.carolinalanterns.com*) sells gas lanterns based on designs from downtown's historic district.

SIDE TRIPS FROM CHARLESTON

Gardens, parks, and the charming town of Summerville are good reasons to travel a bit farther afield for day trips.

MONCKS CORNER

30 mi northwest of Charleston on U.S. 52.

This town is a gateway to a number of attractions in Santee Cooper Country. Named for the two rivers that form a 171,000-acre basin, the area brims with outdoor pleasures centered on the basin and nearby Lakes Marion and Moultrie.

Explore the inky swamp waters of **Cypress Gardens** in a complimentary flat-bottom boat; walk along paths lined with moss-draped cypress trees, azaleas, camellias, daffodils, wisteria, and dogwood; and marvel at the clouds of butterflies in the butterfly house. The swamp garden was created from what was once the freshwater reserve of the vast Dean Hall rice plantation. It's about 24 mi north of Charleston via U.S. 52, between Goose Creek and Moncks Corner. ⊠*3030 Cypress Gardens Rd.* ☎*843/553–0515* 🖃*$10* ⊗*Daily 9–5; last admission at 4.*

Mepkin Abbey is an active Trappist monastery overlooking the Cooper River. The site was the former plantation home of Henry Laurens and, later, of publisher Henry Luce and wife Clare Boothe Luce. You can tour the gardens and abbey or even stay here for a spiritual retreat—one- to six-night stays are open to anyone, including married couples, willing to observe the rules of the abbey and who don't mind spartan accommodations. (Reservations are required, and donations are greatly appreciated). The gift shop carries items the monks have produced—soaps, honey, and sweets—and eggs farmed on the premises. Tours depart at 11:30 and 3. ⊠*1098 Mepkin Abbey Rd., off Dr. Evans Rd.* 🕾*843/761–8509* ⊕*www.mepkinabbey.org* ⊠*Grounds free; tours $5* ⊙*Tues.–Fri. and Sun. 9–4:30, Sat. 9–4.*

☙ On the banks of the Old Santee Canal is the **Old Santee Canal Park,** which you can explore on foot or by canoe. The park includes a 19th-century plantation house. The on-site Berkeley Museum focuses on cultural and natural history. ⊠*900 Stony Landing Rd., off Rembert C. Dennis Blvd.* 🕾*843/899–5200* ⊕*www.oldsanteecanalpark.org* ⊠*$3* ⊙*Daily 9–5.*

Francis Marion National Forest consists of 250,000 acres of swamps, vast oaks and pines, and little lakes thought to have been formed by falling meteors. It's a good place for picnicking, hiking, camping, horseback riding, boating, and swimming. ⊠*U.S. 52* 🕾*843/336–3248* ⊠*Free* ⊙*Daily 9–4:30.*

For more information about area lakes and facilities, contact **Santee Cooper Counties Promotion Commission & Visitors Center** ⊠*9302 Old Hwy. 6, Drawer 40, Santee, 29142* 🕾*803/854–2131* ⊕*www.santeecoopercountry.org.*

WHERE TO STAY

$–$$$ ☒ **Rice Hope Plantation.** On a former rice plantation outside of Moncks Corner, this inn overlooks the Cooper River. The grounds, studded with live oaks, were designed by landscape architect Loutrell Briggs. Antiques and reproductions fill the big, sprawling house with five working fireplaces. Guest rooms have wood floors and four-poster beds. This is not a white-pillared mansion, though; it's a more modest farmhouse. ⊠*206 Rice Hope Dr., Moncks Corner, 29461* 🕾*843/849–9000 or 800/569–4038* ⊕*www. ricehope.com* ⤶*4 rooms, 1 suite* ⚘*In-hotel: tennis court, water sports, no-smoking rooms* ⊟*AE, MC, V* ⊚*BP.*

SUMMERVILLE

25 mi northwest of Charleston via I–26 and Rte. 165.

Victorian homes, many of which are listed on the National Register of Historic Places, line the public park. Colorful gardens brimming with camellias, azaleas, and wisteria abound. Downtown and residential streets curve around tall pines, as a local ordinance prohibits cutting them down. Visit for a stroll in the park, or to go antiquing on the downtown shopping square. Summerville was originally built by wealthy planters.

For more information about Summerville, stop by the **Greater Summerville/Dorchester County Chamber of Commerce and Visitor Center** (✉402 N. Main St., 29484 ☎843/873–2931 ⊕www.summervilletourism.com).

WHERE TO STAY & EAT

★ Fodor'sChoice ✕⊡ **Woodlands Resort & Inn.** With the distinct feel
$$$$ of an English country estate, this Relais & Châteaux property has individually decorated rooms with nice touches like Frette linens. The service and quality of the accommodations are exceptional. In the kitchen, Chef Tarver King is proving himself with every challenging, multicourse menu. Wine pairings by long-term sommelier Stéphane Peltier are perfect. Get here soon, as this little gem is about to grow. An expansion plan includes a destination spa, an indoor pool, and many, many more rooms. ✉125 Parsons Rd., 29483 ☎843/875–2600 or 800/774–9999 ⊟843/875–2603 ⊕www.woodlandsinn.com ⇨10 rooms, 9 suites ⌂In-room: safe, VCR, dial-up. In-hotel: restaurant, tennis courts, pool, bicycles, no-smoking rooms ⊟AE, D, DC, MC, V ⊚EP.

CHARLESTON ESSENTIALS

TRANSPORTATION

BY AIR

Charleston International Airport, about 12 mi west of downtown, is served by American Eagle, Continental, Delta, United Express, Northwest, and US Airways.

Wings Air, a commuter airline that flies to and from Atlanta, operates out of Mount Pleasant Regional Airport and the Charleston Executive Airport. Private planes can also use Charleston Executive Airport.

Several cab companies serve the airport, including the Charleston Black Cab Company, which has London-style taxis with uniformed drivers that cost $40 for two passengers to downtown. Airport Ground Transportation arranges shuttles, which cost $14 per person to downtown.

If you want to add a little excitement to your life, you can arrange for an executive sedan, a stretch limo, or even a super-stretch limo to pick you up at the airport. A Star Limousine has the largest and most varied fleet in town.

Airport Contacts Charleston Executive Airport (✉2700 Fort Trenholm Rd., John's Island ☎877/754–7285). **Charleston International Airport** (✉5500 International Blvd., North Charleston ☎843/767–1100). **Mt. Pleasant Regional Airport** (✉700 Airport Rd., Mount Pleasant ☎843/884–8837).

Airport Transfers Airport Ground Transportation (☎843/767–1100). **A Star Limousine** (☎843/745–6279). **Charleston Black Cab Company** (☎843/216–2627).

BY BOAT & FERRY
Boaters—many traveling the Intracoastal Waterway—dock at Ashley Marina and City Marina, in Charleston Harbor, or at Wild Dunes Yacht Harbor, on the Isle of Palms. The Charleston Water Taxi is a delightful way to travel between Charleston and Mount Pleasant. Some people take the $8 round-trip journey for fun. It departs from the Charleston Maritime Center, half a block south of Adger's Wharf.

Contacts Ashley Marina (✉Lockwood Blvd., Medical University of South Carolina ☎843/722–1996). **Charleston Water Taxi** (✉Charleston Maritime Center, 10 Wharfside St., Upper King ☎843/330–2989). **City Marina** (✉Lockwood Blvd., Medical University of South Carolina ☎843/723–5098).

BY BUS
Greyhound connects Charleston with other destinations. The Charleston Area Regional Transportation Authority, the city's public bus system, takes passengers around the city and to the suburbs. Bus 11, which goes to the airport, is convenient for travelers. CARTA operates DASH, which runs buses that look like vintage trolleys along three downtown routes. A single ride is $1.25, and a day-long pass is $4. You should have exact change.

Contacts CARTA (✉3664 Leeds Ave., North Charleston ☎843/747–0922 ⊕www.ridecarta.com). **Charleston Bus Station** (✉3610 Dorcester Rd., North Charleston ☎843/744–4247). **Greyhound** (☎843/744–4247 or 800/231–2222 ⊕www.greyhound.com).

BY CAR

Interstate 26 traverses the state from northwest to southeast and terminates at Charleston. U.S. 17, the coastal road, also passes through Charleston. Interstate 526, also called the Mark Clark Expressway, runs primarily east–west, connecting the West Ashley area, North Charleston, Daniel Island, and Mount Pleasant.

Contacts **Alamo** (☎843/767-4417 ⊕www.alamo.com). **Avis** (☎843/767-7030 ⊕www.avis.com). **Budget** (☎843/577-5195 ⊕www.budget.com). **Hertz** (☎843/767-4552 ⊕www.hertz.com). **National** (☎843/767-3078 ⊕www.nationalcar.com).

BY TAXI

Fares within the city average about $5 per trip. Reputable companies include Safety Cab and Yellow Cab, which are available 24 hours a day. Charleston Black Cab Company vehicles line up near Charleston Place.

Charleston Rickshaw Company will take you anywhere in the historic district for $7 to $12.

Contacts **Charleston Black Cab Company** (☎843/216-2627). **Charleston Rickshaw Company** (✉21 George St., Market area ☎843/723-5685). **Safety Cab** (☎843/722-4066). **Yellow Cab** (☎843/577-6565).

BY TRAIN

Amtrak has service from such major cities as New York, Philadelphia, Washington, Richmond, Savannah, and Miami. The Amtrak station is somewhat isolated, but a visible police presence means there are few reports of crime in the area. Taxis meet every train; a ride to downtown averages $25.

Contacts **Amtrak** (✉4565 Gaynor Ave., North Charleston ☎843/744-8264 or 800/872-7245 ⊕www.amtrak.com).

CONTACTS & RESOURCES

BANKS & EXCHANGE SERVICES

As in most cities, banks are open weekdays 9 to 5. There are countless branches in the downtown area, all with ATMs.

Contacts **BB&T** (✉151 Meeting St., Ansonborough ☎843/720-5100). **Bank of America** (✉544 King St., Upper King ☎843/720-4913). **Bank of South Carolina** (✉256 Meeting St., Ansonborough ☎843/724-1500).

EMERGENCIES

Medical University of South Carolina Hospital and Roper Hospital have 24-hour emergency rooms. Roper Hospital recently completed a multimillion dollar renovation of its emergency room.

Emergency Services Ambulance, police (☎*911*).

Hospitals Medical University of South Carolina Hospital (✉*169 Ashley Ave., Medical University of South Carolina* ☎*843/792–2300*). **Roper Hospital** (✉*316 Calhoun St., Upper King* ☎*843/724–2000*).

Late-Night Pharmacy Eckerds (✉*261 Calhoun St., Upper King* ☎*843/805–6022*).

INTERNET, MAIL & SHIPPING

The main post office is downtown on Broad Street, while a major branch is at West Ashley. To ship packages, FedEx Kinkos has a downtown branch and another at West Ashley. The UPS Store has locations in Mount Pleasant and West Ashley.

Most area lodgings have in-room data ports or in-room broadband, and some have wireless connections in the rooms or public areas. Internet cafés are rare, but many coffee shops, including Starbucks, will let you use their wireless connection for a fee. The FedEx Kinko's branch on Orleans Road has computers you can use for 25¢ a minute.

Post Offices Downtown Station (✉*83 Broad St., South of Broad* ☎*843/577–0690*). **West Ashley Station** (✉*78 Sycamore St., West Ashley* ☎*843/766–4031*).

Contacts FedEx Kinkos (✉*73 St. Philip St., Upper King* ☎*843/723–5130* ✉*873 Orleans Rd., West Ashley* ☎*843/571–4746*). **UPS Store** (✉*1000 Johnnie Dodds Blvd., Mount Pleasant* ☎*843/856–9099* ✉*1836 Ashley River Rd., West Ashley* ☎*843/763–6894*).

MEDIA

The major daily newspaper is the *Post and Courier*. The Preview section in Thursday editions lists weekend events. *Charleston City Paper* is a free weekly that has gained a large, mostly young, following. It gives a rundown of local nightspots and has good restaurant listings.

Contacts The Post and Courier (☎*843/577-7111* ⊕*www.charleston.net*). **Charleston City Paper** (☎*843/577-5304* ⊕*www.charlestoncitypaper.com*).

TOUR OPTIONS

AIR TOURS

Flying High Over Charleston provides aerial tours of the city and surrounding areas. Trips begin at $60 per person.

Contact Flying High Over Charleston (✉ *Mercury Air Center, W. Aviation Ave., North Charleston* ☎ *843/569–6148* ⊕ *www.flyinghighovercharleston.com*).

BOAT TOURS

Charleston Harbor Tours offers tours that give the history of the harbor. Spiritline Cruises, which runs the ferry to Fort Sumter, also offers harbor tours and dinner cruises. The latter leave from Patriots Point Marina in Mount Pleasant and include a three-course dinner and dancing to a live band. Sandlapper Tours has tours focused on regional history, coastal wildlife, and ghostly lore.

Contacts Charleston Harbor Tours (✉ *Charleston Maritime Center, 10 Wharfside St., Upper King* ☎ *843/722–1691* ⊕ *www.charlestonharbortours.com*). **Sandlapper Tours** (✉ *Charleston Maritime Center, 10 Wharfside St., Upper King* ☎ *843/849–8687* ⊕ *www.sandlappertours.com*). **Spiritline Cruises** (✉ *360 Concord St, Market area* ☎ *843/881–7337 or 800/789–3678* ⊕ *www.spiritlinecruises.com*).

BUS TOURS

Adventure Sightseeing leads bus tours of the historic district. Associated Guides of Historic Charleston pairs local guides with visiting tour groups. Doin' the Charleston, a van tour, makes a stop at the Battery. Sites and Insights is a van tour that covers downtown and nearby islands. Gullah Tours focuses on sights significant to African-American culture. Chai Y'All shares stories and sights of Jewish interest.

Contacts Adventure Sightseeing (☎ *843/762–0088 or 800/722–5394* ⊕ *www.touringcharleston.com*). **Associated Guides of Historic Charleston** (☎ *843/724–6419* ⊕ *www.historiccharleston.org*). **Chai Y'All** (☎ *843/556–0664*). **Doin' the Charleston** (☎ *843/763–1233 or 800/647–4487* ⊕ *www.dointhecharlestontours.com*). **Gullah Tours** (☎ *843/763-7551* ⊕ *www.gullahtours.com*). **Sites and Insights** (☎ *843/762–0051* ⊕ *www.sitesandinsightstours.com*).

CARRIAGE TOURS

Carriage tours are a great way to see Charleston. Carolina Polo & Carriage Company, Old South Carriage Company, and Palmetto Carriage Tours run horse- and mule-drawn carriage tours of the historic district. Each tour, which follows one of four routes, lasts about one hour. Most carriages queue up at North Market and Anson streets. Charleston Carriage and Polo, which picks up passengers at the Doubletree Guest Suites Historic Charleston on Church Street, has a historically authentic carriage that is sought after for private tours and wedding parties.

Contacts Charleston Carriage & Polo Company (☎843/577–6767 ⊕www.cpcc.com). **Old South Carriage Company** (☎843/723–9712 ⊕www.oldsouthcarriagetours.com). **Palmetto Carriage Tours** (☎843/723–8145).

ECOTOURS

Barrier Island Ecotours, at the Isle of Palms Marina, runs three-hour pontoon-boat tours to a barrier island. Coastal Expeditions has half-day and full-day naturalist-led kayak tours on local rivers. Charleston Explorers leads educational boat tours that are great for kids.

Contacts Barrier Island Ecotours (⊠Isle of Palms Marina, off U.S. 17, Isle of Palms ☎843/886–5000 ⊕www.nature-tours.com). **Charleston Explorers** (⊠40 Patriots Point Rd., Mount Pleasant ☎843/723–5656 ⊕www.charlestonexplorers.org). **Coastal Expeditions** (⊠514-B Mill St., Mount Pleasant ☎843/884–7684 ⊕www. coastalexpeditions.com).

PRIVATE GUIDES

To hire a private guide to lead you around the city and outlying plantations, contact Charleston's Finest Historic Tours. Janice Kahn has been leading customized tours for more than 30 years. Christine Waggoner, of Promenade with Christine, offers tours in French and English.

Contacts Charleston's Finest Historic Tours (☎843/577–3311). **Janice Kahn** (☎843/556–0664). **Promenade with Christine** (☎843/971–9364 or 843/200–1766).

WALKING TOURS

Walking tours on various topics—horticulture, slavery, or women's history—are given by Charleston Strolls and the Original Charleston Walks. Bulldog Tours has walks that explore the city's supernatural side. Listen to the infamous tales of lost souls with Ghosts of Charleston, which travel to historic graveyards.

Military history buffs should consider Jack Thompson's Civil War Walking Tour. The food-oriented tours by Carolina Food Pros explore culinary strongholds—gourmet grocers, butcher shops, and restaurants, sampling all along the way.

Contacts **Bulldog Tours** (⊠*40 N. Market St., Market area* ☎*843/568–3315* ⊕*www.cobblestonewalkingtours.com*). **Carolina Food Pros** (⊠*701 E. Bay St., Market area* ☎*843/723–3366* ⊕*www. carolinafoodpros.com*). **Charleston Strolls** (⊠*Charleston Pl., 130 Market St., Market area* ☎*843/766–2080* ⊕*www.charlestonstrolls. com*). **Ghosts of Charleston** (⊠*184 E. Bay St., French Quarter* ☎*843/723–1670 or 800/723–1670*). **Jack Thompson's Civil War Walking Tour** (⊠*Mills House Hotel, 115 Meeting St., Market area* ☎*843/722–7033*). **Original Charleston Walks** (⊠*58½ Broad St., South of Broad* ☎*843/577–3800 or 800/729–3420*).

VISITOR INFORMATION

The Charleston Area Convention & Visitors Bureau runs the Charleston Visitor Center, which has information about the city as well as Kiawah Island, Seabrook Island, Mount Pleasant, North Charleston, Edisto Island, Summerville, and the Isle of Palms. The Historic Charleston Foundation and the Preservation Society of Charleston have information on house tours.

Tourist Information **Charleston Visitor Center** (⊠*375 Meeting St., Upper King* ⌕*423 King St., 29403* ☎*843/853–8000 or 800/868–8118* ⊕*www.charlestoncvb.com*). **Historic Charleston Foundation** (⌕*Box 1120, 29402* ☎*843/723–1623* ⊕*www.historic-charleston.org*). **Preservation Society of Charleston** (⌕*Box 521, 29402* ☎*843/722–4630* ⊕*www.preservationsociety.org*).

Hilton Head

WORD OF MOUTH

"Fripp, especially at south end, has a wide beach. During high tide north beach disappears. Fripp can be traversed on foot in about 30 minutes, if the marsh deer get out of your way. They're everywhere. Enjoy."

—Lex1

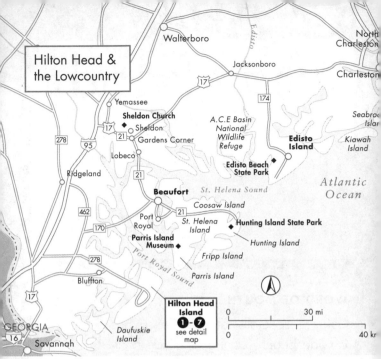

Hilton Head &
the Lowcountry

Updated by Eileen Robinson Smith

The action-packed island of Hilton Head anchors the southern tip of South Carolina's coastline and attracts 2.5 million visitors each year. Although it historically has drawn an upscale clientele, and it still does, you'll find that the crowd here is much more diverse than you might think. Although it has more than its fair share of millionaires (you might run into director Ron Howard at the Starbucks, for instance), it also attracts families in search of a good beach.

This half-tame, half-wild island is home to more than 25 world-class golf courses and even more resorts, hotels, and top restaurants. Still, it's managed development thanks to building restrictions that aim to marry progress with environmental protection.

EXPLORING HILTON HEAD

Hilton Head is just north of the South Carolina–Georgia border. It's so close to Savannah that they share an airport. This part of the state is best explored by car, as its points of interest spread over a flat coastal plain that is a mix of wooded areas, marshes, and sea islands, the latter of which

HILTON HEAD TOP 4

Beachcombing: This island has 12 mi of ocean beaches. You can swim, soak up the sun, or walk along the sand. The differential between the tides leaves a multitude of shells, sand dollars, and starfish.

Challenging Golf: Hilton Head's nickname is "Golf Island," and its many challenging courses have an international reputation.

Serving up Tennis: One of the nation's top tennis destinations, with academies run by legends like Stan Smith, former Wimbleton champion.

Staying Put: This semitropical island has been a resort destination for decades and it has all of the desired amenities for visitors: a vast array of lodgings, an endless supply of restaurants, and excellent shopping.

are sometimes accessible only by boat or ferry. Take U.S. 170 and 17 to get from one key spot to another. It's a pretty drive that winds through small towns and over old bridges. Charleston, the Queen Belle of the South, is at the northern end of the region.

ABOUT THE RESTAURANTS
Given the proximity to the Atlantic and small farms on the mainland, most locally owned restaurant menus are still heavily influenced by the catch of the day and seasonal field harvests. But things are changing. There are numerous national chain restaurants and high-end spots in addition to the down-home holes-in-the-wall. Many restaurants open at 11 and don't close until 9 or 10, but some take a break between 2:30 and 6. During the height of the summer season, book ahead on weekends.

ABOUT THE HOTELS
Hilton Head is known as one of the best vacation spots on the East Coast, and its hotels are a testimony to the reputation. The island is covered in resorts and hotels, or you can rent beachfront or golf-course-view villas, cottages, and mansions. Here, and on private islands, expect the most modern conveniences and world-class service at the priciest places. Clean, updated rooms and friendly staff are everywhere—even at lower-rate establishments—this is the South, after all. Staying in cooler months, for extended periods of time, or commuting from nearby Bluffton, where

there are some new limited-service properties, chains like Hampton Inn, can mean better deals.

The region's high season lasts from spring through summer (June through August), plus holiday and festival weekends. Hilton Head is the most demanding in which to score a good deal, or even a room—unless you plan ahead. The choicest locations are booked a year to six months in advance, almost year-round, but booking agencies can help you make room reservations, and in winter the crowds thin, rates drop.

WHAT IT COSTS				
RESTAURANTS				
$$$$	$$$	$$	$	¢
over $22	$17–$22	$12–$16	$7–$11	under $7
HOTELS				
over $220	$161–$220	$111–$160	$70–$110	under $70

Restaurant prices are for a main course at dinner. Hotel prices are for two people in a standard double room in high season.

TIMING

The high season follows typical beach-town cycles, with May through August and holidays year-round being the busiest and most costly. However, as local guides will tell you, thanks to the Lowcountry's mostly moderate temperatures year-round, tourists are ever-present. Spring is the most glorious time to visit.

HILTON HEAD ISLAND

No matter how many golf courses pepper its landscape, Hilton Head will always be a semitropical barrier island. That means the 12 mi of beaches are lined with towering pines, palmetto trees, and wind-sculpted live oaks; the interior is a blend of oak and pine woodlands and meandering lagoons. Rental villas, lavish private houses, and luxury hotels line the coast as well.

Since the 1950s, resorts like Sea Pines, Palmetto Dunes, and Port Royal have sprung up all over. Although the gated resorts are private residential communities, all have public restaurants, marinas, shopping areas, and recreational facilities. All are secured, and cannot be toured unless arrangements are made at the visitor office near the main gate of each plantation. Hilton Head prides itself on strict laws that keep light pollution to a minimum. ■TIP→**The lack of streetlights makes it difficult to find your way at night, so be sure to get good directions.**

EXPLORING HILTON HEAD

Driving Hilton Head by car or tour bus is the only way to get around. Off Interstate 95, take Exit 8 onto U.S. 278, which leads you through Bluffton and then onto Hilton Head proper. A 5¾-mi Cross Island Parkway toll bridge ($1) is just off 278, and makes it easy to bypass traffic and reach the south end of the island, where most of the resort areas and hotels are. Know that U.S. 278 can slow to a standstill at rush hour and during holiday weekends, and the signs are so discreet that it's easy to get lost without explicit directions. ■TIP→**Be careful of putting the-pedal-to-the-metal, particularly on the Cross Island Parkway. The speed limits change dramatically.**

AROUND IN CIRCLES Locals call the island's many traffic circles the "tourist's nemesis." So they won't be your undoing, get very precise directions. And if you miss a turn, don't brake violently, just go around again.

WHAT TO SEE

❷ **Audubon-Newhall Preserve,** in the south, is 50 acres of pristine forest, where native plant life is tagged and identified. There are trails, a self-guided tour, and seasonal walks. ✉*Palmetto Bay Rd., near southern base of Cross Island Pkwy., South End* ☎*843/842–9246* ⊕*www.hiltonhead-audubon.org* ✑*Free* ☉*Daily dawn–dusk.*

★ **Fodor'sChoice Bluffton.** Tucked away from the resorts, charm-
❹ ing Bluffton has several old homes and churches, a growing artists' colony, and oak-lined streets dripping with moss. You could grab Southern-style picnic food and head to the boat dock at the end of Pritchard Street for great views. There are interesting little shops around, too. ✉*Route 4◄ 8 mi northwest on U.S. 278.*

❶ **Coastal Discovery Museum.** Here you find two types of ͼ manent exhibits—depicting Native American island li͜

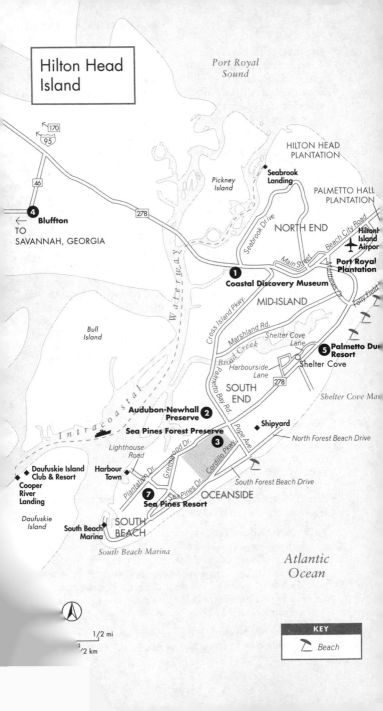

sea island biodiversity—along with various temporary displays. The museum also sponsors historical and natural history tours of Native American sites, forts, and plantations as well as kayak trips, turtle watches, birding treks, and visits to wildlife preserves. ✉ *100 William Hilton Pkwy., North End* ☎ *843/689–6767* ⊕ *www.coastaldiscovery.org* ✒ *Free* ☉ *Mon.–Sat. 9–5, Sun. 10–3.*

❺ **Palmetto Dunes Resort.** This complex is home to the renowned Rod Laver Tennis Center, a good stretch of beach, three golf courses, and several oceanfront rental villa complexes. The oceanfront Hilton Head Marriott Beach & Golf Resort and the Hilton Resort are also on this property. ✉ *Queens Folly Rd. at U.S. 278, Mid-Island* ☎ *800/845–8160* ⊕ *www. palmettodunesresort.com.*

❻ **Port Royal Plantation.** The main draws here are the posh Westin Resort, which is on the beach, three PGA-championship golf courses, and Port Royal racquet club, with 16 tennis courts. ✉ *2 Grasslawn Ave., Mid-Island* ☎ *843/681–4000* ⊕ *www.portroyalplantation.com.*

❸ **Sea Pines Forest Preserve.** At this 605-acre public wilderness tract, walking trails take you past a stocked fishing pond, waterfowl pond, and a 3,400-year-old Indian shell ring. Pick up the extensive activity guide at the Sea Pines Welcome Center to take advantage of goings-on—moonlight hayrides, storytelling around campfires, and alligator- and bird-watching boat tours. The preserve is part of the grounds at Sea Pines Resort. ✉ *Off U.S. 278, Sea Pines Resort, South End* ☎ *843/363–4530* ⊕ *www.seapines.com* ✒ *$5 per car* ☉ *Daily dawn–dusk.*

★ Fodor'sChoice **Sea Pines Resort.** The oldest and best known of
❼ Hilton Head's developments, this resort occupies 4,500 thickly wooded acres with three golf courses, tennis clubs, stables, a fine beach, and shopping plazas. The focus of Sea Pines is **Harbour Town,** a charming marina with a luxury boutique hotel, shops, restaurants, some condominiums, and the landmark Hilton Head Lighthouse. A free trolley takes visitors around the resort. ✉ *Off U.S. 278, South End* ☎ *843/363–4530* ⊕ *www.seapines.com* ✒ *$5 per car.*

OFF THE BEATEN PATH **Daufuskie Island.** From Hilton Head you can take a 45-minute ferry ride to nearby Daufuskie Island, the setting for Pat Conroy's novel *The Water Is Wide,* which was made into the movie *Conrack.* A few descendants of former slaves

PAMPER YOURSELF

The low-key **Faces** (✉*The Village at Wexford, 1000 William Hilton Pkwy., North End* ☎*843/785–3075* ⊕*www. facesdayspa.com*) has been pampering loyal clients for 20 years. The **Spa at Main Street Inn** (✉*2200 Main St., Hilton Head* ☎*843/681–3001* ⊕*www.mainstreetinn.com*) has holistic massages that will put you in another zone. The **Spa at Palmetto Bluffs** (✉*476 Mount Pelia Rd., Bluff-* *ton* ☎*843/7066500* ⊕*www. palmettobluffresort.com*) has been dubbed the "celebrity spa" by locals, for this two-story facility is the ultimate pamper palace.

live on small farms here, among remnants of churches, homes, and schools—all reminders of antebellum times. Once on the island, you can rent a golf cart or take guided tours that include sights such as a 200-year-old cemetery, former slave quarters, a local winery, and the Haig Point Lighthouse. The scenic boat ride and the physically beautiful island itself will become etched in your memory bank.

Staying at the Daufuskie Island Club & Resort (✉*Embarkation Center, 421 Squire Pope Rd., North End* ☎*843/341–4820 or 800/648–6778* ⊕*www.daufuskieresort.com*)—with an ocean-front inn, cottages, golf courses, tennis, spa, pools, water sports, and several restaurants—is a wonderful getaway. **Calibogue Cruises** (✉*Broad Creek Marina, 164B Palmetto Bay Rd., Mid-Island* ☎*843/342–8687*) has several Daufuskie tour options, including guided tours with lunch and gospel-music performances starting at $40. **Vagabond Cruises** (✉*Harbour Town Marina, South End* ☎*843/785–2662* ⊕*www.vagabondcruise. com*) conducts daytime boat rides, from dolphin tours to runs to Savannah, sails on the Stars & Stripes, of America's Cup fame, and dinner cruises.

SPORTS & THE OUTDOORS

BEACHES

Although resort beach access is reserved for guests and residents, there are four public entrances to Hilton Head's 12 mi of ocean beach. The two main parking spots are off U.S. 278 at Coligny Circle in the South End, near the Holiday Inn, and on Folly Field Road, Mid-Island. Both have changing facilities. South of Folly Field Road, Mid-Island along U.S. 278, Bradley Beach Road and Singleton Road lead to beaches where parking space is limited. ■TIP→A delightful stroll on the beach can end with an unpleasant surprise if you don't put your towels, shoes, and other earthly possessions way up on the sand. Tides here can fluctuate as much as 7 feet. Check the tide chart at your hotel.

BIKING

There are more than 40 mi of public paths that crisscross Hilton Head island, and pedaling is popular along the firmly packed beach. ■TIP→Bikes with wide tires are a must if you want to ride on the beach. They can save you a spill should you hit loose sand on the trails.

Bicycles can be rented at most hotels and resorts. You can also rent bicycles from the **Hilton Head Bicycle Company** (⊠112 Arrow Rd., South End ☎843/686–6888 ⊕www. hiltonheadbicycle.com). **South Beach Cycles** (⊠Sea Pines Resort, off U.S. 278, South End ☎843/671–2453 ⊕www. southbeachracquetclub.com) rents bikes, helmets, tandems, and adult tricycles. **Pedals Bicycles.** ⊠71 Pope Ave., South End ☎843/842–5522.

HOT WHEELS An amazing array of bicycles can be hired, from beach cruisers to mountain bikes to bicycles built for two. Many can be delivered to your hotel, along with helmets, baskets, locks, child carriers, and whatever else you might need. There are 40 mi of trails, as well as 12 mi of hard-packed beach, so the possibilities are endless.

CANOEING & KAYAKING

Outside Hilton Head (⊠Sea Pines Resort, off U.S. 278, South End ⊠Shelter Cove Lane at U.S. 278, Mid-Island ☎843/686–6996 or 800/686–6996 ⊕www.outsidehilton-head.com) is an ecologically sensitive company that rents canoes and kayaks; it also runs nature tours and dolphin-watching excursions.

GOLF

Hilton Head is nicknamed "Golf Island" for good reason: the island itself has 24 championship courses (most semi-private), and the outlying area has 16 more. Each offers its own packages, some of which are great deals. Almost all charge the most in the morning and lower the rates as the day goes on. Some offer lower rates in the hot summer months. ■TIP→ **The dress code on island golf courses does not permit blue jeans, gym shorts, or jogging shorts. Men's shirts must have collars.**

Arthur Hills at Palmetto Hall. A player favorite from the renowned designer Arthur Hills, this course has his trademark: undulating fairways. The course, punctuated with lakes, gently flows across the island's rolling hills, winding around moss-draped oaks and towering pines. The clubhouse is a replica of an antebellum greathouse. ⊠*108 Fort Howell Dr., Mid-Island* ☎*843/689–5891 or 800/827–3006* ☎*843/689–9205* ⊕*www.golfisland.com* ⌂*Reservations essential* ⚑*18 holes. 6,918 yds. Par 72. Greens fee: $99–$75–$65* ☞*Facilities: Driving range, putting green, pitching area, golf carts, rental clubs, pro-shop, golf academy/lessons, restaurant, bar.*

Country Club of Hilton Head. Although it's part of a country club, the course is open for public play. A well-kept secret, it's never overcrowded. In 2005 it was a U.S. Open–qualifying site. ⊠*70 Skull Creek Dr. N, North End* ☎*843/681–4653 or 888/465–3475* ☎*843/689–9976* ⊕*www.golfisland. com* ⌂*Reservations essential* ⚑*18 holes. 6,919 yds. Par 72. Greens fee: $89–$69–$49* ☞*Facilities: Driving range, putting green, pitching area, golf carts, pull carts, rental clubs, pro-shop, golf academy/lessons, restaurant, bar.*

★ **Fodor's**Choice **Harbour Town Golf Links.** Many golfers say this is one of those must-play-before-you-die courses. It's extremely well known because it has hosted the Verizon Heritage Classic every spring for the last three decades. Designed by Pete Dye, the layout is reminiscent of Scottish courses of old. The Golf Academy is ranked among the top 10 in the country. ⊠*Sea Pines Resort, 11 Lighthouse Lane, South End* ☎*843/842–8484 or 800/955–8337* ☎*843/363–8372* ⊕*www.golfisland.com* ⌂*Reservations essential* ⚑*18 holes. 6,973 yds. Par 71. Greens fee: $270–$230* ☞*Facilities: Driving range, putting green, pitching area, golf carts, pull carts, caddies, rental clubs, pro-shop, golf academy/lessons, restaurant, bar.*

Old South Golf Links. This course has scenic holes with marshland and views of the Intracoastal Waterway. ✉*50 Buckingham Plant Dr., North End* ☎*843/785–5353* 🖷*843/837–7375* ⊕*www.golfisland.com* ⚲*Reservations essential* ⚑*18 holes. 6,772 yds. Par 72. Greens fee: $50–$90* ☞*Facilities: Driving range, putting green, pitching area, golf carts, rental clubs, pro-shop, golf academy/ lessons, restaurant, bar.*

Robert Trent Jones at Palmetto Dunes. This course is one of the island's most popular layouts. Its beauty and character are accentuated by the par-5, 10th hole, which offers a panoramic view of the ocean. It's one of only two oceanfront holes on Hilton Head. ✉*7 Robert Trent Jones Way, North End* ☎*843/785–1138* 🖷*843/785–3220* ⊕*www.golfisland. com* ⚲*Reservations essential* ⚑*18 holes. 7,005 yds. Par 72. Greens fee: $59–$105* ☞*Facilities: Driving range, putting green, pitching area, golf carts, rental clubs, pro-shop, golf academy/lessons, restaurant, bar.*

HORSEBACK RIDING

☾ **Lawton Stables** (✉*Sea Pines Resort, Plantation, off U.S.*
★ *278, South End* ☎*843/671–2586*) gives riding lessons and pony rides, in addition to having horseback tours through the Sea Pines Forest Preserve.

TENNIS

There are more than 300 courts on Hilton Head. **Port Royal** (✉*15 Wimbledon Ct., North End* ☎*843/686–8803* ⊕*www.heritagegolfgroup.com*) has 16 courts, including two grass. **Sea Pines Racquet Club** (✉*Sea Pines Resort, off U.S. 278, 32 Greenwood Dr., South End* ☎*843/363–4495*) has 23 courts, instructional programs, and a pro-shop. **Palmetto Dunes Tennis Center** (✉*6 Trent Jones La., Mid-Island* ☎*843/785–1152* ⊕*www.palmettodunes.com*) welcomes nonguests. Highly rated **Van der Meer Tennis Center/ Shipyard Racquet Club** (✉*Shipyard Plantation, 19 de Allyon Rd., Mid-Island* ☎*843/686–8804* ⊕*www.vandermeer. com*) is recognized for tennis instruction. Four of its 28 courts are covered.

WHERE TO EAT

$$$$ ✗**Aqua.** A good bit was spent on creating the ambience here—the waterfall on the first level, the fireplace lounge adjacent to the second-story dining room. The food—particularly the shellfish—and portions are commendable, the

wine list up with the trends, the servers savvy. Grazing is the way to go: the oysters with champagne mignonette or chili-lime remoulade; the delicious sashimi; the bibb and red-leaf salad with macadamias dressed with orange-miso vinaigrette. (Forget the spring rolls.) A late-night menu is served from 10 to midnight. ⊠*10 Forest Beach Dr., South End* ☎*843/341–3331* ☐*AE, MC, V* ☉*No lunch.*

$$$-$$$$ ✕**Old Fort Pub.** Overlooking the sweeping marshlands of ★ Skull Creek, this romantic restaurant has almost panoramic views. It just may be the island's best overall dining experience, for the building is old enough to have personality, as are the professional waiters. The kitchen serves flavorful food, like the appetizer of roasted calamari with sun-dried tomatoes and olives. Entrées like duck confit in rhubarb sauce, and fillet with shitake mushrooms hit the spot. The wine list is extensive, and there's outdoor seating plus a third-floor porch for toasting the sunset. Sunday brunch includes a mimosa. ⊠*65 Skull Creek Dr., North End* ☎*843/681–2386* ☐*AE, D, DC, MC, V* ☉*No lunch.*

$$$-$$$$ ✕**Redfish.** The "naked" catch of the day—seafood grilled with olive oil, lime, and garlic—stands out here; it's a welcome change from the fried fare at many other local spots. Caribbean and Cuban flavors pervade the rest of the menu in dishes such as red trout with Boursin-cheese grits; *tasso* (a spicy cured ham) in a cream sauce spiked with amaretto, Tabasco, and Worcestershire; and Dominican braised pork, roasted with bananas, chilis, and coconut. Its wine cellar is full with some 1,000 bottles and there's a retail wineshop. Although its commercial strip location isn't inspired, the lively crowd sitting amid candlelight, subdued artwork, dark furniture, and white linens more than makes up for this typical island shortcoming. However, some locals have signed off this place, saying the food and service is not worth the elevated prices. ⊠*8 Archer Rd., corner Palmetto Bay Rd., South End* ☎*843/686–3388* ☐*AE, D, MC, V* ☉*No lunch Sun.*

$$-$$$$ ✕**Brick Oven Café.** Velvet drapes, dramatic chandeliers, and '40s lounge-style entertainment—on top of good, reasonably priced food served late—make this an *in* place. It's a refreshingly quirky joint on an island that is more luxe than funky and the menu is equally eclectic: appetizers include sweet-potato and lobster cakes or shrimp and pork spring rolls; entrées are wood-fired pizzas, roasted veggie sandwiches, and veal meat loaf. The wine list has a good range

and pricing. ⊠*Park Plaza, Greenwood Dr., South End* ☎*843/686–2233* ⚑*Reservations essential* ▭*AE, D, DC, MC, V* ☺*No lunch.*

$–$$$$ ✕**Truffles Cafe.** When a restaurant survives here for more than 20 years, there's a reason. This place has personable, hands-on owners; prices low enough to keep the islanders coming all year, and food that is fresh and flavorful. There's none of the namesake truffles, but there's grilled salmon with a mango-barbecue glaze and—if you're gonna be bad—barbecued baby back ribs. ⊠*Sea Pines Center, 71 Lighthouse Rd.* ☎*843/671–6138* ▭*AE, MC, V.*

¢–$$ ✕**Kenny B's French Quarter Café.** Surrounded by Mardi Gras memorabilia, Kenny himself cooks up jambalaya, gumbo, and muffaletta sandwiches. His wife runs the dining room, serving hungry working folks golden fried oyster po' boys topped with real remoulade sauce. Go for the Sunday buffet brunch; there's chicory coffee, perfect beignets, spicy omelets, and various Benedicts. A local haunt for nearly 10 years, this place in a shopping center is open from morning until 9 PM. ⊠*Bi-Lo Circle, 70 Pope Ave., Mid-Island* ☎*843/785–3315* ▭*AE, D, MC, V* ☺*No dinner Sun.*

¢–$$ ✕**Mi Tierra.** At this friendly Mexican restaurant, freshness is the key to tasty fare like fried-fish tacos. Next door, Baja Tacos—run by the same people—is a simple taco stand with counter service, café tables, and a condiments bar with fresh salsas and relishes. Down a *cerveza* (beer) as you watch Mexican *telenovelas* (soap operas). ⊠*160 Fairfield Sq., North End* ☎*843/342–3409* ▭*MC, V.*

¢ ✕**Signe's Heaven Bound Bakery & Café.** Mornings find locals ★ rolling in for the deep-dish French toast, crispy polenta, and whole-wheat waffles. For 34 years, European-born Signe has been feeding islanders soups (the chilled cucumber has pureed watermelon, green apples, and mint), curried chicken salad, and loaded hot and cold sandwiches. The beach bag ($10 for a cold sandwich, pasta or fresh fruit, chips, a beverage, and cookie) is a great deal. The key-lime bread pudding is amazing, as are the melt-in-your mouth cakes and the rave-worthy breads, especially the Italian ciabatta. Dine in the new room, with original art by—who else?—Signe. ⊠*93 Arrow Rd., South End* ☎*843/785–9118* ▭*AE, D, MC, V* ☺*Closed Sun. No dinner.*

WHERE TO STAY

$$$$ 🖵 **Crowne Plaza Hilton Head Island Beach Resort.** Decorated in
a nautical theme and set in a luxuriant garden, the Crowne
Plaza is appropriately resplendent. It's the centerpiece of
Shipyard Plantation, which means guests have access to all
its amenities. However, this resort has the fewest oceanfront
rooms of the majors and is the farthest from the water.
Its latticed bridge and beach pavilion have seen many an
island wedding. ✉ *130 Shipyard Dr., Shipyard Plantation,
Mid-Island, 29928* 🕾 *843/842–2400 or 800/334–1881*
🖷 *843/785–8463* ⊕ *www.crowneplazaresort.com* ⤳ *331
rooms, 9 suites* ⚬ *In-room: refrigerators. In-hotel: restaurants, golf courses, pools, gym, bicycles, public Wi-Fi, children's programs (ages 3–12), no-smoking rooms* ⊟ *AE, D,
DC, MC, V* ⦿ *EP.*

$$$$ 🖵 **Disney's Hilton Head Island Resort.** Disney's typical cheery
☾ colors and whimsical designs create a look that's part
★ Southern beach resort, part Adirondack hideaway. The villas here have fully furnished dining, living, and sleeping
areas, as well as porches with rocking chairs and picnic
tables. It's on a little islet in Broad Creek; many units have
marsh or marina views. The smallest villa is a studio, the
largest has three bedrooms, four baths, and space to sleep a
dozen. The resort has a fishing pier and a lively beach club
a mile from the accommodations (shuttle service provided).
Kids are kept happy and busy, be it crabbing or roasting
marshmallows. Surprisingly, it's popular with couples unac-
companied by children. ✉ *22 Harbourside La., Mid-Island,
29928* 🕾 *843/341–4100 or 407/939–7540* 🖷 *843/341–
4130* ⊕ *www.dvcmagic.com* ⤳ *102 units* ⚬ *In-room: some
kitchens, dial-up. In-hotel: 2 restaurants, pools, gym, water
sports, bicycles, children's programs (ages 3–16), laundry
service, no-smoking rooms* ⊟ *AE, MC, V* ⦿ *EP.*

$$$$ 🖵 **Hilton Head Marriott Beach & Golf Resort.** Marriott's stan-
☾ dard rooms get a tropical twist at this palm-enveloped
resort: sunny yellow-and-green floral fabrics and cherry furnishings are part of the peppy decor. All guest rooms have
private balconies, writing desks, and down comforters. The
granddaddy of the island's resorts, it's looking good after a
$27 million renovation that includes revamped pool areas
and restaurants. Kids love the real sand castle in the lobby.
To take in the sea views, you can lounge by the pool or
lunch at the exceptional outdoor snack bar. ✉ *1 Hotel Circle, Palmetto Dunes, Mid-Island, 29928* 🕾 *843/686–8400*

or 800/228–9292 ⊠*843/686–8450* ⊕*www.hiltonheadmarriott.com* ⊃*476 rooms, 36 suites* ⌂*In-room: some kitchens. In-hotel: restaurant, bar, golf courses, tennis courts, pools, gym, beachfront, water sports, bicycles, public Wi-Fi, children's programs (ages 3–12), concierge, no-smoking rooms* ⊟*AE, D, DC, MC, V* ◉*EP.*

$$$$ ⌷**Hilton Oceanfront Resort.** There's a Caribbean sensibility to this five-story chain hotel; the grounds are beautifully landscaped with deciduous and evergreen bushes, and palms run along the beach. All the rooms face the ocean and are decorated with elegant wood furnishings, such as hand-carved armoires. Warm reds accent neutral beiges and creams in the linens and upholstery. Its lounge, called Regatta, is a happening nightspot. ⊠*23 Ocean La., Mid-Island* ⊄*Box 6165, 29938* ☎*843/842–8000 or 800/845–8001* ⊠*843/842–4988* ⊕*www.hiltonheadhilton.com* ⊃*303 studios, 20 suites* ⌂*In-room: kitchens, dial-up. In-hotel: restaurants, golf courses, pools, gym, water sports, bicycles, public Wi-Fi, children's programs (ages 5–12), no-smoking rooms* ⊟*AE, D, DC, MC, V* ◉*EP.*

$$$$ ⌷**The Inn at Harbour Town.** The most buzz-worthy of Hilton
★ Head's properties is this European-style boutique hotel. A proper staff, clad in kilts, pampers you with British service and a dose of Southern charm. Butlers are on hand any time of the day or night, and the kitchen delivers around the clock. The spacious guest rooms, decorated with neutral palettes, have luxurious touches like Frette bed linens, which are turned down for you each night. Harbour Town Grill serves some of the best steaks on the island. ⊠*Lighthouse La., off U.S. 278, Sea Pines South End, 29926* ☎*843/363–8100 or 888/807–6873* ⊕*www.seapines.com* ⊃*60 rooms* ⌂*In-room: refrigerators, dial-up. In-hotel: restaurant, golf courses, tennis courts, bicycles, laundry service, concierge, public Wi-Fi, no-smoking rooms* ⊟*AE, D, DC, MC, V* ◉*EP.*

★ **Fodor$Choice** ⌷**The Inn at Palmetto Bluff.** Fifteen minutes
$$$$ from Hilton Head is the Lowcountry's most luxurious new resort. This 22,000-acre property has been transformed into a perfect replica of a small island town, complete with its own clapboard church. As a chauffeured golf cart takes you to your cottages, you'll pass the clubhouse, which resembles a mighty antebellum greathouse. All of the cottages are generously sized—even the one-bedroom cottages have more than 1,100 square feet of space. The decor is

coastal chic, with sumptuous bedding, gas fireplaces, surround-sound home theaters, and marvelous bathroom suites with steam showers. Your screened-in porch puts you immediately in touch with nature. The spa puts you close to heaven with its pampering treatments. ⊠*476 Mount Pelia Rd., Bluffton, 29910* ☎*843/706–6500 or 866/706–6565* 🖷*843/706–6550* ⊕*www.palmettobluffresort.com* ⟿*50 cottages* ⌂*In-room: refrigerator, dial-up. In-hotel: 3 restaurants, bar, golf course, pool, water sports, bicycles, concierge, no smoking rooms* ▭*AE, MC, V* ¶⊙*EP.*

$$$$ 🖃**Westin Resort, Hilton Head Island.** A circular drive winds
★ around a metal sculpture of long-legged marsh birds as you approach this luxury resort. The lush landscape lies on the island's quietest, least inhabited stretch of sand. Guest rooms, most with ocean views from the balconies, have homey touches, crown molding, and contemporary furnishings. If you need space to spread out, there are two- and three-bedroom villas. The service is efficient and caring. Expect additional pampering touches when a spa opens in mid-2007. ⊠*2 Grass Lawn Ave., North End, 29928* ☎*843/681–4000 or 800/228–3000* 🖷*843/681–1087* ⊕*www.westin.com* ⟿*412 rooms, 29 suites* ⌂*In-room: dial-up. In-hotel: 3 restaurants, golf courses, tennis courts, pools, gym, beachfront, bicycles, children's programs (ages 4–12), concierge, no-smoking rooms* ▭*AE, D, DC, MC, V* ¶⊙*EP.*

$$$–$$$$ 🖃**Holiday Inn Oceanfront Resort.** This high-rise, on one of the island's busiest beaches, is within walking distance of shops and restaurants. Standard rooms are spacious and furnished in a contemporary style; golf and tennis packages are available. The outdoor Tiki Hut lounge, a poolside bar, is hugely popular. ⊠*S. Forest Beach Dr., South End* ⌓*Box 5728, 29938* ☎*843/785–5126 or 800/423–9897* 🖷*843/785–6678* ⊕*www.hihiltonhead.com* ⟿*201 rooms* ⌂*In-room: refrigerators, dial-up. In-hotel: restaurant, bar, pool, gym, bicycles, public Wi-Fi, children's programs (ages 3–12), no-smoking rooms* ▭*AE, D, DC, MC, V* ¶⊙*EP.*

★ **Fodor**ʹₛChoice 🖃**Main Street Inn & Spa.** This Italianate villa
$$$–$$$$ has stucco facades ornamented with lions' heads, elaborate ironwork, and shuttered doors. Staying here is like being a guest at a rich friend's estate. Guest rooms have velvet and silk brocade linens, feather duvets, and porcelain and brass sinks. An ample breakfast buffet is served in a petite, sunny dining room. In the afternoon there's complemen-

tary gourmet coffee and homemade cookies in the formal garden. The spa offers treatments ranging from traditional Swedish massages to Indian Kyria massages. ✉2200 Main St., North End, 29926 ☎843/681–3001 or 800/471–3001 📠843/681–5541 ⊕www.mainstreetinn.com ⤳33 rooms ♿In-hotel: pool, spa, no-smoking rooms ⊟AE, MC, V, Dis ⊠BP.

$$ ⌂**Hampton Inn.** This hotel, sheltered from the noise and traffic, is a good choice if you have kids. The two-bedroom family suites are surprisingly upscale; the parents' rooms are tastefully appointed, and the kids' room are *cool* enough to have foosball tables. King-size studios with sleeper sofas are another alternative for families. Breakfast is as Southern as country gravy and biscuits or as European as Belgian waffles. ✉1 Dillon Rd., Mid-Island, 29926 ☎843/681–7900 📠843/681–4330 ⊕www.hampton-inn. com ⤳115 rooms, 7 suites ♿In-room: dial-up. In-hotel: pool, public Wi-Fi, no-smoking rooms ⊟AE, D, DC, MC, V ⊠BP.

$$ ⌂**Park Lane Hotel & Suites.** The island's only all-suites property, Park Lane has a friendly feel, since many guests stay for weeks. Each suite has a full kitchen, so there's no need to eat out for every meal. You can cool in the pool after heating up on the tennis courts. The public beach is 2 mi away. ✉12 Park Lane, South End, 29928 ☎843/686–5700 📠843/686-5700 ⊕www.hiltonheadparklanehotel. com ⤳156 suites ♿In-room: kitchen, dial-up. In-hotel: tennis court, pool, bicycles, public Wi-Fi, no-smoking rooms ⊟AE, D, MC, V ⊠BP.

NIGHTLIFE & THE ARTS

THE ARTS

In warm weather free outdoor concerts are held at Harbour Town and Shelter Cove Harbour; at the latter fireworks light up the night Tuesday from June to August. Guitarist Gregg Russell has been playing for children under Harbour Town's mighty Liberty Oak tree for decades. He begins strumming nightly at 8, except on Saturday.

The **Native Islander Gullah Celebration** (☎843/689–9314 ⊕www.gullahcelebration.com) takes place in February and showcases Gullah life through arts, music, and theater.

The **Arts Center of Coastal Carolina** (✉Shelter Cove La., Mid-Island ☎843/686–3945 ⊕www.artscenter-hhi.org) has a gallery and a theater with programs for young people. The Hallelujah Singers, Gullah performers, appear regularly.

NIGHTLIFE

Hilton Head has always been a party place, and now more than ever. Bars, like everything else in Hilton Head, are often in strip malls.

Reggae bands play at **Big Bamboo** (⊠*Coligny Plaza, N. Forest Beach Dr., South End* ☎*843/686–3443*), a bar with a South Pacific theme. The **Hilton Head Brewing Co.** (⊠*Hilton Head Plaza, Greenwood Dr., South End* ☎*843/785–2739*) lets you shake your groove thing to '70s-era disco on Wednesday. There's live music on Friday and karaoke on Saturday. **Monkey Business** (⊠*Park Plaza, Greenwood Dr., South End* ☎*843/686–3545*) is a dance club popular with young professionals. On Friday there's live beach music.

The latest hot spot, **Santa Fe Cafe** (⊠*Plantation Center in Palmetto Dunes, 700 Plantation Center, North End* ☎*843/785–3838*) is where you can lounge about in front of the fireplace or sip top-shelf margaritas on the rooftop. **Turtle's** (⊠*2 Grass Lawn Ave.* ☎*843/681–4000*) appeals to anyone who still likes to hold their partner when they dance.

SHOPPING

ART GALLERIES

Linda Hartough Gallery (⊠*Harbour Town, 140 Lighthouse Rd., South End* ☎*843/671–6500*) is all about golf. There's everything from landscapes of courses to gold balls to pillows embroidered with sayings like "Queen of the Green." The **Red Piano Art Gallery** (⊠*220 Cordillo Pkwy., Mid-Island* ☎*843/785–2318*) showcases 19th- and 20th-century works by regional and national artists.

JEWELRY

The **Bird's Nest** (⊠*Coligny Plaza, Coligny Circle and N. Forest Beach Dr., South End* ☎*843/785–3737*) sells locally made shell and sand-dollar jewelry, as well as island-theme charms. The **Goldsmith Shop** (⊠*3 Lagoon Rd., Mid-Island* ☎*843/785–2538*) carries classic jewelry and island charms. **Forsythe Jewelers** (⊠*71 Lighthouse Rd., South End* ☎*843/342–3663*) is the island's leading jewelry store.

NATURE

The **Audubon Nature Store** (⊠*The Village at Wexford, U.S. 278, Mid-Island* ☎*843/785–4311*) has gifts with a wildlife theme. **Outside Hilton Head** (⊠*The Plaza at Shelter Cove, U.S. 278, Mid-Island* ☎*843/686–6996 or 800/686–6996*) sells Pawleys Island hammocks (first made in the late 1800s) and other items that let you enjoy the great outdoors.

HILTON HEAD ESSENTIALS

TRANSPORTATION

4

BY AIR

Hilton Head Island Airport is served by US Airways Express. Most travelers use the Savannah/Hilton Head International Airport, about an hour from Hilton Head, which is served by AirTran, American Eagle, Continental Express, Delta, Northwest, United Express, and US Airways.

Contacts **Hilton Head Island Airport** (⊠*120 Beach City Rd., Hilton Head, SC* ☎*843/689–5400* ⊕*www.hiltonheadairport.com*). **Savannah/Hilton Head International Airport** (⊠*400 Airways Ave., Savannah, GA* ☎*912/964–0514* ⊕*www.savannahairport.com*).

BY BOAT & FERRY

Hilton Head is accessible via the Intracoastal Waterway, with docking available at Harbour Town Yacht Basin, Hilton Head Boathouse, and Shelter Cove Harbour.

Contacts **Harbour Yacht Basin** (☎*843/671–2704*). **Hilton Head Boathouse** (☎*843/681–2628*). **Shelter Cove Harbor** (☎*843/842–7001*).

BY CAR

Hilton Head Island is 19 mi east of Interstate 95 (Exit 8 off Interstate 95S, Exit 8 off Interstate 95N). If you're heading to the southern end of the island, your best bet to save time and avoid traffic is to take the Toll Expressway. The cost is $1 each way. Beaufort is 25 mi east of Interstate 95, on U.S. 21.

BY TAXI

At Your Service, Gray Line Lowcountry Adventures, and Yellow Cab are good options in Hilton Head.

Contacts **At Your Service** (☎*843/837–3783*). **Gray Line Lowcountry Adventures** (☎*843/681–8212*).

BY TRAIN

Amtrak gets you as close as Savannah or Yemassee. Gray Line Lowcountry Adventures will send a limo to pick you up at a cost of $66 per hour.

Contacts Savannah Amtrak Station (✉ *2611 Seaboard Coastline Dr., Savannah* ☎ *912/234–2611 or 800/872–7245* ⊕ *www.amtrak. com*). **Gray Line Lowcountry Adventures** (☎ *843/681–8212*).

CONTACTS & RESOURCES

BANKS & EXCHANGE SERVICES

Banks have slightly different hours, but most are open on weekdays. Bank of America in the North End and Harbourside Community Bank in Mid-Island also have limited Saturday hours.

Contacts Bank of America (✉ *59 Pope Ave., South End* ☎ *843/342– 1076*). **Harbourside Community Bank** (✉ *852 William Hilton Pkwy., Mid-Island* ☎ *843/341–1201*). **SunTrust Bank** (✉ *2 Greenwood Dr., South End* ☎ *843/341–2100*). **Wachovia Bank** (✉ *200 Merchant St., North End* ☎ *843/686–9601*).

EMERGENCIES

Emergency medical service is available at the Hilton Head Medical Center and Clinics. There are no 24-hour pharmacies, but CVS is open until 10 PM.

Emergency Services Ambulance, fire, police (☎ *911*).

Hospitals Hilton Head Regional Medical Center (✉ *25 Hospital Center Blvd., Mid-Island, Hilton Head Island* ☎ *843/681–6122*).

Late-Night Pharmacies CVS (✉ *10 Pope Ave., South End, Hilton Head Island* ☎ *843/785–7786*).

INTERNET, MAIL & SHIPPING

There are several Internet cafés, including Internet Café & Sundries in the South End, as well as numerous coffee shops and restaurants with free wireless connections. Nearly all hotels also have some way to get you wired.

There are two major post offices on Hilton Head, one in the South End and one on the North End.

Internet Cafés Internet Café & Sundries (✉ *1 N. Forest Dr., South End, Hilton Head Island* ☎ *843/785–6600*).

Post Offices Fairfield Station Post Office (✉ *213 William Hilton Pkwy., North End, Hilton Head Island* ☎ *843/682–3002*). **Hilton Head**

Island Main Post Office (✉*10 Bow Circle, South End, Hilton Head Island* ☎*843/785–7002*).

TOUR OPTIONS

Boat Tours Adventure Cruises (✉*Shelter Cove Marina, 9 Shelter Cove Lane, Mid-Island, Hilton Head Island* ☎*843/785–4558* ⊕*www.hiltonheadisland.com*). **H2O Sports** (✉*Harbour Town Marina, 149 Lighthouse Rd., South End, Hilton Head Island* ☎*843/363–2628* ⊕*www.h2osportsonline.com*). **Low Country Nature Tours** (✉*Shelter Cover Marina, Shelter Cove Lane, Mid-Island, Hilton Head Island* ☎*843/683–0187* ⊕*www.lowcountrynaturetours.com*).

VISITOR INFORMATION

In Hilton Head your best bet for local information is to stop by the Welcome Center, on the island side of the bridge that connects Hilton Head to Bluffton.

Tourist Information Welcome Center of Hilton Head (✉*100 William Hilton Pkwy., 29938* ☎*843/689–6302 or 800/523–3373* ⊕*www.hiltonheadisland.org*).

Savannah & Charleston Essentials

PLANNING TOOLS, EXPERT INSIGHT, GREAT CONTACTS

There are planners and there are those who, excuse the pun, fly by the seat of their pants. We happily place ourselves among the planners. Our writers and editors try to anticipate all the issues you may face before and during any journey, and then they do their research. This section is the product of their efforts. Use it to get excited about your trip to Savannah & Charleston, to inform your travel planning, or to guide you on the road should the seat of your pants start to feel threadbare.

GETTING STARTED

We're really proud of our Web site: Fodors.com is a great place to begin any journey. Scan Travel Wire for suggested itineraries, travel deals, restaurant and hotel openings, and other up-to-the-minute info. Check out Booking to research prices and book plane tickets, hotel rooms, rental cars, and vacation packages. Head to Talk for on-the-ground pointers from travelers who frequent our message boards. You can also link to loads of other travel-related resources.

❚ RESOURCES

ONLINE TRAVEL TOOLS

In addition to the Web sites listed below, for more information on events in Savannah & Charleston try visiting the Web sites of major newspapers and alternative newsweeklies in the area. Also take a look at the Web sites listed for regional and local tourism offices in the Essentials sections throughout each chapter.

ALL ABOUT SAVANNAH & CHARLESTON

Civil War Traveler (⊕*www.civilwartraveler.com*) has information about Civil War sites in the Carolinas and Georgia. **Doc South** (⊕*docsouth.unc.edu*) is a vast collection of historical documents and archives on Southern history, culture, and literature. **Dr. Beach** (⊕*www.drbeach.org*) is Dr. Stephen Leatherman's take

> ### WORD OF MOUTH
>
> After your trip, be sure to rate the places you visited and share your experiences and travel tips with us and other Fodorites in Travel Ratings and Talk on www.fodors.com.

on the best beaches in the Carolinas and Georgia and other states. The online edition of **Southern Living** (⊕*www.southernliving.com*) has many articles on travel, attractions, gardens, and people in the region.

Art & Culture Gullah Culture (⊕www.pbs.org/now/arts/gullah.html), from the PBS program with Bill Moyers, is a good introduction to Gullah life and culture. **Southern High Craft Guild** (⊕www.southernhighlandguild.org) represents more than 900 craftspeople in the Southeast.

Southern Literary Review (⊕www.southernlitreview.com) has biographical and bibliographical information on scores of Southern writers, including those hailing from the Carolinas and Georgia.

Golf Georgia State Park Golf Courses (⊕www.georgiagolf.com) has detailed information on Georgia's public golf courses. **Golf Guide** (⊕www.golfguideweb.com) has links to most golf courses in the Carolinas and Georgia. **Golf Link** (⊕www.golflink.com) offers information on nearly all the golf courses in the region. Public golf courses in South Carolina can be researched on **South Carolina Golf Trail** (⊕www.scgolftrail.com).

Safety Transportation Security Administration (TSA; ⊕www.tsa.gov)

Time Zones Timeanddate.com (⊕www.timeanddate.com/worldclock) can help you figure out the correct time anywhere.

Weather Accuweather.com (⊕www.accuweather.com) is an independent weather-forecasting service with good coverage of hurricanes. **Weather.com** (⊕www.weather.com) is the Web site for the Weather Channel.

Other Resources CIA World Factbook (⊕www.odci.gov/cia/publications/factbook/index.html) has profiles of every country in the world. It's a good source if you need some quick facts and figures.

VISITOR INFORMATION

Going online is the fastest way to get visitor information. All of the state tourism offices listed below have excellent Web sites, with maps and other travel information that you can browse.

Contacts Georgia Department of Industry, Trade and Tourism (✉285 Peachtree Center Ave., NE Marquis Tower II, Suite 1100, Atlanta, GA 30303 ☎404/656–3553 or 800/847–4842 ⎙404/651–9462 ⊕www.georgia.org). **South Carolina Department of Parks, Recreation, and Tourism** (✉1205 ⋯dleton St., Suite 106, Columbia, ⋯9201 ☎803/734–0122 or

888/727–6453 ⎙803/734–0138 ⊕www.travelsc.com).

∎ THINGS TO CONSIDER

GEAR

The Carolinas and Georgia are hot and humid in summer and sunny and mild in winter. Smart but casual attire works fine almost everywhere. A few chic restaurants in both Savannah and Charleston prefer more elegant dress, and tradition-minded resorts along the coast still require jackets and ties for men for dinner. For colder months pack a lightweight coat, slacks, and sweaters. Keeping summer's humidity in mind, pack absorbent natural fabrics that breathe; bring an umbrella, but leave the plastic raincoat at home. You'll want a jacket or sweater for summer evenings and for too-cool air-conditioning. And don't forget insect repellent.

TRIP INSURANCE

What kind of coverage do you honestly need? Do you need trip insurance at all? Take a deep breath and read on.

We believe that comprehensive trip insurance is especially valuable if you're booking a very expensive or complicated trip (particularly to an isolated region) or if you're booking far in advance. Who knows what could happen six months down the road? But whether or not you get insurance has more to do with how comfortable you are assuming all that risk yourself.

Comprehensive travel policies typically cover trip-cancellation and interruption, letting you cancel or cut your trip short because of a personal emergency, illness, or, in some cases, acts of terrorism in your destination. Such policies also cover evacuation and medical care. Some also cover you for trip delays because of bad weather or mechanical problems as well as for lost or delayed baggage. Another type of coverage to look for is financial default—that is, when your trip is disrupted because a tour operator, airline, or cruise line goes out of business. Generally you must buy this when you book your trip or shortly thereafter, and it's only available to you if your operator isn't on a list of excluded companies.

If you're going abroad, consider buying medical-only coverage at the very least. Neither Medicare nor some private insurers cover medical expenses anywhere outside of the United States (including time aboard a cruise ship, even if it leaves from a U.S. port). Medical-only policies typically reimburse you for medical care (excluding that related to preexisting conditions) and hospitalization abroad, and provide for evacuation. You still have to pay the bills and await reimbursement from the insurer, though.

Expect comprehensive travel insurance policies to cost about 4% to 7% or 8% of the total price of your trip (it's more like 8%–12% if you're over age 70). A medical-only policy may or may not be cheaper than a comprehensive policy. Always read the fine print of your policy to make sure that you're covered for the risks that are of most concern to you. Compare several policies to make sure you're getting the best price and range of coverage available.

Trip Insurance Resources

INSURANCE COMPARISON SITES		
Insure My Trip.com	800/487–4722	www.insuremytrip.com
Square Mouth.com	800/240–0369	www.quotetravelinsurance.com
Comprehensive Travel Insurers		
Access America	866/807–3982	www.accessamerica.com
CSA Travel Protection	800/873–9855	www.csatravelprotection.com
HTH Worldwide	610/254–8700 or 888/243–2358	www.hthworldwide.com
Travelex Insurance	888/457–4602	www.travelex-insurance.com
Travel Guard International	715/345–0505 or 800/826–4919	www.travelguard.com
Travel Insured International	800/243–3174	www.travelinsured.com
MEDICAL-ONLY INSURERS		
International Medical Group	800/628–4664	www.imglobal.com
International SOS	215/942–8000 or 713/521–7611	www.internationalsos.com
Wallach & Company	800/237–6615 or 504/687–3166	www.wallach.com

BOOKING YOUR TRIP

Unless your cousin is a travel agent, you're probably among the millions of people who make most of their travel arrangements online.

But have you ever wondered just what the differences are between an online travel agent (a Web site through which you make reservations instead of going directly to the airline, hotel, or car-rental company), a discounter (a firm that does a high volume of business with a hotel chain or airline and accordingly gets good prices), a wholesaler (one that makes cheap reservations in bulk and then resells them to people like you), and an aggregator (one that compares all the offerings so you don't have to)?

Is it truly better to book directly on an airline or hotel Web site? And when does a real live travel agent come in handy?

■ ONLINE

You really have to shop around. A travel wholesaler such as Hotels.com or HotelClub.net can be a source of good rates, as can discounters such as Hotwire or Priceline, particularly if you can bid for your hotel room or airfare. Indeed, such sites sometimes have deals that are unavailable elsewhere. They do, however, tend to work only with hotel chains (which makes them just plain useless for getting hotel reservations outside of major cities) or big airlines (so that often leaves out upstarts like jetBlue and some foreign carriers like Air India).

Also, with discounters and wholesalers you must generally prepay, and everything is nonrefundable. And before you fork over the dough, be sure to check the terms and conditions, so you know what a given company will do for you if there's a problem and what you'll have to deal with on your own.

■TIP→ To be absolutely sure everything was processed correctly, confirm reservations made through online travel agents, discounters, and wholesalers directly with your hotel before leaving home.

Booking engines like Expedia, Travelocity, and Orbitz are actually travel agents, albeit high-volume, online ones. And airline travel packagers like American Airlines Vacations and Virgin Vacations—well, they're travel agents, too. But they may still not work with all the world's hotels.

An aggregator site will search many sites and pull the best prices for airfares, hotels, and rental cars from them. Most aggregators compare the major travel-booking sites such as Expedia, Travelocity, and Orbitz; some also look at airline Web sites, though rarely the sites of smaller budget airlines. Some aggregators also compare other travel products, including complex packages—a good thing, as you can sometimes get the best overall deal by booking an air-and-hotel package.

▌ WITH A TRAVEL AGENT

If you use an agent—brick-and-mortar or virtual—you'll pay a fee for the service. And know that the service you get from some online agents isn't comprehensive. For example Expedia and Travelocity don't search for prices on budget airlines like jetBlue, Southwest, or small foreign carriers. That said, some agents (online or not) *do* have access to fares that are difficult to find otherwise, and the savings can more than make up for any surcharge.

A knowledgeable brick-and-mortar travel agent can be a godsend if you're booking a cruise, a package trip that's not available to you directly, an air pass, or a complicated itinerary including several overseas flights. What's more, travel agents that specialize in a destination may have exclusive access to certain deals and insider information on things such as charter flights. Agents who specialize in types of travelers (senior citizens, gays and lesbians, naturists) or types of trips (cruises, luxury travel, safaris) can also be invaluable.

■TIP→**Remember that Expedia, Travelocity, and Orbitz are travel agents, not just booking engines. To resolve any problems with a reservation made through these companies, contact them first.**

A top-notch agent planning your trip to Russia will make sure you get the correct visa application and complete it on time; the one booking your cruise may get you a cabin upgrade or arrange to have bottle of champagne chilling in your cabin when you embark. And complain about the surcharges all you like, but when things don't work out the way you'd hoped, it's nice to have an agent to put things right.

If you're flying into the Carolinas and Georgia, renting a car, traveling to multiple destinations, and staying at several different hotels, you may find that working with a travel agent could save you time, and possibly money. However, if you're visiting only one or two destinations, you may find it preferable to make reservations on your own.

Agent Resources American Society of Travel Agents (☎703/739–2782 ⊕www.travelsense.org).

▌ ACCOMMODATIONS

With the exception of Savannah and Charleston, most lodging rates in the region fall at or below the national average. They do vary a great deal seasonally, however—coastal resorts tend to have significantly higher rates in summer. All major chains are

Online Booking Resources

AGGREGATORS

Kayak	www.kayak.com;	also looks at cruises and vacation packages.
Mobissimo	www.mobissimo. com	
Qixo	www.qixo.com	also compares cruises, vacation packages, and even travel insurance.
Sidestep	www.sidestep.com	also compares vacation packages and lists travel deals.
Travelgrove	www.travelgrove. com	also compares cruises and packages.

Booking Engines

Cheap Tickets	www.cheaptickets. com	a discounter.
Expedia	www.expedia.com	a large online agency that charges a booking fee for airline tickets.
Hotwire	www.hotwire.com	a discounter.
lastminute.com	www.lastminute. com	specializes in last-minute travel the main site is for the U.K., but it has a link to a U.S. site.
Onetravel.com	www.onetravel. com	a discounter for hotels, car rentals, airfares, and packages.
Orbitz	www.orbitz.com	charges a booking fee for airline tickets, but gives a clear breakdown of fees and taxes before you book.
Travel.com	www.travel.com	allows you to compare its rates with those of other booking engines.
Travelocity	www.travelocity. com	charges a booking fee for airline tickets, but promises good problem resolution.

ONLINE ACCOMMODATIONS

Hotelbook.com	www.hotelbook. com	focuses on independent hotels worldwide.
Hotel Club	www.hotelclub.net	good for major cities worldwide.
Hotels.com	www.hotels.com	a big Expedia-owned wholesaler that offers rooms in hotels all over the world.

well represented in this part of the country, both in cities and suburbs, and interstates are lined with inexpensive to moderate chains. It's not uncommon to find clean but extremely basic chains offering double rooms for as little as $25 to $40 nightly along the busiest highways.

The lodgings listed are the cream of the crop in each price category. Properties indicated by ✕▣ are lodging establishments whose restaurant warrants a special trip. Facilities that are available are listed—but not any extra costs associated with those facilities. When pricing accommodations, always ask what's included and what costs extra.

CATEGORY	COST
$$$$	over $220
$$$	$161–$220
$$	$111–$160
$	$70–$110
¢	under $70

All prices are for a standard double room in high season, based on the European Plan (EP) and excluding tax and service charges

▮TIP➔ Assume that hotels operate on the European Plan (EP, no meals) unless we specify that they use the Breakfast Plan (BP, with full breakfast), Continental Plan (CP, Continental breakfast), Full American Plan (FAP, all meals), Modified American Plan (MAP, breakfast and dinner) or are all-inclusive (AI, all meals and most activities).

APARTMENT & HOUSE RENTALS

The far-flung resort areas of the region are filled with rental properties—everything from cabins to luxury homes. Most often these properties, whether part of a huge corporation or individually owned, are professionally managed; such businesses have become an industry unto themselves.

Hatteras Realty, Midgett Realty, and Sun Realty, and handle properties on North Carolina's Outer Banks. Island Realty focuses on the Charleston and Isle of Palms area in South Carolina. Hilton Head Rentals and Resort Rentals of Hilton Head Island offer rentals on Hilton Head.

▮ ONLINE BOOKING RESOURCES

Contacts Hilton Head Rentals (☎800/368–5975 ⊕www. hiltonheadrentals.com). **Interhome** (☎954/791–8282 or 800/882–6864 ⊕www.interhome.us). **Island Realty** (☎843/886–8144 or 800/707–6421 ⊕www.islandrealty.com).

Resort Rentals of Hilton Head Island (☎800/845–7017 or 843/686–6008 ⊕www.resortrentalshhi.com).

Vacation Home Rentals Worldwide (☎201/767–9393 or 800/633–3284 ⊕www.vhrww.com). **Villas International** (☎415/499–9490 or 800/221–2260 ⊕www.villasintl.com).

BED & BREAKFASTS

Historic B&Bs and inns are found everywhere in the region and include quite a few former plantation houses and lavish Southern estates. In many rural or less touristy areas, B&Bs offer an affordable and homey alternative to chain properties, but in tourism-dependent destinations you can expect to pay, for a historic inn, about the same as or more than for a full-service hotel. Many of the South's finest restaurants are also found in country inns.

Reservation Services Bed & Breakfast.com (☎512/322–2710 or 800/462–2632 ⊕www.bedandbreakfast.com) also sends out an online newsletter. **Bed & Breakfast Inns Online** (☎615/868–1946 or 800/215–7365 ⊕www.bbonline.com). **BnB Finder.com** (☎212/432–7693 or 888/547–8226 ⊕www.bnbfinder.com).

Local Associations Association of Historic Inns of Savannah (☎912/233–1833 ⊕www.historicinnsofsavannah.com). **Romantic Inns of Savannah** (☎No phone ⊕www.romanticinnsofsavannah.com). **South Carolina Bed & Breakfast Association** (☎No phone ⊕www.southcarolinabedandbreakfast.com).

HOTELS

In summer, especially July and August, hotel rooms in coastal areas can be hard to come by unless you book well advance.

All hotels listed in this book have private baths unless otherwise noted.

▌ RENTAL CARS

When you reserve a car, ask about cancellation penalties, taxes, drop-off charges (if you're planning to pick up the car in one city and leave it in another), and surcharges (for being under or over a certain age, for additional drivers, or for driving across state or country borders or beyond a specific distance from your point of rental). All these things can add substantially to your costs. Request car seats and extras such as GPS when you book.

Rates are sometimes—but not always—better if you book in advance or reserve through a rental agency's Web site. There are other reasons to book ahead, though: for popular destinations, during busy times of the year, or to ensure that you get certain types of cars (vans, SUVs, exotic sports cars).

▌ TIP→ **Make sure that a confirmed reservation guarantees you a car. Agencies sometimes overbook, particularly for busy weekends and holiday periods.**

It's important to reserve a car well in advance of your expected arrival. Rental rates vary from city to city, but are generally lowest in larger cities where there's a lot of competition. Economy cars cost between $27 and $61 per day, and luxury cars go for $70 to $198. Weekend rates are generally much lower than those on weekdays, and weekly rates usually offer big discounts. Rates are also seasonal, with th highest rates coming during peak travel times. Local factors can also affect rates; for example, a big convention can suck up most of the rental-car inventory and boost rates for those remaining.

Some off-airport locations offer lower rates, and their lots are only minutes from the terminal via complimentary shuttle. Also ask whether certain frequent-flyer, American Automobile Association (AAA), corporate, or other such promotions are accepted and whether the rates might be lower the day before or after you had originally intended to travel.

In some cases you can find that the same agency offers a region's cheapest luxury car rates but priciest economy cars, or that the cheapest agency in one city may have high rates in another. It pays to check around. Also, although an economy car is almost always your cheapest option, agencies sometimes offer upgrade specials that cost only a dollar or two more per day. Think carefully about how much and where you'll be using the car before choosing among economy, compact, standard, luxury, and premium; it may be worth the extra few dollars per day for a more substantial vehicle if you're traveling long distances, driving over rugged terrain, traveling with more than a couple of passengers, or using the car extensively. If you're traveling winter, you may want to pay little extra for a four-wheel-e vehicle.

CAR RENTAL RESOURCES

Automobile Associations U.S.: American Automobile Association (AAA ☎315/797–5000 ⊕www. aaa.com); most contact with the organization is through state and regional members. **National Automobile Club** (☎650/294–7000 ⊕www.thenac.com); membership is open to California residents only.

Local Agencies Armada (☎770/416–7996 ⊕www.arma-davans.com). **Triangle Rent A Car** (☎919/840–3400 ⊕www.triangle-rentacar.com).

Major Agencies Alamo (☎800/522–9696 ⊕www.alamo.com). **Avis** (☎800/331–1084 ⊕www.avis.com). **Budget** (☎800/472–3325 ⊕www.budget.com). **Hertz** (☎800/654–3001 ⊕www.hertz.com). **National Car Rental** (☎800/227–7368 ⊕www.nationalcar.com).

CAR-RENTAL INSURANCE

Everyone who rents a car wonders whether the insurance that the rental companies offer is worth the expense. No one—including us—has a simple answer. It all depends on how much regular insurance you have, how comfortable you are with risk, and whether money is an issue.

If you own a car and carry comprehensive car insurance for both collision and liability, your personal auto insurance will probably cover a rental, but read your policy's fine print to be sure. If you don't have auto insurance, then you should probably buy the collision- or loss-damage waiver (CDW or LDW) from the rental company. This eliminates your liability for damage to the car.

Some credit cards offer CDW coverage, but it's usually supplemental to your own insurance and rarely covers SUVs, minivans, luxury models, and the like. If your coverage is secondary, you may still be liable for loss-of-use costs from the car-rental company (again, read the fine print). But no credit-card insurance is valid unless you use that card for *all* transactions, from reserving to paying the final bill.

■TIP→Diners Club offers primary CDW coverage on all rentals reserved and paid for with the card. This means that Diners Club's company—not your own car insurance—pays in case of an accident. It *doesn't* mean that your car-insurance company won't raise your rates once it discovers you had an accident.

You may also be offered supplemental liability coverage; the car-rental company is required to carry a minimal level of liability coverage insuring all renters, but it's rarely enough to cover claims in a really serious accident if you're at fault. Your own auto-insurance policy will protect you if you own a car; if you don't, you have to decide whether you are willing to take the risk.

U.S. rental companies sell CDWs and LDWs for about $15 to $25 a day; supplemental liability is usually more than $10 a day.

The car-rental company may offer you all sorts of other policies, but they're rarely worth the cost. Personal accident insurance, which is basic hospitalization coverage, is an especially egregious rip-off if you already have health insurance.

■TIP→You can decline the insurance from the rental company and purchase it through a third-party provider such as Travel Guard (www.travelguard.com)—$9 per day for $35,000 of coverage. That's sometimes just under half the price of the CDW offered by some car-rental companies.

■ VACATION PACKAGES

Packages *are not* guided excursions. Packages combine airfare, accommodations, and perhaps a rental car or other extras (theater tickets, guided excursions, boat trips, reserved entry to popular museums, transit passes), but they let you do your own thing. During busy periods packages may be your only option, as flights and rooms may be sold out otherwise.

Most visitors to Charleston and Savannah travel independently, usually by car. For many such travelers, package rates aren't available or don't offer enough flexibility. However, visitors planning to fly in and rent a car may want to look at the flight/hotel/rental car packages now routinely offered by online travel companies. These may—or may not—be better deals than buying each one individually. Many o the region's visitor information centers have sections on their Web sites listing local packages. The American Automobile Association offices—there are 24 in the Carolinas and nine in Georgia—often offer discounted admissions to local attractions to members.

Organizations American Society of Travel Agents (ASTA ☎703/739–2782 or 800/965–2782 ⊕www.astanet.com). **United States Tour Operators Association** (USTOA ☎212/599–6599 ⊕www.ustoa.com).

■TIP➡Local tourism boards can provide information about lesser-known and small-niche operators that sell packages to only a few destinations.

▎ GUIDED TOURS

Most of this region attracts visitors traveling independently, usually by car. But some areas—notably Savannah—get a number of escorted bus tours. Collette Tours has several tours of Charleston, Savannah, and other coastal communities. The escorted tours operate in spring and fall, with prices from $1,100 per person. You stay at first-class hotels and the price includes most breakfasts and dinners. Presley Tours has five- to eight-day tours of Charleston, Savannah, and other places along the coast. Most tours are $800 to $1,100 per person. A large tour company called Tauck has an eight-day tour of Charleston, Savannah, ▯yll Island, and Hilton Head,

staying at such high-end hotels as the Westin Resort on Hilton Head. The cost is $2,080 per person.

Recommended Companies Collette Tours (☎800/942–3301 ⊕www.escortedcollettetours.com). **Presley Tours** (☎800/621–6100 ⊕www.presleytours.com). **Tauck** (☎800/788–7885 ⊕www.tauck.com).

GETTING STARTED / BOOKING YOUR TRIP / TRANSPORTATION / ON THE GROUND

TRANSPORTATION

▌ BY AIR

If you're flying into the Carolinas or Georgia, chances are you'll pass through Hartsfield-Jackson Atlanta International Airport. It's by far the most popular airport in the region, and is the busiest in the world, at least in terms of number of passengers—more than 85 million annually. (Chicago's O'Hare International Airport claims to be the busiest in terms of number of flights.)

Flying time to Atlanta is 4½ hours from Los Angeles, 2½ hours from New York, 2 hours from Chicago, 2 hours from Dallas, and 9 hours from London. By plane, Charleston, Hilton Head, and Savannah are all about an hour east–southeast of Atlanta.

Airlines & Airports Airline and Airport Links.com (⊕www.airlineandairportlinks.com) has links to many of the world's airlines and airports.

Airline Security Issues Transportation Security Administration (⊕www.tsa.gov) has answers for almost every question that might come up.

AIRPORTS

For the most part, fares tend to be lower at the region's major airports, but you can sometimes find good deals at smaller airports such as South Carolina's Charleston International (CHS)

and Georgia's Savannah/Hilton Head International (SAV). It can be difficult to find direct flights to these smaller airports if you're flying in from outside the region. You may decide it's easier to fly into Hartsfield-Jackson Atlanta International Airport (ATL).

Airport Information Charleston International Airport (⊠5500 International Blvd., North Charleston, SC ☎843/767-1100 ⊕www.chs-airport.com). **Hartsfield-Jackson Atlanta International Airport** (⊠6000 N. Terminal Pkwy., Hapeville, GA ☎404/530-7300 ⊕www.atlanta-airport.com). **Savannah/Hilton Head International Airport** (⊠400 Airways Ave., West Chatham, GA ☎912/964-0514 ⊕www.savannahairport.com).

FLIGHTS

Hartsfield-Jackson Atlanta International Airport is the primary hub of Delta Airlines and AirTran Airways. Altogether, about two dozen domestic and international airlines fly into Atlanta. Commuter airlines, including US Airways Express, Continental Express, Delta Connection, and United Express have service to many smaller airports in South Carolina and Georgia.

Airline Contacts Alaska Airlines (☎800/252-7522 or 206/433-3100 ⊕www.alaskaair.com). **American Airlines** (☎800/433-7300 ⊕www.aa.com). **ATA** (☎800/435-9282 or 317/282-8308 ⊕www.ata.

com). **Continental Airlines** (☎800/523–3273 for U.S. and Mexico reservations, 800/231–0856 for international reservations ⊕www.continental.com). **Delta Airlines** (☎800/221–1212 for U.S. reservations, 800/241–4141 for international reservations ⊕www.delta.com). **Northwest Airlines** (☎800/225–2525 ⊕www.nwa.com). **Southwest Airlines** (☎800/435–9792 ⊕www.southwest.com). **Spirit Airlines** (☎800/772–7117 or 586/791–7300 ⊕www.spiritair.com). **United Airlines** (☎800/864–8331 for U.S. reservations, 800/538–2929 for international reservations ⊕www.united.com). **USAirways** (☎800/428–4322 for U.S. and Canada reservations, 800/622–1015 for international reservations ⊕www.usairways.com).

Smaller Airlines AirTran (☎770/994–8258 or 800/247–8726 ⊕www.airtran.com). **Midwest Express** (☎800/452–2022 ⊕www.midwestairlines.com).

▌ BY CAR

A car is your most practical and economical means of traveling around the region. Savannah, Charleston, and other smaller communities can also be explored fairly easily on foot or by using public transit and cabs, but a car is helpful to reach many of the most intriguing attractions, which are not always downtown.

Although you'll make the best ~ne traveling along the South's ~ensive network of interstate ~ways, keep in mind that U.S.

and state highways offer some delightful scenery and the opportunity to stumble on funky roadside diners, leafy state parks, and historic town squares. Although the area is rural, it's still densely populated, so you'll rarely drive for more than 20 or 30 mi without passing roadside services, such as gas stations, restaurants, and ATMs.

▌ BY TRAIN

Several Amtrak routes pass through the region. Three trains, the *Palmetto*, the *Silver Meteor*, and the *Silver Star* make the daily run between New York and Miami via Charleston and Savannah.

Information Amtrak (☎800/872–7245 ⊕www.amtrak.com).

ON THE GROUND

▌ EATING OUT

The increase of international flavors in the region reflects the tastes and backgrounds of the people who have flooded into the region over the past couple of decades. Bagels are as common nowadays as biscuits, and, especially in urban areas, it can be harder to find country cooking than a plate of hummus. For the most part, though, you can still find plenty of traditional Southern staples—barbecue, fried chicken, greens, and the like.

A new wave of restaurants in Charleston and Savannah serves innovative versions of Lowcountry cooking, with lighter takes on traditional dishes. Outside of the many resort areas along the coast, dining costs in the region are often lower than those in the North.

Vegetarians will have no trouble finding attractive places to eat, although in small towns they may have to stick with pizza.

The restaurants we list are the cream of the crop in each price category. Properties indicated by ✕☒ are lodging establishments whose restaurant warrants a special trip.

MEALS & MEALTIMES

The Southern tradition of Sunday dinner—usually a midday meal—has morphed to some degree, at least in urban areas, to Sunday brunch. For many this meal follows midmorning church services, so be advised that restaurants will often be very busy through the middle of the day. In smaller towns, many restaurants are closed on Sunday.

Southerners tend to eat on the early side, with lunch crowds beginning to appear before noon. The peak time for dinner is around 7. Only in big cities will you find much in the way of late-night dining.

Unless otherwise noted, the restaurants listed in this guide are open daily for lunch and dinner.

CATEGORY	COST
$$$$	over $22
$$$	$17–$22
$$	$12–$16
$	$7–$11
¢	under $7

All prices are per person for a main course at dinner.

RESERVATIONS & DRESS

Regardless of where you are, it's a good idea to make a reservation if you can. In some places (Hong Kong, for example), it's expected. We only mention them specifically when reservations are essential (there's no other way you'll ever get a table) or when they are not accepted. For popular restaurants, book as far ahead as you can (often 30 days), and reconfirm as soon as you arrive. (Large parties should always call ahead to check the reservations policy.) We mention dress only when men are required to wear a jacket or a jacket and tie.

For the most part, restaurants in the Carolinas and Georgia tend to be informal. A coat and tie are rarely required, except in a few of the fanciest places. You'll be safe almost anywhere if you show up in business-casual clothes.

WINES, BEER & SPIRITS

Blue laws—legislation forbidding sales on Sunday—have a history in this region dating to the 1600s. These bans are still observed in many rural areas, particularly with regard to alcohol sales. Liquor stores are closed on Sunday in the region, although beer and wine generally can be purchased in grocery stores or convenience stores. In the Carolinas, beer and wine can't be sold anywhere on Sunday mornings.

...crobreweries are common all ...the region, and the list of ...pots includes Charleston. ...are two dozen breweries

BE A CORRESPONDENT!

Was the service stellar or not up to snuff? Did the food give you shivers of delight or leave you cold? Did the prices and portions make you happy or sad? Rate restaurants and write your own reviews in Travel Ratings or start a discussion about your favorite places in Travel Talk on www.fodors.com. Your comments might even appear in our books. Yes, you, too, can be a correspondent!

in South Carolina, and about a dozen in Georgia, where state laws on beer distribution have crimped the growth of microbreweries.

▌ HOURS OF OPERATION

Banks and post offices are usually open weekdays from 9 to 5 (often to 6 on Friday) and frequently Saturday morning. In rural areas, post offices often close for lunch. In Georgia, in addition to national holidays, government offices are closed on Confederate Memorial Day (usually the fourth Monday in April) and Robert E. Lee's Birthday (January 19 but usually celebrated the day after Thanksgiving). South Carolina also celebrates Confederate Memorial Day, but on May 10.

Museums typically operate Tuesday through Saturday from 10 to 5, and Sunday from 1 to 5. Many museums and state-run tourist attractions are closed Monday.

From Monday to Saturday, shops in urban and suburban areas open at 9 or 10 and close anywhere from 6 to 10; on Sunday, they frequently don't open until noon and close at 5 or 6. Many supermarkets in urban and suburban communities are open 24 hours; they often contain pharmacies and banks with extended hours.

▮ MONEY

Although the cost of living remains fairly low in most parts of the South, travel-related costs (such as dining, lodging, and transportation) have become increasingly steep. And tourist attractions are pricey, too. Costs can also be dear in resort communities throughout the Carolinas and Georgia.

Prices throughout this guide are given for adults. Substantially reduced fees are almost always available for children, students, and senior citizens.

CREDIT CARDS

Throughout this guide, the following abbreviations are used: **AE**, American Express; **D**, Discover; **DC**, Diners Club; **MC**, MasterCard; and **V**, Visa.

It's a good idea to inform your credit-card company before you travel, especially if you're going abroad and don't travel internationally very often. Otherwise, the credit-card company might put a hold on your card owing to unusual activity—not a good thing halfway through

your trip. Record all your credit-card numbers—as well as the phone numbers to call if your cards are lost or stolen—in a safe place, so you're prepared should something go wrong. Both MasterCard and Visa have general numbers you can call (collect if you're abroad) if your card is lost, but you're better off calling the number of your issuing bank, since MasterCard and Visa usually just transfer you to your bank; your bank's number is usually printed on your card.

Reporting Lost Cards American Express (☎800/528–4800 in U.S., 336/393–1111 collect from abroad ⊕www.americanexpress.com). **Diners Club** (☎800/234–6377 in U.S., 303/799–1504 collect from abroad ⊕www.dinersclub.com). **Discover** (☎800/347–2683 in U.S., 801/902–3100 collect from abroad ⊕www.discovercard.com). **MasterCard** (☎800/627–8372 in U.S., 636/722–7111 collect from abroad ⊕www.mastercard.com). **Visa** (☎800/847–2911 in U.S., 410/581–9994 collect from abroad ⊕www.visa.com).

▮ SAFETY

In general, South Carolina and Georgia are safe destinations for travelers. Most rural and suburban areas have low crime rates. However, some of the region's larger cities have significantly higher crime rates than the national average. Savannah and Charlotte have crime rates that top the national average.

TAXES

Sales taxes are 4% in Georgia and 5% in South Carolina. Some counties or cities may impose an additional sales tax of 1% to 3%. Most municipalities also levy a lodging tax (usually exempting small inns) and sometimes a restaurant tax. The hotel taxes in the South can be rather steep: more than 10% in Georgia. Taxes and fees on car rentals, especially if rented from an airport, can easily add 30% or more to your bill.

TIME

Georgia and South Carolina fall in the eastern standard time (EST) zone, which is the same as New York and Florida, making it three hours ahead of California.

TIPPING

Tipping in South Carolina and Georgia is essentially the same as tipping anywhere else in the United States. Hotel chambermaids should be tipped $1 to $3 a night for inexpensive and moderate hotels and up to $5 a night per guest for high-end properties. A concierge typically receives anywhere from $5 to $25, depending on the favor requested. Room-service waiters get 10% to 15% (look to see if it's already included on the bill), and $1 to $2 per bag is customary for bellhops, porters, and skycaps. Tips aren't necessary, though they're still accepted, if the hotel includes a service fee in its package price.

INDEX

A

African-American history sites, 16–17, 18, 21, 51–52, 55–56, 73, 88–89, 94, 96
Aiken-Rhett House, 88
Air travel, 181–182
Charleston area, 140–141
Coastal Isles, 76
Hilton Head, 167
Savannah, 39
Altamaha River, 53
Andolini's Pizza ✕, 115–116
Andrew Low House, 11
Andrew Pinckney Inn 🖼, 126
Anson ✕, 112
Ansonborough Inn 🖼, 125
Aqua ✕, 157–158
Aquarium, 87
Ashley Inn 🖼, 125
Audubon-Newhall Preserve, 151
Avery Research Center for African-American History and Culture, 88

B

Ballastone Inn 🖼, 31–32
Banks
Charleston area, 142
Coastal Isles, 77
Hilton Head, 166
Savannah, 41
Baseball, 96
Basket ladies, 94
Battery, 90–91
BB&T Charleston Food + Wine Festival, 132
Beach Institute African-American Cultural Center, 16–17
Beachcomber BBQ and Grill ✕, 61
Beaches, 98, 155
Beachview Club 🖼, 69

Bed & Breakfast Inn 🖼, 32–33
Belford's Steak and Seafood ✕, 25
Bella's Italian Café ✕, 29
Bennie's Red Barn ✕, 60
Biking, 24, 57–58, 66, 98, 155
Bistro Savannah ✕, 26
Blossom ✕, 114
Blue Heron Inn 🖼, 54
Bluffton, 151
Boat and ferry travel
Charleston area, 141
Coastal Isles, 76–77
Hilton Head, 165
Savannah, 39–40
Boathouse Restaurant ✕, 116
Boating, kayaking, and sailing, 23, 52, 59, 73, 99, 155
Booking the trip, 173–180
Boone Hall Plantation and Garden, 93
Boulevard Diner ✕, 115
Brick Oven Café ✕, 158–159
Brickhill Bluff △, 74
Broad Street Guesthouse 🖼, 126–127
Bubba Gump ✕, 117
Buccaneer Beach Resort 🖼, 70
Bus travel
Charleston area, 141
Savannah, 40
Business hours, 184–185

C

Camping, 55, 70, 74
Cannonboro Inn 🖼, 125
Cape Romain National Wildlife Refuge, 94
Car rental, 177–179
Car travel, 182
Charleston area, 142
Coastal Isles, 77

Hilton Head, 165
Savannah, 40
CARGO Portside Grill ✕, 59
Carolina's ✕, 112
Cathedral of St. John the Baptist, 17
Cemeteries, 11
Charles Pinckney National Historic Site, 94
Charles Towne Landing State Historic Site, 96
Charleston Crab House ✕, 116–117
Charleston Grill ✕, 111–112, 133
Charleston Harbor Resort & Marina 🖼, 120
Charleston Marriott 🖼, 120–121
Charleston Museum, 84
Charleston Place 🖼, 84, 119
Charleston Visitors Center, 85
Children
Charleston area, 84, 85–86, 87, 91–92, 93, 94, 95–96, 139
Coastal Isles, 56, 57, 58, 67, 68, 73
Hilton Head, 157, 160–161
Savannah, 22
Children's Museum of the Lowcountry, 84
Chippewa Square, 11
Christ Episcopal Church, 57
Christie's ✕, 59
Churches
Charleston, 85, 86, 87–88, 89, 91
Coastal Isles, 57
Savannah, 13, 17, 19
Circa 1886 ✕, 103
Circular Congregati Church, 85

NOTES